BY
DESIGN

BY DESIGN

Interviews with Film Production Designers

VINCENT LoBRUTTO

PRAEGER

Westport, Connecticut
London

#25677129

Library of Congress Cataloging-in-Publication Data

LoBrutto, Vincent.
  By design : interviews with film production designers / Vincent
LoBrutto.
      p.   cm.
  Includes bibliographical references and index.
  ISBN 0–275–94030–6.—ISBN 0–275–94031–4 (pbk.)
  1. Motion picture art directors—Interviews.   2. Motion pictures—
Setting and scenery.   I. Title.
PN1995.9.A74L6   1992
791.43'0232—dc20   92–5849

British Library Cataloguing in Publication Data is available.

Library of Congress Catalog Card Number: 92–5849
ISBN: 0–275–94030–6
ISBN: 0–275–94031–4 (pbk.)

First published in 1992

Praeger Publishers, 88 Post Road West, Westport, CT 06881
An imprint of Greenwood Publishing Group, Inc.

Printed in the United States of America

The paper used in this book complies with the
Permanent Paper Standard issued by the National
Information Standards Organization (Z39.48–1984).

10 9 8 7 6 5 4 3 2 1

To

Harriet Morrison,

my wife

"If two people dream the same dream,
it ceases to be an illusion."
—*Philip K. Dick*

Contents

Contents

Acknowledgments

I would like to thank my family and friends for all the support they have given me during this project. My parents, Rose and Anthony LoBrutto, continue to encourage my work and are a constant source of inspiration. My children, Rebecca and Alex Morrison, generously demonstrate their pride and recognition of my achievements at a time in their lives when they are tenaciously pursuing their own goals. My wife, Harriet Morrison, has contributed countless hours of her time and intelligence toward making this project a reality. She has helped to locate and contact people, has worn the many hats of researcher, chauffeur, and adviser, and has given her impeccable taste and attention to the manuscript. I am forever grateful to her for keeping our personal lives on an even course. This book and its author would not be the same without her presence.

I express my appreciation to all those who assisted me in contacting interviewees: Lindsey Besant of Sandra Marsh Management; The Gersh Agency; Craig Jacobson, Esq.; Triad Artists, Inc.; ICM–New York; and the Society of Motion Picture Art Directors–Local 876.

I want to thank everyone at Praeger Publishers for the constant support and careful attention they provide. Particular thanks go to my editor, Anne Kiefer, for overseeing the many facets involved in realizing this project. The book was given expert care by project editor John Roberts, assistant production editor Andrew Schub, and copy editor Susan Cox.

I am especially indebted to the twenty production designers who gave so much of their valuable time to discuss their working lives, and explore the art and craft of film production design. My respect and gratitude to all.

My thanks also go to Dean Tavoularis for his time in talking to me about film production design.

I respectfully recognize the passing of Gene Callahan, John DeCuir, and Anton Furst, three gifted production designers who were not able to share their wisdom with me.

I also thank Saal and Deborah Lesser for their special support, Morty and Leila Marks, John Howard, Peter Halfon of The Eggers Group, David B. Eagan, AIA, the reference room at the Mount Vernon Public Library, the Sarah Lawrence College Library, and the Margaret Herrick Library.

This book was written using WordPerfect 5.1. My thanks are extended to the patient and knowledgeable staff on the WordPerfect Hotline for always answering my questions.

Filmmaking is a collaborative process and so is a book of interviews; again, I would like to thank all who have contributed to this project—your participation helped to bring this book to fruition.

Introduction

The purpose of this book is to let production designers speak in their own voices about the art and craft of feature film production design.

Although the results of their efforts are visible on the screen, a mysterious veil hangs over the magnitude of the production designer's role in the filmmaking process.

A production designer is responsible for the visual look of the film. In its fullest definition, this extends to translating the script into visual metaphors, creating a color palette, establishing architectural and period details, selecting locations, designing and decorating sets, coordinating the costumes, make-up, and hair styles into a pictorial scheme, and collaborating with the director and director of photography to define how the film should be conceived and photographed.

The production designer researches the world in which the film takes place to capture a sense of authenticity and render the director's vision to celluloid reality.

Production designers use sketches, illustrations, models, and complex production storyboards to plan every shot from microscopic to macroscopic detail. They have tremendous financial accountability and are expected to produce a complete environment for a film within a restricted budget.

The significance of the production designer has changed dramatically over the course of film history. During the Hollywood studio era, supervising art directors ran the art departments. They created a house style in art direction that gave each studio's product a distinctive image. The supervising art director assigned each film to an art director who was responsible for designing and building the scenery and sets.

The advent of the production designer occurred in 1939 when producer David O. Selznick awarded the title to William Cameron Menzies for his work on *Gone with the Wind*. Selznick recognized that Menzies did much more than design the sets; he created a blueprint for shooting the picture by storyboarding the entire film. His detailed work incorporated color and style, structured each scene, and encompassed the framing, composition and camera movement for each shot in the film. Menzies's contribution helped expand the function of the art director beyond the creation of sets and scenery to responsibility for the entire visualization of a motion picture.

The production designers in this book represent a myriad range of approaches and techniques. They come from various backgrounds and disciplines, and their work reflects a panorama of filmmaking styles. The interviews are presented in an order that attempts to convey a historical scope and sense of the development of the craft.

Production design is an art and craft embedded in the core of the filmmaking process. Production designers utilize imagination and technique, illusion and reality, and apply discipline and financial restraint to enhance the script and the director's intent visually by creating images out of ideas and purpose out of the images.

BY
DESIGN

Robert Boyle

Robert Boyle graduated as an architecture student from the University of Southern California during the Depression. He worked for three architects in three months, and all were suffering the effects of the economic hard times. These circumstances prompted Boyle to seek work as a bit player at RKO, where he met the supervising art director, Van Nest Polglase. Polglase referred him to Paramount, and he was hired by supervising art director Hans Dreier.

Boyle's work caught the eye of Alfred Hitchcock, who asked him to storyboard *Saboteur*, thus launching a long relationship that led to the films *Shadow of a Doubt*, *North by Northwest*, *The Birds*, and *Marnie*.

Robert Boyle is in his sixth decade as a designer with over seventy films to his credit. He has been nominated for the Academy Award for best art direction—set decoration four times for *North by Northwest*, *Gaily Gaily*, *Fiddler on the Roof*, and *The Shootist*. In addition to his collaboration with Alfred Hitchcock, he has joined forces with many fine directors, including Richard Brooks, J. Lee Thompson, Norman Jewison, Sam Fuller, Don Siegel, Budd Boetticher, and Hal Ashby.

Boyle's career spans the golden age of the studio system. He is a master craftsman who has helped create some of the cinema's greatest illusions. On the studio stage floor, he recreated the Statue of Liberty for *Saboteur*, Mount Rushmore for *North by Northwest*, and the terror of a massive bird rebellion in *The Birds*.

Robert Boyle continues designing motion pictures while training future filmmakers as a teacher at the American Film Institute.

1942 *Saboteur*
1943 *Flesh and Fantasy*
      Shadow of a Doubt
      Good Morning Judge
      White Savage
1946 *Nocturne*
1947 *They Won't Believe Me*
      Ride the Pink Horse
1948 *Another Part of the Forest*
      An Act of Murder
      For the Love of Mary
1949 *The Gal Who Took the West*
      Abandoned
      The Western Story
1950 *Buccaneer Girl*
      Sierra
      Louisa
      The Milkman
      Mystery Submarine
1951 *Iron Man*
      Mark of the Renegade
      The Lady Pays Off
      Weekend with Father
1952 *Bronco Buster*
      Lost in Alaska
      Yankee Buccaneer
      Back at the Front
1953 *Girls in the Night*
      The Beast from 20,000 Fathoms
      Gunsmoke
      Abbott and Costello Go to Mars
      Ma and Pa Kettle on Vacation
      It Came from Outer Space
      East of Sumatra
1954 *Ma and Pa Kettle at Home*
      Ride Clear of Diablo
      Johnny Dark
1955 *Chief Crazy Horse*

The Private War of Major Benson
Kiss of Fire
Lady Godiva
Running Wild
1956 *Never Say Goodbye*
A Day of Fury
Congo Crossing
1957 *The Night Runner*
The Brothers Rico
Operation Mad Ball
1958 *Wild Heritage*
Buchanan Rides Alone
1959 *The Crimson Kimono*
*North by Northwest**
1962 *Cape Fear*
1963 *The Birds*
The Thrill of It All
1964 *Marnie*
1965 *Do Not Disturb*
The Reward
1966 *The Russians Are Coming, the Russians Are Coming*
1967 *Fitzwilly*
How to Succeed in Business Without Really Trying
In Cold Blood
1968 *The Thomas Crown Affair*
1969 *Gaily Gaily**
1970 *The Landlord*
1971 *Fiddler on the Roof**
1972 *Portnoy's Complaint*
1974 *Mame*
1975 *Bite the Bullet*
1976 *Leadbelly*
*The Shootist**
W. C. Fields and Me
1978 *The Big Fix*
1979 *Winter Kills*
1980 *Private Benjamin*
1982 *The Best Little Whorehouse in Texas*

Lookin' to Get Out
1983   *Table for Five*
       Staying Alive
1984   *Rhinestone*
       No Small Affair
1985   *Explorers*
1986   *Jumpin' Jack Flash*
1987   *Dragnet*
1989   *Troop Beverly Hills*

* Academy Award nomination for best achievement in art direction–set decoration.

What is your background? How did you become involved in the film business?
    I wasn't intending to get into film at all when I went to college. I went to USC and graduated in architecture at a time that was very depressed. USC was one of the good architectural schools, and I was able to get a job with an architect. I worked for about a month and he went broke. I worked for three architects in a period of about three months, all of whom went broke. I needed money to live on. I had been interested in theater and was a member of the National Collegiate Players at USC. I hadn't given much thought to film, but through USC you could get jobs as bit players and extras in films. The pay was minimal but I took what I could get. One day at RKO, dressed as an Annapolis cadet waiting to say, "Good night, sir," I looked around and thought, "Well, they build sets; they must have to draw them." So I went to the office of the supervising art director, Van Polglase, and he said, "Have you anything to show?" I said, "I have school projects." I looked around the office and saw all these sketches. I went home and worked all night. I made about fifteen sketches, one right after another, of what I thought a movie set was like. The next day I took those sketches and my school projects into Van, and he said, "They're interesting. I don't have anything right now, but I have a friend over at Paramount." He called Wiard Ihnen at Paramount, and a date was arranged for as soon as I finished the bit part. After three days I finally said my, "Good night, sir," and went over to see Wiard Ihnen, who introduced me to the supervising art director, Hans Dreier. I went to work, and I never looked back.
    In addition to being a great art director in his own right, Hans Dreier was the supervising art director for Paramount during Hollywood's golden era. What was he like?
    Hans Dreier was a Prussian; he had come over from UFA with Ernst Lubitsch, Fritz Lang, and that group. We had a wonderful, real intellectual in Hans Dreier, more so than Cedric Gibbons and all the rest of them in town. Hans Dreier was more of a realist. He was a strong force

who gathered together some oddball characters for art directors. A lot of his people at Paramount were architects like Wiard himself and Robert Odell, but some of the best ones were fine artists like Robert Usher. It was marvelous. Hans had a variety of people, and he would cast them according to the picture.

What were the working conditions at Paramount?

Mostly, we worked under the controlled environment of a studio. It was all designed; we never went out and looked for locations. I still prefer the studio. I don't think it's economical at all to go out on the streets. Nowadays, it's almost impossible to work on city streets. Cities don't want you, residential communities hate you, and the sun comes up in the east and sets in the west, so the light's changing all day long. Why fight that? In the studio, you have control of the light. My most productive years in film were with Hitchcock. He disliked the location chaos and preferred to have control. The only way you could really have the security of control was in the studio situation.

Can you describe how art departments were set up during the studio era?

It was very, very easy to work in the studio in those days, because each studio had a complete complex of arts and crafts and a lot of equipment. Each studio had a staff shop with sculptors, and all the plaster work was done there. Each studio had a paint department and a construction department. They had property departments that were like museums. Each studio went to Europe every year and bought millions of dollars worth of antiques and props that were just there for you to check out. Each studio had a matte department that took care of matte paintings. All of this was within three hundred yards of your office, so you had no problem. You'd come to work in the morning, get your people drawing and drafting, then make the tour of all the departments where work was going on, and end up on your set, where you might have something being built. You could do all this in a very short time. You could do a whole picture.

There was also location work. You'd make your long shot on location, but you didn't have a whole company standing around on a street waiting for you to move the cameras in for the close shot as somebody knocks on the door. In those days if we were shooting in New York on a street, we would shoot somebody driving up to a building in a cab and the next shot you're in the studio. The front door was built to match the location and be a part of the studio-built interior. What you saw out the windows of the interior were painted or photographic backings. We always used to do our own location scouting. Now we have location managers, but in the early days that was the job of the art department and I would sometimes go off for weeks. We had to go through all of that photographing and sending it back to Hollywood. We didn't have fax machines in those days. I thought it was good, because now there is a tendency to pick locations that are more convenient for everybody rather than what's right for the film.

What was the house style in art direction at the various studios?

At MGM it was make everybody feel good. Gibbons and those people didn't care about realism. At MGM shop girls lived in penthouses, but Paramount was very realistic. Richard Day and the people at Fox had a kind of romantic view of life, but it was very sweet, very nice. Fox was doing lovely things, and Richard Day was marvelous. He could do gritty things like *On the Waterfront*, too. Then there were the smaller studios like Universal—you could never depend on their being in any one place at any one time. They did mostly Westerns, then strange things like Ma and Pa Kettles and Abbott and Costello pictures, then *All Quiet on the Western Front*, then the horror cycle. Warner Brothers had their big, flashy musicals and then their gangster periods. Each studio had a kind of a stamp.

Who maintained the look of a studio's house style?

A lot of that was the supervising art directors. The look of a film actually came from the art department. These supervising art directors selected art directors who had a certain kind of a feel. At MGM Cedric Gibbons had people who did his bidding. Their art directors were marvelous, they were expert, they did great things, but they did the bidding of Cedric Gibbons. They couldn't vary from his stamp; they knew where they were.

What was the MGM style under Cedric Gibbons?

It was overblown; it was a kind of modern fairyland. It was all Andy Hardy time; the small towns were lovely. There was one kind of studio stamp if you worked for Cedric Gibbons and another if you worked for Hans Dreier. Obviously, you were influenced by the director, particularly somebody who had the taste of an Ernst Lubitsch or the precision of a Fritz Lang, where everything was Germanic. Of course, if you worked for Julien Duvivier, it was something else. It was, "Oui, oui, monsieur," but you did your own interpretation. The MGM stamp was dictated not only by Cedric Gibbons, but by Louis B. Mayer himself.

Do you think a studio-era mogul like Louis B. Mayer had a substantial impact on the look of a studio's films?

Oh yes, they were sort of generally hated, but I think a lot of people look back with some nostalgia and wish they had some of that unifying force.

How did the art director get assigned to a particular movie?

The supervising art directors had a big office, they read all the scripts, and they assigned you. If a director was particularly happy with somebody, they would request him and usually the supervisor would handle that.

What was the set up at the Paramount art department?

We took one floor of the production building, and we had a big drafting room at the rear where a lot of the work was done. Walter Tyler, Henry Bumstead, Al Nozaki, Boris Leven, and myself were assistants. I was never an art director under Hans Dreier. I became an assistant art director on several pictures, but in those days we called ourselves draftsmen, not even draftspersons, because except for Dorothea Holt, I don't know of any women involved in our area. Then there were the art directors: Johnny Goodman, Ernst Fegte, Bob Usher—a lot of very talented designers and each completely different from the other—a pretty interesting group of guys. Bob Usher later became a monk.

How did the art directors feel about sharing credits on the film with the supervising art director?

There were a lot of complaints about the supervising art director in those days. We all objected to sharing credit with somebody who didn't do any of the work. Once you got assigned, they did nothing on the film. You might take a few drawings into Cedric Gibbons or Hans Dreier and say this is what I plan to do. Generally, you were let alone. Their function was being in charge. There's no longer such a thing as a supervising art director. We got rid of them. Everybody recognized that it was very unfair.

What is your approach to designing in black and white?

Black and white is a little harder to do than color. The difference is you can separate the planes with color, but with black and white you have to separate the planes with values. The cameraman's job in a black and white film is the difficult one, because you separate the planes with light, particularly when you are trying to indicate depth. Anybody can go out and snap a color shot and the planes will just naturally separate by the intensity of the color, but in black and white you have to do it all with value. You have to assess whether a yellow and a light red are going to be different enough in values to separate the planes. There may be a red room in the foreground and behind that you'll have a light gray, and that will separate the planes and help the cameraman. Josef Von Sternberg worked in black and white with a painter on the set all the time. If a very expensive piece of furniture wasn't dark enough, he sprayed it black.

Your first credit is on Saboteur. *It also was the beginning of a long association with Alfred Hitchcock. How did you come to work on the film?*

I wasn't an art director. I was doing some sketching. In those days we weren't tied down to any one thing. You would do illustration, drafting—you did a little bit of everything including supervising on the set. On *Saboteur*, Hitchcock wanted somebody who would do storyboards. I had more of a theatrical background than a lot of art directors, and I also had done storyboards at Paramount. I guess I worked more like a director in that sense, and that's what Hitchcock wanted.

What was it like to work on Saboteur?

Oh, it was the hardest job I ever had. There were a lot of sets, and we had no money. It was done at Universal. In fact, the war broke out when we were working on it; that was when the Japanese bombed Pearl Harbor. We were doing a film about war plants, and suddenly we couldn't get into any war plants for the film; everything had to be synthesized.

Where did you create the military factory?

Right on the lot at Universal. We used one of their storage bins with sliding doors for the factory, and everything inside was a painted backing.

Were the sequences with the truck on the road done in the studio?

Yes, right on Stage Twelve.

What materials did you use to construct the road?

That was mostly paint because it was a concrete floor. Then, we brought in dirt to outline it. When the road got back to where we had miniatures, we had to put a ramp up to accommodate the horizon. By changing some rocks and sagebrush, we had the circus caravan on the same stage. We had two real trucks in the front and a couple of small ones. As we went way back, we had small painted trucks cut out of plywood. We kept diminishing this way down. In the front we had full-sized people, then shorter people, and in the back we had midgets. In those days the little people in Hollywood made a good living doing things like that. I remember a film that had a scene of Washington at Valley Forge, and the soldiers in the background were all midgets because we didn't have the space. It was done on the stage so we had to do a lot of reduced miniatures. That was forced perspective.

How would you define forced perspective, and how is it created?

You're achieving a large space in a limited space. You bring the background up, and you force everything smaller. For the circus caravan scene in *Saboteur*, we not only used midgets in the background, we went beyond that. We had cut-out figures where the arms move, and we had little lights on the arms. They were supposed to be policemen with flashlights way in the background. It was at night, and you could do things like that. I think it was very effective. Those were standard ways of working in those days.

What did you shoot at the Plaza Hotel in New York for North by Northwest?

All we did at the Plaza was the exterior—the entrance by the desk clerk and the telephones in the lobby. We did the rooms in Hollywood. The long hotel corridor was a painted backing of the extension of the corridor we built, and the actors came around in front of the painted backing and over to the room.

That's a forced perspective, isn't it?

That's a forced perspective in a scenic painting. Then we took the same backing and used that for the reverse angle shot. Gibbons had the best scenic artists in the world, no question about it; that was MGM's real claim. There's a story at MGM that they had a set with a road in front of a house. The road went up a slight ramp on a scenic painting, and a horse bolted on the set and ran right through the backing—the horse thought it was real. If you had birds on a big stage, they would fly right into the backing.

Were you influenced by Frank Lloyd Wright when you designed the house that overlooked Mount Rushmore in North by Northwest?

Every architect is influenced by Frank Lloyd Wright. Most people don't realize that the house was all on Stage Five over at MGM. I knew we had to have a house where Cary Grant would be in a precarious position if he was discovered; he had no way out. It also had to be a position where he could see everything in the house: he had to see her bedroom, he had to see the living room, he had to see the balcony over the living room, and he had to be able to get down and get away. It had to be a kind of jungle gym for Cary Grant. So this was not a house we could find. The Fallingwater house, which Frank Lloyd Wright designed, was partly cantilevered, but that wasn't what interested me; it was the stonework in the Fallingwater house, which was horizontal striated stone. That was perfect for somebody to get a handhold and climb up; that's why I selected it. I was really influenced by the handholds. Fallingwater jutted out over a little stream. I made the Mount Rushmore house more extravagant, and I really jutted it out. Of course, in actuality, there is no such place around Mount Rushmore. We did certain tricks, which helped. The long shot of Cary Grant going up to the house was done on a back lot. All we had was a road, and the house was a matte painting. Then there's a closer shot, which is another matte in which you see the maid actually close the window and close the curtain. That piece of film was shot on the stage where we had the actual set. The maid closed the curtain, and then that was reduced and put in the matte. So that's a composite piece of filmmaking there. All the split screen and composite shots used to be done in the studio; now they're all done by special photographic houses like Industrial Light and Magic.

Where was the famous crop duster scene created?

The idea of the scene was very simple—agoraphobia. Hitch wanted to find Cary Grant in a situation where there was no place to hide, so we needed an absolutely flat landscape. I surely thought we'd find it in South Dakota—the plains state—and if we didn't do that, we could drop down to Kansas. So when we were in South Dakota, I went around in an airplane trying to find a place. It looked flat from the air, but you'd get down and that country's all rolling; even Kansas rolls. I was about to give up, and when we got back to Hollywood I said, "My God, Hitch, I was raised on the flattest piece of ground in the world in the San

Joaquin Valley—the Tulare Lake Basin. I used to go there all the time. Wait a minute." I got on the phone; the same day I went up out of Bakersfield, and sure enough, it was what we were looking for.

Was there anything physically done to the location to change it at all?

We planted the corn. There was no corn field there. Then we had bits of studio sets for the bullet hits and where Cary Grant ducks down to escape. That was done in the studio with rear projection.

The climax of North by Northwest *takes place on Mount Rushmore. How was this accomplished?*

We did all of that on the stage. The Department of the Interior said, "We're not going to give you permission to photograph on Mount Rushmore and make fun of the statues." Hitchcock wasn't making fun of the statues, he just wanted to do the scene. But they wouldn't give permission for motion picture photography. They would allow stills. The cable car used by Gutzon Borglum, the sculptor, no longer existed, so it was necessary, aided by ropes, to climb to the top of the mountain where we found rusted cable and a windlass attached to a bosun's chair, which made still photography possible. I was lowered by these cables and was able to photograph in all directions every ten feet down the faces of each of the Presidents. It was, perhaps, the most frightening and dangerous experience in my career as a production designer. We needed the photographs to follow Cary Grant and Eva Marie Saint on a whole course right down to the shoulder. The heads you saw were the photographs I made going down Mount Rushmore. We'd get a long shot and print the actors into it. We only had little pieces of sets. The set pieces needed were just large enough to cover the action and were placed as foregrounds only, in front of the rear projected photos. We built the shoulder, which was in front of a tremendous scenic backing. It was at least a hundred feet long and thirty-six feet high. It was one of the best scenic backings I had ever seen. It still exists at J. C. Baskings. It was a visual effects job. In those days, that was the art department's bailiwick. Now you go to ILM or one of those companies that subcontract special visual effects.

How is a scenic painting done?

In Hollywood the scenic artist used a scenic loft, which allows the hanging canvas to be raised and lowered as needed by the painter. The loft is big and tall; it's like standing in a fly gallery in a theater with the backing being raised and lowered.

What is the function of scenic backings?

I think they are very, very important. I consider openings, entrances, doors, windows, all these orifices in a particular set as the opening onto life and onto the world of the characters. I don't like to forget that there's a world out there, so what you see through the windows and the doors is very important, because that's where the people come from, into the area that you're dramatizing. There's been a tendency in the last several years to overexpose out the window to save money. Very often you'll just see a white nothing, and some cameramen have done that because they don't want the trouble of lighting the backing. If you don't want to see out of the windows, I prefer they close the curtains or the blinds, but don't give me a white space. The cameraman's argument is if you photograph toward a window, it will overexpose because the camera and the film cannot accommodate the light contrast. The human eye sees out of the windows; it's just photography that can't. That is why I use scenic backings, which can be photographed. One must be reminded that there is a life outside of a particular place. I keep hammering on it. Let's remember there's a world and what's happening is happening in that world.

You designed the original Cape Fear *in 1962. The climax of the film takes place on the Cape Fear River. It involves interiors and exteriors of a houseboat, and much of it takes place on the water and in a swamp. Where was that sequence created?*

We actually went to the Cape Fear River and worked out of Wilmington, North Carolina. We had the exterior of the houseboat on the Cape Fear River in Wilmington, but we built the interior in the studio. The big fight at the end in the swamp between Gregory Peck and Robert Mitchum was done on the back lot lake at Universal Studios at night. We had taken fiberglass casts of cypress trees and built them on the lake there at Universal. We had to bulkhead off the whole area so we could heat the water, because we were working at night under very miserable conditions. The current was created by firehoses under the water.

The exterior of the pet shop in the opening shot of The Birds *is on a street in San Francisco. Was that built on location?*

No, I always use that as an example of how to get from a location to a set. Tippi Hedren crosses the street in San Francisco. She passes a poster on a newsstand, and that's a patch match because we take that same poster and put it on a stage. As you pan over to the bird shop, it's now on the stage. It looks like a continuous shot, but it is a patch match. You've segued into the actual set.

Marnie *is the story of a psychologically disturbed young woman. How did you use color to create the atmosphere for her psychological state?*

The main thing was the color red. What we were trying to do was get those colors which evoked certain feelings in Hitchcock. He had a lot of phobias, but he could put them up on the screen—that's part of the Hitchcock touch. I think he felt red related to his own fears. All of his heroines are blondes. I think he felt a blonde was a lady, and dark hair was somebody of a lesser status. He liked green; he didn't like blue.

We used blue, of course—you can't get away from it—but he preferred
green. He felt there was a certain kind of green that was elegant, like
coach green. He even related it to royalty.

So you almost had to work as a color psychologist.

Yes, right.

What is your process for designing a set?

Of course, the first part of the process is the script. I read the script
and very often make quick studies—little sketches—sometimes on the
page opposite the one I'm reading. Then I say, "Where do the people
move, do they come in, and in what manner do they come in? Is this
for suspense reasons or are we just being objective and introducing
people to a particular place?" Then I can begin to do my plot of how
people move in the space, because their movement in the space and the
image size is very important. Whether you see somebody in a big head
close-up or full figure is terribly important. Sometimes you need air and
space around people to make a particular point. Let's say you want to
show a young woman in a big city and show her loneliness. You can
see her sit by the window and show tears running down her cheek, or
you get her out in a big crowd and get a big shot where she's lost in
the crowd. Somehow or another you're going to relate that to italicized
loneliness and work it from there. Now you've got some ammunition
because one director says, "Well, I like the big shot with her lost in the
crowd," and the other one says, "No, I like her to be lonely and hear
some sounds of the city or maybe somebody across the way is playing
music, and I want to be on a big head close-up." These are things that
would be a director's choice. Maybe we've established the neighborhood. If it's in the city, we put another apartment building across the
way outside the window. What's out there has to indicate the kind of
world she's in. Whatever that world is depends on the script. It's very
simple; you plot the action, and this all has to be done in real collaboration with the director. I think the big thing is communication because
it is a collaborative art. I don't care how many auteurs there are around.
Let them try it on their own; they can't. You need a space that's designed
for this particular project. I avoid anybody who says they're the auteur.
The director I would consider in some ways an auteur would be Hitchcock, but he availed himself of all the best help he could get. He was
so secure in his own ability and achievements—you knew this was a
Hitchcock picture. He would listen to his chauffeur; it never bothered
him.

*What is the next step after you have worked out your ideas for the design on
paper?*

Then we have a lot of wonderful help; we have illustrators and set
designers to lay out in graphic form, miniatures, diminished perspective,
mattes, et cetera. All of these have to be drawn and built. I've worked

with the dean of matte painters, Albert Whitlock, many years and have great respect for this highly specialized art.

How would you proceed to work with Albert Whitlock on a matte painting for a set you designed?

It starts with the production designer's concept, and then you get somebody who's such a wonderful painter as Whitlock, and he takes it a step further and makes it better. Suppose it's a big building, a house, or a mansion that you can't afford to build. You're going to build the door of the mansion, and everything else is painted. You make a sketch of the whole composition and you give it to Albert, who adds his own special flavor to it, and it invariably becomes better.

On the screen, the finished result of Whitlock's work usually looks so detailed. Are the paintings very detailed?

No, it's not photographic; it's almost like an Impressionist painting. Some of his paintings are just daubs and dibbles. It's like the pointillist system—the vibration of the paint. There are things that happen with brush strokes. His work is so different and so marvelously alive. That's why I like painted backings instead of photographic blow-ups for what you see out the windows. Personally, I don't like the hard, sharp quality of a photograph because it's dead. Unless a photograph is done by an artist who manages to compose it in such a way that it begins to live, it's a snapshot. As a backing, it has deadness. A painted scenic work has a kind of vibration that happens with paint and doesn't happen with photographic emulsion. There's a big difference. To bring a photograph alive takes a good artist. Otherwise photography can be very dead—truly a still.

What is a hard backing?

Ted Haworth very often does hard backings—cutouts on which he mounts the photographs on plywood. What he gets from that is one plane, and the sky and everything is another plane. So the cutouts are on plywood, and the sky will probably be on cloth. I think Ted does it almost more than anyone else. He's very good at it.

Can a canvas backing be lit from behind, or is it always lit from the front?

Both. In a night scene, the back of the canvas will be painted black, except for those parts you want to project light through—a lighted window or a street light, for instance. Then you will light from back. The light will go through the canvas and give the impression of a lighted window. There are a lot of things you can do. You can even add lights on the front; it can be lit from the front. Bringing life to it is the important thing. I've used photographic blow-ups many times. There are times when they're more convenient. A painted backing needs a little more space to light it. If you haven't got much stage space and you want to work close, you could almost put the photographic backing right on the window and light it.

What is a translight?

It is a translucent photograph that's just like a huge blown-up slide. I have the negative made very sharp—as sharp a negative as you can— but when the print is made, I like to throw it just a little out of focus, because you need that softness; otherwise it's going to be hard. The people who print them hate to do that, because if they keep them for rental, then the next guy says, "I don't like that; it's out of focus." You can't throw a painted backing out of focus, so you put a gauze in front of it, because if something is supposed to be a quarter of a mile away, it's going to need to be softened.

The backgrounds in a Hitchcock film are often on rear-screen projection. Why did Hitchcock shoot the long shots and medium shots of a scene on location, and then shoot the close-ups of the same scene in the studio using rear-screen projection?

That's the only way Hitchcock liked to work. He only wanted to use the rear projection system. He hated locations. He didn't want to spend an extra minute there. Also, when he was dealing with actors, he wanted to be in a controlled situation. He always felt on location he lost control to some degree. There was always a noise you didn't want, an airplane overhead, or the light was not right. He didn't like the inconvenience. If it was too cold or too hot he was miserable, and he wanted his creature comforts—he insisted on them. A lot of the young directors don't mind sitting on a hood of a car and shooting. Everybody has a different system—all kinds of ways to make movies—and there's room for all kinds of movies.

You often have a ceiling on your interior sets, and they usually have a visually dynamic beam structure. What is your philosophy about ceilings?

I like ceilings because that's another dimension to any room. Ceilings are terribly important. Michelangelo recognized that and so did the Pope. I think it is a very important part of the room. Ceilings are some- times a big problem with cameramen. Cameramen hate ceilings. My argument is in these days where you go out and shoot a location, you never complain when they put you in a little room and say, "Shoot it." Then they get marvelous light, bounce light, all kinds of things that are great. One of the problems about Hollywood lighting is every set is rimmed with a scaffold. All the light comes in from the top, and all the actors have this white halo. The light is always coming down. If it's bounce light, the light is coming from a source, hitting the floor going up and around. By the time it hits anything, it's quite diffused. The scaffolding made it easy for the electricians and the grips to work high and get out of the way of the camera, but you get on a location and they work it out. I like to nail the top down if I can, but sometimes you're with a cameraman who says, "Well, it's going to take me another day to light it," and they'll outmaneuver you.

Hitchcock's principal cameraman, Robert Burks, liked to work with a ceiling, didn't he?

Yes, Bob and I had a long relationship, and we could talk out almost anything. He was very malleable and very good. Now a lot of these cameramen are very good. They manage to work with location lighting, but they still would like to hang the lights up high. The beam is kind of traditional in Hollywood because you hide lights. Also, if you put in a beam, you could put a ceiling in back, but you could take the front ceiling off. So, although I prefer to nail them on, most ceilings are demountable because you have to be a bit cooperative with the cine-matographer. If you're not showing the ceiling, why have it in, but generally, I like it because then you're prepared for everything.

Do you consider the costume department part of the art department?

Yes, the art department is the umbrella, and the production designer is the umbrella head for the visual, physical aspects of the film. Since you have to coordinate the costumes with the sets, you've got to ac-commodate for color and the values—dark against light or light against dark. I personally work very closely with the costume designer.

How do you work with the set decorator?

The decorator is particularly important in Hollywood. The decorator is valuable and should be a part of the team. There's the decorator, the costume designer, the property master—these are all people who have to be coordinated. The position of the production designer is in seeing that it is a collaborative effort, making sure it has a unity when it's all finished. The costumer can't go off and design costumes and the dec-orator say, "This is what I want," when you have gone over the whole project from reading the script to conferring with the director. If a dec-orator wants to go off on his or her own, that's of no value. It must be done in very close collaboration. At the beginning of any picture, I usually have several days where I just go through the property depart-ment. If it's a modern or contemporary picture, I go with the decorator to stores where you can either rent or buy pieces. Very often you're working with somebody you've worked with before, so you understand each other. The decorator is essentially somebody who has taste but is able to adapt. You have to forget yourself a lot. You're interpreting the character. I know a very good decorator who worked with me who felt if he could be a method decorator and put himself into the characters—that would be it.

On reflection, having studied architecture at USC, can you perceive how your education ultimately prepared you for your career as a production designer?

I was fortunate; I went to school in the classic period. We were mem-bers of the Paris Beaux Arts, so this meant a very traditional background, but at the same time, foreign students were coming in with new thoughts on the international style of Walter Gropius, which they had gotten from the Bauhaus, so we were on the threshold of change. When we went into movies, we found this invaluable, because movies are inclined to use a mix of traditional and modern backgrounds. We had to be very eclectic. Except for a basic sense of structure, there's nothing you find in school that really prepares you for production design any more than studying a course in literature is exactly what you need to become a screenwriter. You have to take the skills you collect along the way and adapt them to the whole collaborative art of filmmaking, which is all dependent upon one thing: that script. We're creating a physical environment. I have to say physical environment rather than architecture or background or sets; it's a total physical environment that interprets the script. What you're doing is designing spaces for action; that's what we're really trying to do.

There really is nothing that you're going to learn in a school to prepare you to build a cardboard shack under an overpass in a modern urban setting. You don't learn that in school, but you learn it because you go to see how the homeless live. You note that, because even in a homeless cardboard carton there's a sense of structure, so your architectural background plays on that. You don't have to be an architect; you can come from fine arts, but fine arts has its own rules of structure and composition. Everything has to have a workable standard. You have to feel that it *can be* unless the script says do something that *can't be*. If the script says this is about a homeless person, you better do it within the parameters of the logic of the homeless. I always start with the economics of the characters. Very often they are not indicated in the script. You read a script. The first thing I ask is how much do these people make, what can they afford, because economics are the basis of our lives. Then I want to know who their friends are. I want to know what their educational background is: Did they go to college, did they drop out of high school, are they from the streets, or are they more earthy, country people? Then there's that whole range of sexual choice: Are they heterosexual or homosexual? You have to know all this before you can sit down with a pencil and start to draw. At one point, it's your picture; you are the director. You can't design a film if you don't work from the director's viewpoint. It's very easy to make films that show off design. The problem is to exert some discipline. Essentially, if we are worthy of the name *production designer*, we are responsible for the main look of the environment of the film. My concern is for interpreting the film.

2

Ted Haworth

Ted Haworth entered show business when a stage production in Cleveland, Ohio, featuring his brother-in-law, Wallace Ford, required a twelve-year-old actor. Haworth's family has a fertile heritage in the theater. In addition to Wallace Ford, who went on to be one of Hollywood's venerable character actors, his uncle Joseph Haworth was a leading Shakespearean actor, and his father was a playwright.

When his family moved to California in 1936, Ted Haworth, then in his last year of high school, decided not to pursue a life in the theater. He had always loved to draw and paint, so he began to study art at night.

In 1940, Haworth began to work in film as a production illustrator. His burgeoning talent was nourished by the production designers Gordon Wiles and William Cameron Menzies. Under Menzies's tutelage, Haworth learned how to conceive a film shot for shot by creating a detailed production storyboard, which the director could use as a blueprint to shoot a film.

Menzies introduced Haworth to Alfred Hitchcock, a director who preplanned his films down to the smallest detail. Haworth immediately gained Hitchcock's respect as the art director on *Strangers on a Train*. When the director fell behind schedule, he asked Haworth to design and direct the second unit on the classic carousel sequence, which is the climax of the film.

In addition to Hitchcock, Haworth has worked with many fine directors, including William Wyler, John Huston, Robert Wise, Richard Brooks, Joshua Logan, Sidney Pollack, John Frankenheimer, and Paul Mazursky. He has had long, artistically fulfilling relationships with directors Don Siegel and Sam Peckinpah and the writer Paddy Chayefsky. He designed *Batteries Not Included* for executive producer Steven Spielberg and worked with Spielberg to rebuild a section of the historic Universal Studios lot destroyed by fire in 1990.

The production designer of over fifty films, Haworth has designed such classics as *Some Like It Hot, The Longest Day, Invasion of the Body Snatchers, The Professionals, Marty,* for which he received an Academy Award nomination, and *Sayonara,* for which he received the Oscar for best art direction–set decoration. He has been in the film industry for six decades.

In addition to his long list of credits, Haworth has continued to use his considerable skill a production illustrator, designing continuity storyboards for such films as *War of the Worlds, Stalag 17, War Games,* and *Brainstorm.*

Although the work of Ted Haworth can be seen in his fine art direction, there is a hidden artistry in the thousands of production illustrations and storyboards that have come from Haworth's fine hand and are a universe unto themselves. These creations reveal the wondrous promise of the films to come.

1951 *Strangers on a Train*
1952 *Mutiny*
1953 *I Confess*
      His Majesty O'Keefe
1955 *Marty**
1956 *Friendly Persuasion*
      Four Girls in Town
      Invasion of the Body Snatchers
1957 *Sayonara***
1958 *I Want to Live*
      The Goddess
      The Naked and the Dead
1959 *Middle of the Night*
      Some Like It Hot
1960 *Pepe*
      Who Was That Lady?
1961 *The Outsider*
1962 *Escape from East Berlin*
      The Longest Day
1964 *Ride the Wild Surf*

Wild and Wonderful

What a Way to Go!

1965 *The Glory Guys*

1966 *The Professionals*

Seconds

Maya

1967 *The Way West*

1968 *Half a Sixpence*

Villa Rides

1969 *Those Daring Young Men in Their Jaunty Jalopies*

1970 *The Kremlin Letter*

1971 *The Beguiled*

1972 *Jeremiah Johnson*

The Getaway

Junior Bonner

1973 *Pat Garrett and Billy the Kid*

1974 *Claudine*

Harry and Tonto

1976 *The Killer Elite*

The Sailor Who Fell from Grace with the Sea

1977 *Telefon*

Cross of Iron

1978 *Somebody Killed Her Husband*

1979 *When You Comin' Back, Red Ryder?*

Bloodline

1980 *Rough Cut*

1981 *Carbon Copy*

Death Hunt

1982 *Jinxed*

1983 *The Osterman Weekend*

1984 *Blame It on the Night*

1985 *The Legend of Billie Jean*

1986 *Poltergeist II: The Other Side*

1987 *Batteries Not Included*

1992 *Mr. Baseball*

*Academy Award nomination for best achievement in art direction–set decoration.

**Academy Award for best achievement in art direction–set decoration.

What skills do you think are necessary to be a good production designer?

It's a happy cross between an illustrator, an architect, and an engineer. Without a drawing skill you can call yourself a production designer, but in fact you're really not.

What do these skills offer to the director of a film?

The director doesn't always have the luxury to sit and concentrate on exactly what he wants to do with a sequence. With the director's encouragement, the production designer can create the best sequence in the picture out of what was the worst sequence in the picture. If they get along wonderfully well, the production designer gets the chance to really illuminate the director's best notions of what he would like to do with one scene. He can come up with a totally fresh and different concept—a way of opening or closing the picture or taking a sequence that especially troubles the director. The storyboard is a springboard to what the director wants. The production designer can research what the director has in the script and put it all together in a workable, cutable sequence. It's a great opportunity for production designers to share that awful load a director has with finishing the screenplay, casting, and the budget. Along with the cameraman, the production designer usually can come up with quite a handsome picture, something memorable that people take with them out of the theater.

How did you first get involved in show business?

My father had been a playwright in Cleveland, Ohio. My uncle was Joseph Haworth, one of the great Shakespearean leading men at the turn of the century. I started as an actor on the stage when I was twelve years old. My brother-in-law was Wallace Ford, and I got into a production with him in Cleveland, Ohio, that needed a twelve-year-old boy.

How did you become a production designer?

I had been painting and drawing for years. My family came out to California in 1936, and I was in the last year of high school. I didn't like acting. I didn't want to follow in that path. So I started to draw more and more. I studied at night school. I did a lot of portraits and illustrated some books. I loved the idea of illustrations for films. I started as an illustrator around 1940 and just never stopped. I would storyboard with the director, and eventually he would say, "Why aren't you production designing this picture? I'd rather have you than the man I've got." I began to work directly with the directors, not for art directors. Then I met a wonderful production designer, Gordon Wiles, who had a very serious form of cancer. The King Brothers kept paying him even though he was in the hospital. So I would take my sketches over to the hospital and show them to him. He used to look at my sketches and say, "Oh, I could do card tricks with those." He would tell me things I should do with the sketches. After he died, I went to work for Bill Menzies, and

Bill kept saying to people of consequence in the business he couldn't do the picture but they ought to give me a break. It got back to Hitchcock and to people who took me out of the small independent field and gave me bigger and bigger features to do.

Do you credit Menzies with trailblazing the profession of the production designer as we now know it?

Menzies told me how it all started. When he was very young, he would start drawing a sled in the snow, and then he would not be happy with finishing the sketch. He'd have to go and get an ironing board and put it on the top step and go down the steps, because he said, "I had to know what it felt like before I could draw it." Then, he would go back and finish the sketch. He didn't have to have snow; he could always make something out of nothing. If an art director was to design a front door of a church, they would go to great lengths to make the tallest door you ever saw or do some trick with it to make it look outstanding, and then hope the cameraman or the director would say, "We love that set-up; that's exactly the shot we want." Menzies would do a door that was three inches thick, had a piece of iron on it, and maybe a key sticking out of it, but the door would only be ten feet high because you would want the camera to be reasonably close to the actor coming out of the door. Then to insinuate this was a church, he'd have a little platform of stone steps, all of this tailored to the camera, not forty or a hundred feet back, which you would have to jump cut to get into. As the door creaked open, pigeons would fly out. You thought you saw a door a hundred feet high, but you didn't. The feeling and the whole notion of a church was there.

The directors that Menzies worked for would not want to be on the stage without Bill there. They would not want to shoot a difficult scene without sketches. Bill literally would trim the shot to exactly what he wanted to show and spend the money on. If the cameraman said, "Well, couldn't we dolly into this?" that was the set-up and the director gave Menzies carte blanche. He had that power; he had that ability. The director never failed to make the most of it. They would inspire Bill. He could take the most ordinary thing in a picture and make it so cinematically fascinating. He had a way of dividing the motion picture screen, taking big patterns, and using those patterns for foreground and background. In the simplest of close-ups, you had the longest of long shots combined. Bill Menzies's philosophy was that if you were going to show a close-up, make it closer than any close-up has ever been. If you are going to make a long shot, make it a longer long shot than anyone else has ever done. Nobody could do what he did, just nobody. There were a lot of people who illustrated every bit as well as Menzies—David Hall, Harland Fraser—but the first use of the title of production designer was when David O. Selznick gave Menzies the credit on *Gone with the Wind*. At that time, Menzies was not in the Society of Motion Picture Art Directors, and after *Gone with the Wind*, they realized what an advantage it would be if they could get him to join. Bill wasn't about to join except they offered him a lifetime honorary membership in acknowledgment of all of his wonderful work. The minute that Bill joined, all of the art directors suddenly became production designers. Now they more or less owned the title, because Bill was a member of their society. All the top art directors felt they could do what Menzies did. Well, there was only one person who could do what Menzies did, and that was William Cameron Menzies.

You worked with Alfred Hitchcock on Strangers on a Train *and* I Confess. *He was a director known for extensive preplanning. How did Hitchcock communicate ideas to you?*

His way of communicating was to sit down and literally draw three lines and say, "Do you have the idea?" He would never go any further than he had to, to get the composition in your mind. He had a great sense of line—that was his language. When I met Menzies and Hitch I found out right away that if I followed the pattern they laid out, I did the best sketch I ever made in my life. It was visual excitement. When you look at a floor plan or a piece of architecture, it's not visually exciting. It's what's happening to it that makes it visually exciting. Those lines had composition; they had light and dark. Hitch didn't spend an ounce of time more than he had to to convey the idea.

How did you work with Hitchcock on the design for an interior set?

I would make sketches, and Hitch would approve or not approve them. Hitch was one of the few directors who knew *exactly* what it was going to be by the time he went on the set. He would say, "I need space here because when two people are angry, they almost always distance themselves from each other and start yelling." You knew he wanted to have a staircase connected to the staircase upstairs, the scale of the staircase, the look of it. You knew at what point on the staircase Hitch was going to stop the actor to look back at the dog, at what point you wanted the actor to get up to the door of the bedroom he is going to start to open, and at what point you cut to a set that is down on the stage floor and how you match the two together. Hitch kept it alive in your mind. He would say, "I would imagine if I were to open that door, there would be a staircase going down three or four steps, but since we don't have the actress doing that, you would have pictures on the wall and no hole for her to walk down into." He could look at a plan and wouldn't let you spend the money on digging a hole in the stage floor. He'd go over and open the door, and say, "Just as I suspicioned." He would sit down and think about what he wanted to do with the set in detail. He would say, "Everybody get lost for a few minutes," and chase everybody out of the room but never the art director. He was just an absolute gem to work for.

How did Hitchcock feel about having a ceiling on an interior set?

Hitch would not allow them to build a set without a ceiling, because he felt it was always best to play the actors against the simplest and most dramatic background. He always wanted to make it look like the actor's every move and gesture was clear and wasn't compounded by a busy background. Bob Burks and other cameramen moved just as fast if there was a ceiling or not. A lot of times a ceiling tempts them to do a more natural look rather than overlighting for any eventuality.

The ceiling is also a natural way of getting light into the room.

Yes, by bouncing a single source of light off the ceiling, it does a pretty good job of painting a room with light. Now with fast film, it's even an easier task. You just don't need that hot, heavy, overlit look. Hitch and Menzies would go crazy with things they could do today.

Where were the train sequences for Strangers on a Train *filmed?*

We built everything for the interior of the train in the studio, and they were all photographed against a process screen. We didn't do anything on a real train.

What was your involvement on the process work for the film?

I would do the process plates with the cameraman, Fred Koenkamp, because the first unit wasn't needed for that. Koenkamp was just a pleasure to work with, because he knew every trick in optical printing, process, and blue screen that had been invented at that time. He was what we called the Stage Five cameraman who did all of those difficult shots. Since Hitch had picked all of the set-ups and angles, they weren't malleable, they were tenacious and fixed. Koenkamp and I knew that, so there was no room for saying, "Well, maybe it ought to be a little freer and looser."

Were all the sets for the train built next to each other on the stage?

They usually are because the sequence belongs together. They tried their best to keep continuity as close as possible, so they could move from one set to the other.

How often were you on set while Hitchcock was shooting?

I would try to be with the shooting crew twenty minutes of every day. I'm usually on what they are going to do next rather than where they are shooting. When they were shooting, if I could afford to be there, I was there.

During the climactic scene in Strangers on a Train, *Farley Granger and Robert Walker fight on a carousel that has gone awry. How were you involved in the creation of this scene?*

Hitch was a week behind schedule, and we were coming closer and closer to doing that sequence. The studio called him in and said, "We've

got to get back on schedule. We're going to recommend something."
He said, "I've long since determined that Mr. Haworth will do the second
unit. Nobody is to interfere with that." That was the end of all of the
guys they probably had been lining up for weeks to direct this sequence.
He said, "Mr. Koenkamp will be the cameraman. I shall have them on
one stage, and I shall be across the street on another stage. When I
finish with Bobby Walker and Farley Granger, I'll send them over. They'll
change costumes, shoot the scene, and then send them back to me
immediately." He then told me I had to do it. I said, "Hitch, why do
you have this faith in me? I'm not a member of the Directors Guild
anymore. I let my dues go." He said, "I shall oblige you on that. When
you're ready to shoot, I'll stand by the stage door. I won't interfere with
a thing you've been doing, and I'll just say roll 'em and action. When
you're done, you can say cut or hold your hand up and I'll say cut."
Every shot he wanted to make in that sequence was painstakingly laid
out. When he got all done with the preproduction, I knew all the details
that went into it. I studied how the merry-go-round could break down.
I had to make sure that the practical way the merry-go-round goes off
its tilt could be incorporated in just one shot. I did that sequence all by
myself; they were his sketches—his determination of what I should
shoot—but I did it. Hitch had directed everything from the guy climbing
underneath the speeding merry-go-round up to the merry-go-round
breaking down and collapsing. The minute the two actors got on the
merry-go-round, it was my turn to take them and do exactly what Hitchcock asked me to do: the horse's hoof coming down on the actor's face,
the madness of the points of view. It was all wonderful.

How many shots were there in the carousel sequence?
Ninety to 110 separate shots.

*What parts of the carousel set did Hitchcock have to work with for the shots
he directed?*
We had the full-size carousel, so that Hitch could jump people on and
off the moving carousel. The man crawling underneath the carousel was
shot out on the ranch where we had the whole carnival set.

*What elements of the set did you use to shoot the fight sequence on the moving
carousel?*
The minute we got on the merry-go-round, we were not on a real
merry-go-round. Everything was photographed against a process
screen. The carousel wasn't turning. We just had the sections of it we
needed; then we could do anything we wanted. We controlled the area
we wanted and were photographing it against all of the fast background
movement on the process screen. Sometimes we'd just be moving the
inside area or just three horses in the background that could go as fast
or as slow as we wanted. The speed of the editing made everything
look like the merry-go-round went faster and faster. When Farley Gran-

ger was holding onto the rail of the merry go-round and his body was hanging off, I had a platform that went in and just hung right underneath. The carousel that collapsed and broke was a miniature that we built.

Was Hitchcock very specific about what lens should be used for a particular shot?

Hitch always had a philosophy about a point of view shot, which I had to adapt to. He never wanted the actor to be further away than the person looking at them, so he used a 70mm lens. He sat opposite me at a desk once and said, "I'll teach you about a point of view. Look at me with a 25mm lens. Now, tell me if I get bigger or smaller." I said, "You're smaller." He said, "Well, put a 50mm on it." I said, "You're a little smaller, but not so small." He said, "Put a 70mm on it." I put a 70mm on it and he said, "I'm the same size, aren't I?" It was really incredible. If people are talking to each other and you do an individual shot of what is supposed to be one person's point of view, it will have to be a 70mm lens. So you have this indulgence of continuity that is just incredible.

How did you capture the authentic atmosphere of New York City on Marty?

The budget was only $350,000. United Artists didn't have any faith in the picture at all. The producer Harold Hecht said to me, "I want you to do everything in your power to get Paddy Chayefsky and the director Delbert Mann to shoot the picture entirely in California." Paddy and Delbert came to Los Angeles from New York to see what I had found in the way of locations. On the first day I said, "Paddy, don't nail me on these locations. You're seeing the most look-alike locations I can show you, but I am dead against doing the picture in California. You can't get that New York look here." So I showed them the locations and we went back to Harold, who said, "Well boys, how do you feel?" Paddy, being such a fox, turned around and said, "Well, Ted will tell you how we feel." I looked at them and I said, "Look Harold, this picture is dead if we don't go to New York for a week—it's dead. Paddy and Del didn't convince me of it. I know I can do everything when it comes to interiors—I can do the front porch of the house, the church, the dance hall—but there are thirty-nine sets in this picture, and unless you set them with the exterior moments, you're not going to believe it. If you don't believe it, this picture is doomed—it's not television." Harold said, "Well, who's fighting going to New York?" So we did a week's work in New York, and all the rest was done on a soundstage over at Goldwyn Studios. The sets ended up costing $57,000. Paddy loved and knew New York so well. I'm capable of doing that wonderful look of New York, but only at the inspiration of somebody like Paddy who says, "We've got to have it. Don't let them tell you there isn't money for this set or we only want three walls—I'll get the money. Every time I walk on a set of Ted Haworth's, I want to feel that I'm back in New York," and boy, he got it. On every picture we did together in New York, Paddy would take me around and show me all these places. I must have done ten to fifteen bar and nightclub sets for *Bachelor Party*, and every one of them is someplace that Paddy and I sat and talked in.

Where did you get the idea for the design of the pods in Invasion of the Body Snatchers?

I got the idea one night when I was sitting at a friend's house, looking at a pair of drapes which had a sort of a skeleton of leaves in autumn on them. I went home that night, and I made the first pod. My wife had just had a baby, and I wanted to give the whole impression of a baby being born, so this slithering image came out and the foam kept pouring out. It was a combination of looking at that curtain, a bubble bath, and of the idea of doing it without special effects. Both the director, Don Siegel, and the producer, Walter Wager, didn't want to have a lot of special optical tricks. They wanted to do everything they could right there and then on the soundstage. I took a bunch of hairpins and put a texture on it with cobwebbing so that you could color it like an autumn leaf. When I got through sculpting, it was like a great big puffed-out autumn leaf. Then I did it on the stage full-size. I had built the lath-and-glass house for the greenhouse, and I set it all up. I had these slats on the roof so that slatted moonlight would come through and give you an atmosphere of the place. Don Siegel said, "I want to feel it's all happening under that table." I said, "I think you're going to feel what's going to happen under the table." They got the camera going and Don said, "Go ahead, let's see your action." The pod started to foam. Don began to watch it and said, "Well, how far is this going to go?" He started to go back and he tipped over a whole table, and this thing was still working. He climbed out of the wreckage and said, "My God, it's just wonderful."

How did you create the illusion that people were being re-created inside the pods?

I took all of the actors, and I cast them with a very fine mold, like a dental plaster, which gave a perfect cast of the entire body from head to toe. The poor actors; we had straws up their nose so they could breathe, and the plaster heats up after a while, it gets very warm. When we were done, we had a perfect likeness of everybody.

How did you work with Don Siegel during the shooting of Invasion of the Body Snatchers?

Don was wonderful to work with. One day he said, "Where's that sketch you made of the living room with the guy sleeping on the couch?" "Oh," I said, "It's someplace in the art department." He said, "We're shooting it. Go get it." I came back ten or fifteen minutes later, and they'd already made the set-up. Don looked at the sketch and said to the cameraman, Elly Fredericks, "Elly, here's the set-up. Pick the camera up and bring it over here." We went right back to the sketch with no wailing from the crew, who was ready to go onto the next set-up. That was our first picture together. It's one of the great horror films of all time. I think the whole picture cost about $320,000. Don and I did many together after that.

You have created production storyboards for many films. How did you work with Paul Mazursky to storyboard the script for Harry and Tonto *prior to shooting the film?*

I was stunned that Paul Mazursky would want production story-boarding on *Harry and Tonto*, because there was so little action. The first thing we did was to find all of the locations for the picture in New York, Chicago, Las Vegas, and the Grand Canyon. Back in the studio, we did the sketches working from photos. Every day at noon, Paul Mazursky would come in and sit down for an hour. He talked about every shot in the picture months ahead of shooting. He would go through one sequence with me. There was never anybody else in the room. We would rough it out almost as you dictate to a secretary. He would bounce things off me and I would mirror them back. Paul was very explicit about the size of the image. He would say, "I'd like to be on those two guys talking," or "I would like to be dollying with them, except you don't feel the dolly; you want to feel that you're going with them. You have to be low enough to get the cat on the sidewalk and high enough just to get the top of his head." He came to a fixed conclusion of what he would do with that location. We'd make pencil notes, and when we got done, I would go into the work and complete it. Paul would come in the next day and look at the sketches as he reread the script. He rarely changed things. When he eventually shot the film, he practically didn't deviate from the storyboard at all. The storyboards were his personal notes. Paul was the most disciplined craftsman I'd come across in years. Paul has a great comprehension of where and how everything will fit. He precuts a picture more than anyone else I know.

How did you work with Mazursky during the shooting of Harry and Tonto?

There wasn't one set built in the whole picture. I would get things ready for him. When we were all ready and he was shooting on a location, he'd send me to the next one. So when he got there, the phone booth was where it was supposed to be; everything that he asked for was just the way he wanted it. A lot of people wanted to get to the next location. Paul said, "Nobody knows what I want except Teddy. Get him there as quick as you can." I was on the plane the next day. When he got all through the picture, he did a marvelous thing for the cameraman and me. The studio said, "Paul, you've gone all across the United States and you've finished seven to ten days ahead of schedule; how have you done it?" Paul said, "Don't give me any credit; the credit belongs to

Teddy Haworth and my cameraman." I thought, "How many guys in 112 Hollywood would do that?" At the end of the picture I was saying goodbye to him, and he put his arms around me and said, "At the end of every picture, I'm ready for the hospital; at this moment I feel like I've been on a vacation. I knew what I was going to do every day, every hour. I know how it's going to go together, and I know people are going to love it. Let me tell you, you've given me one of the greatest treats of my life."

Where did you find the house that was used for the exterior of the Southern Gothic mansion in The Beguiled?

The studio wanted to do the opening of that picture at the Disney ranch, where they build a lot of sets. They insisted that if I were going to production design the picture I go out there with Don Siegel and look at it. So Don and I went out and looked at it. The head of the art department, Alex Golitzen, was with us. We were all going back in this big limo. Don's quiet, I'm quiet, and Alex is saying, "You can take the house down, and as far as the trees are concerned, we can get that long hanging stuff from northern California and put it on all of the trees." Finally I said, "Well, we can get a three-foot-high guy who looks like Clint Eastwood, we'll get a dog to look like a horse, and he'll go riding under those trees." Alex said, "They look almost as good as the trees back in Louisiana." I said, "Those don't look anything like the trees in Louisiana. It looks like a park. It doesn't look like the wilderness in Louisiana during that period. Did they have lawn mowers back in 1860?" Alex was fit to be tied. He said, "You mean you don't want to do the picture?" and I said, "If you're going to do it there, no, Alex, I don't want to do the picture, plain and simple." Don said, "Supposing we gave you a week in Louisiana to find a better exterior of a house and better exteriors for the battle scene, would that change your mind?" I said, "I think I can do it in a day or two; I don't need a week. If I can't find better than that, you've won the case. I just think it's in the best interest of the film." That night a guy was waiting at the airport, took me to his house, and showed me all of the antebellum houses in Louisiana on both sides of the river. I said, "I think they're too much like *Gone with the Wind*." So I went out the next morning; it was so foggy you couldn't see anything. We got to a place where the guy said, "There's a railroad track here. I'm not going to go across those tracks, because we might be hit by a train." So we sat there, and slowly the fog on the Mississippi lifted. We literally went around the block for about a half a mile, and here's this fantastic house. I said, "Well, it's too pretty to photograph from the sunlight side, but from the back side with back light all of the time, it will be just the Gothic touch that we need." So Don came that night, and we went out the next morning. He bought it just like that and told the studio that he wouldn't consider shooting back at the Disney park. So you know my name was mud at Universal for years. When it played in Paris, the lines were around the block.

The Getaway isn't a Western, but it has that dusty atmosphere that gives it a Western quality. How do you get that kind of a look?

That was typical of Sam Peckinpah. He didn't like anything that didn't have a considerable amount of age on it. All age is is dust. In New York it's black; here in California, it's the color of the earth. You would show Sam a wooden wagon some painters had worked on to make it look old, and he would throw a fit if it was not right—the same with costumes. The costume people and the painters had to work like insane people on Peckinpah pictures. In Europe it's called patina. Without patina, Sam just wouldn't shoot it.

What are some of the techniques to age wood?

You paint it over with one coat of a material called asphaltum. It's still wet because asphaltum doesn't dry right away. Then you paint the color of driftwood right over the asphaltum. In a very short period of time, the paints start to mix together, and they bring out all of the texture of the wood with the asphaltum bleeding through so it begins to look more and more like unpainted or raw wood. That's the quickest way to get a log cabin to look seventy, eighty years old. The whole phase in painting today is to go with acrylics because it's so fast, but you can't really age it as well. For the acrylic technique, they try to catch the high points of the wood by painting on top of dry paint with a brush, but it doesn't look the same. It has an entirely different, almost unnatural look to it. You can almost see the brush strokes.

How do you age stone?

With stone you put on a coat of paint that will get into the darkest areas and then a lighter tone. You wipe the stone until it has the natural exterior grain of the texture. The dark sediment settles into the dimples of the stone. I had to create a huge cave for *Poltergeist II*, and it all had to look like natural stone. We did it all with foam, which we carved to look like all of the forms we needed. If you paint through the colors that are underneath and then wipe it, you're revealing two or three different colors. You can get a very natural look, especially where there has been sediment of water running through it. It's just another technique, but today you have to get the older painters in to do that; the younger guys don't want to take the time. Lately, if we have to get a set aged down and they've used acrylics, I have them take about 2 percent India ink, 98 percent water, and spray it on the set. They wash it down so that the natural black tone of age sinks right into the texture of that wall, and you don't have to wipe it—it's got runs where the natural runs would be. I've seen them take two guns, one with the darker tone and one with water, and work it down until it runs the whole length of an exterior building. This India ink is marvelous, because you can take a white jacket and knock it down two tones. You can't even see that with the human eye, but the cameraman won't get a flare off of it anymore. You dodge it, you try to just take the edge off of it.

In Cross of Iron *the bunkers and command centers look like they were really underground. How were they built?*

I got the research in Zagreb for the interiors of the emergency base stations that the Germans had made. They couldn't have been made in concrete, because the Germans were constantly moving or retreating. We took real logs used for underground fortification, and we cast them in fiberglass so they were all lightweight. They were perfectly painted and looked like eight tons of logs, but everything that looked like wood was really fiberglass. I was always very close to a whole group of special effects men, great ones like Augie Lohman. I learned the trick of taking a set and laying it on a foundation of two-by-twelve vertical flooring, but sealed top and bottom with plywood. It was smooth. You could lift the whole thing up with jacks and then put big truck innertubes underneath it, so that when you put the set back down on the innertubes, you could have it absolutely stable just putting braces all around it or absolutely instable by pulling the braces off and relying on the innertubes. Then you could make the set shake, and dust would come down through the rafters and beams creating the illusion of an underground bunker.

The actors really were scared to be under there, because above them, it looked as if we had almost carved it out of the earth itself. It was really claustrophobic. It almost hurt me more to stand and watch it than to be in there, because if anything went wrong it was my stupidity. You couldn't believe the way this stuff would hold together. The minute the shot was finished, they would go in and cinch it up again. You had to do it all day long, and it never came apart.

What was it like to work in the Utah wilderness on Jeremiah Johnson?

The studio said we were insane to try and shoot in the snow. They said, "You're never going to get a shot. It's impossible to work in the snow. It's four and five feet deep at times. You're out of your minds!" Sidney Pollack was determined to get summer, winter, spring, and fall into his picture, so he shot at the end of summer into the beginning of fall and then shot all of the winter sequences until spring. He really got a wonderful kind of an environment out in the wilderness. There were some great locations that we picked where the roads were closed off and there was six feet of snow, but we got these marvelous vehicles called Snowcats. We got four of them and put truck ends on the back end of them, so you could stow all the lamps and generators. We would take off every day in one of those things to any location that was difficult and shot just tremendous footage up in those mountains.

How did you work in snow six feet deep?

I had a lot of problems; I had to invent an awful lot. I had done a picture in Sweden where we went all the way up practically to the pole, so I learned to work in snow. Each experience teaches you things. In *Jeremiah Johnson*, Jeremiah had to ride around the old man's cabin and out of sight. It sounds simple, but the snow is deep and the horse would break its legs. So I said, "Well, if I laid a cyclone fence on top of the snow, could a horse walk on it?" We rolled out a big cyclone fence, and at lunch the horses came over and walked across it. Sidney said, "I think you've got the answer." I said, "We should put it down about six inches so that there is no chance of seeing it. You stake out the exact area you want the horses to go, and when you come back in the morning, that will all be underneath the snow." So we stayed up there right into the darkness and got all of this fence down. We got up the next morning and put a fresh coat of snow all over the fence and flattened it out smooth. It worked like an absolute charm.

How did you design and build all the log cabins that are in the film?

I designed and prebuilt all those cabins before anybody came up, so they could be mobile and put wherever they thought was the best spot. We numbered all of the logs, so they would go right back together. In a day, you could put the cabin there dressed.

Do you think you have a style as a production designer?

I have a strong recognizable style in my sketches, and if I can carry it off into the picture—that's my style. I've been exposed to all styles from Willy Wyler to Otto Preminger to Sam Peckinpah. I know how each of them would do it, and each would do it differently. If I have any style, it's not mine, it's borrowed. It's a piece of all these wonderful people that I've had so much fun with—Don Siegel, Hitch—they all bring that out in you. They let you do what you think is in the best interest of the picture.

How much preproduction time do you get on a film?

Since salaries have gone up and up and up, the preproduction time on a picture becomes less and less. If they can possibly do it, they'll bring in a location manager to find a location.

Do you feel it's important for the production designer to find the locations?

I want to choose it. Whether it's anyplace in the world I want to do 85 percent of the survey. On *Sayonara*, Marlon Brando read the script and said to Josh Logan and Bill Goetz, "If the picture is going to be ready by the third of January, you've got me, and if it isn't ready, forget it." I had from the twenty-third of December until the second of January to be ready to shoot the picture in Japan. That was the challenge of my lifetime. I had to separate what we could do in the studio and what we could do in Kyoto. I was there before the company arrived and started to shoot. I had a chance to get things ready for the director.

In addition to all your years of studio experience, you have also worked on location in many countries all over the world. How has that enriched you as a designer?

Whether it's being left in a garden that has a big iron gate around it and wild elephants are standing up on the hill waiting to get to the lake that you're standing right in front of, or Yugoslavia, or a place like Tokyo or India, what you see in real life starts to tell a story better than the script you're shooting. You go half-mad trying to get some of those things into the picture. It is a terrible challenge, but enrichment-wise I wouldn't have missed a day of it.

What do the many members of the art department contribute to the work of the production designer?

They are a part and a party of the best you can do. There are a lot of wonderful storyboard people and illustrators who are, in fact, production designers. There are wonderful decorators who should be art directors. When you are working with truly gifted set dressers, you realize how vulnerable you are if suddenly they weren't so good. The whole idea can come down like a house of cards. Production designers come up the hard way from the dusty, dirty gravel roads, and in the process, you begin to know the people that are going to make a film wonderful in the director's eyes. They're not going to shortchange you. They're probably going to go in on a weekend when you're not around and add that special touch. They are going to take your sketches and really make it look as good as it can be.

What kind of relationship do you like to have with the director of a film?

Without the director backing you, you can expend an awful amount of energy and waste an awful lot of ideas, but if he is your constant source of communication, usually you can do wonders together. Time and time again, I was asked to take the second unit and many times three or four days with the first unit, because I know almost adamantly what the director will insist on. I don't suddenly want to explore my technique; I want to explore what he's committed himself to. I think the new directors today often don't understand that; they think it's an invasion of their prerogatives. It's not that at all. I go into a picture today not even caring whether I get screen credit anymore, as long as I'm making a contribution. If I'm not making a contribution, I want to find out in the first two weeks so I can get off it and give it to somebody they think will make a contribution. My whole philosophy is: If I can do something to make the audience feel less a spectator and more a participant, then I think I've done what I can do to help the director. It could be anybody—the cameraman or the guy sweeping the stage—if everyone has that motive, there's no glory for oneself. You don't get ulcers when the idea is rejected, because you've tried your best to sell the idea. There is absolutely no bitterness at all; you've tried your best and that's it. I don't wail and say, "Well, when I'm a director, it won't be like that." I'm sure it would be just like that. A director has a vision and is going to try to inspire it in others.

What options does production storyboarding give to the director?

Paul Mazursky, Hitchcock, Spielberg, and Matthew Robbins all have the same mind about the fun of making a picture before it's made. You don't have to be in the editing room at six in the morning or twelve at night. It's the preparation. Hitch always considered that shooting the picture was the most boring part, and he really meant it. The director still has total control. You have done the sketches. Who better could tell the cameraman what the director wants? There are a lot of pictures that I feel I really don't deserve production design credit on, because I didn't control a lot of the set-ups. I really didn't influence the director into executing some of my ideas. I don't feel justified in calling myself a production designer unless I've done storyboards and everything in the world I can possibly do to get the director to make the most of the time I have to give. The more I work with a director, the more I can anticipate him. The more I can anticipate them, the happier they are to have me work with them. On *The Getaway*, Sam Peckinpah was three hundred miles away, and I had to set up the battle action sequence of the picture inside a hotel. Sam arrived and was going to shoot it in the next twenty-four hours. He never changed a bullet hole.

What does it mean to you to be a production designer?

Once you get immersed in it, you get so saturated. I've had three offers from studios to run a studio art department, and I always refused because I said that I give so much to one picture that I've got to have time off in between to recover. I can't be on three pictures with three guys working for me. You become a man in an ivory tower. Who wants to be king of the art department? I wouldn't really have my hand on the pulse of the picture at all. I just want to do whatever is in the best interest of the picture and know that not a lot of people could do better—that's my satisfaction. I don't care what it costs. I did a high dive off a platform into six feet of water in Munich posing as Anne Baxter because she was scared to do it. In *Pepe* I was on the horse under water. I'll do anything if I think it's in the best interest of the film, and I can do it. I'll do anything; I'll act, I'll jump into flaming tanks to get Anne Baxter out, I'd do that tomorrow.

3

Ken Adam

Ken Adam was born in Berlin, Germany, where he was educated at Le College Français. In 1934 he continued his education at the Craigend Park School in Edinburgh and the St. Paul's School in London. After two years of studying architecture at the Bartlett School of London University, Adam worked for the architectural firm of C. W. Glover & Partners. In 1940 he joined the Pioneer Corps, and in 1941 he transferred to the RAF, in which he served as a fighter pilot until 1946.

In 1947, Ken Adam began his film career in England as a draftsman. He worked as an assistant art director on *Obsession* directed by Edward Dmytryk, and in 1953 Adam became an art director on *The Devil's Pass*. For the next six years Ken Adam was art director for such renowned directors as John Ford, Robert Aldrich, and Jacques Tournier. He also worked with the legendary William Cameron Menzies on the 1955 classic, *Around the World in 80 Days*, for which he received his first Academy Award nomination.

Adam's opportunity to become a production designer came in 1959, a year in which he attained that title on three films.

Ken Adam is probably best known as the production designer of seven James Bond films, a series loved and admired all over the world. His achievements on the first Bond film, *Dr. No*, set the standards of futuristic style and perpetual imagination that have become a mainstay of the Bond cycle. His work on *The Spy Who Loved Me* garnered an Oscar nomination. Adam's substantial artistic accomplishments on the Bond films are only one aspect of a long and varied design career that includes two films for director Stanley Kubrick, *Dr. Strangelove* and *Barry Lyndon*, for which he won the Academy Award for best art direction–set decoration.

Adam has demonstrated an expansive visual style in which his ingenious imagination exposes the audience to extraordinary images in such diverse films as *Chitty Chitty Bang Bang, Sleuth, Pennies from Heaven, The Freshman,* and *The Doctor.*

All of Ken Adam's sets have a distinctive and architecturally bold style. Angled ceilings, jutting support beams, and immense scale are characteristic of the many elements that infuse his design concepts. His recent work on *The Doctor,* for which he created a contemporary hospital, transports the viewer into a world of heightened reality, which is an integral part of Adam's work.

1953 *The Devil's Pass*
1955 *Soho Incident.*
1956 *Around the World in 80 Days**
      Child in the House
1957 *V.1*
      Night of the Demon
      Gideon's Day
1958 *Beyond This Place*
1959 *Ten Seconds to Hell*
      The Angry Hills
      The Rough and the Smooth
      In the Nick
      Let's Get Married
1960 *The Trials of Oscar Wilde*
1962 *Dr. No*
1963 *Sodom and Gomorrah*
      In the Cool of the Day
1964 *Dr. Strangelove, or: How I Learned to Stop Worrying and Love the Bomb*
      Woman of Straw
      Goldfinger
1965 *The Ipcress File*
      Thunderball
1966 *Funeral in Berlin*
1967 *You Only Live Twice*
1968 *Chitty Chitty Bang Bang*
1969 *Goodbye, Mr. Chips*

1970 *The Owl and the Pussy Cat*

1971 *Diamonds Are Forever*

1972 *Sleuth*

1973 *The Last of Sheila*

1975 *Barry Lyndon***

1976 *The Seven-Per-Cent Solution*
      Salon Kitty

1977 *The Spy Who Loved Me**

1979 *Moonraker*

1981 *Pennies from Heaven*

1985 *King David*
      Agnes of God

1986 *Crimes of the Heart*

1988 *The Deceivers*

1989 *Dead Bang*

1990 *The Freshman*

1991 *Company Business*
      The Doctor

1992 *Cloak and Diaper*

* Academy Award nomination for best achievement in art direction–set decoration.

** Academy Award for best achievement in art direction–set decoration.

How did you become a production designer?

From early on in my life, I was always drawing or painting. I was fortunate that I knew at the age of fourteen or fifteen that I wanted to be a theater or film designer. When I was about sixteen, I was lucky to meet the art director Vincent Korda, one of the three Korda brothers, and I asked him what to do if I wanted to get into film. He advised me to study architecture, to get a grounding in the history of styles and period. So I went to London University College and studied two years of architecture, which was interfered with by the Second World War. I never really wanted to complete those studies because they were a means to an end. I joined the RAF and then was a fighter pilot until 1946. After my demobilization I tried to get into films, which wasn't very easy in those days because everybody wanted to. Suddenly the glamour and the hero worship of being a fighter pilot had gone. By a stroke of luck I managed to get into films. My sister was working at the U.S. Embassy in London, and a buyer from a small studio came in and asked if she could supply him with some American props for a picture called *No Orchids for Miss Blandish*. She said, "Yes, I think I can do that. I wonder if you can help a young brother of mine who has just come out of the Air Force." He said, "Oh, no problem, let him see the art director of the film." And that's how I got into films as a junior draftsman. That was in 1947; then the whole thing progressed pretty quickly.

Do you think you have a distinctive and recognizable style as a production designer?

Yes, I'd like to think that. When I was brought up in Berlin, I was influenced by the Bauhaus and German Expressionism, and one of the first films that really impressed me as a kid was *The Cabinet of Dr. Caligari*. Once I started expressing myself as a designer, I always leaned toward the choice of the theatrical. I find it dull to do a room as it is. I feel as a designer your function is to give a reality to the public that is real but departs from the dullness which is very often part of the actual place. This style is not only reflected in my modern films but even in some of my period designs. It is nearly always a heightened reality—stylization.

How did you apply this concept of heightened realism to your work as art director on Around the World in 80 Days?

It was the first time I really started experimenting with stylization or heightened reality. I was very fortunate that the associate producer on the picture was William Cameron Menzies, who was the father of production design. Bill was a giant in the field and encouraged me a lot. Every set had to be designed for Todd-AO—the bug-eye lens—and to compose within the enormous frame ratio. We decided to treat the stodgy Reform Club all in black and green. Lloyds of London, the world famous insurer, was entirely in black and white; even the exterior backdrop and the library steps were painted in black and white. Then at a certain moment, the clerks walk through the frame, and they are wearing bright, scarlet red robes. Menzies encouraged this sort of stylization so it was very exciting for me, but we had to be very disciplined to stick to the concept. It was heightened reality. I was very young and most fortunate to have a man like Cameron Menzies. It was the first time I started experimenting, and having him behind my shoulders helped. We became great friends. I think he was very fond of me; so was the producer, Mike Todd, and that encouraged me always to experiment. I feel in any creative field if you want to achieve something, you need a lot of courage—even more in films because it's such a costly process. You have to convince the producers and the director to go along with you, then you have to do it within a certain budget. If you want to say what you feel, then you need the courage of your convictions.

The seven James Bond films you have designed display a great affinity for using materials in a pure form. You've often used glass, marble, steel, and wood in one room. How did you arrive at this design concept?

At the time I started in film in 1947, I hardly saw a slightly ahead-of-time contemporary film; it was really more kitchen-sink realism. The slightly ahead-of-time concept of filmmaking came very early on with the Fritz Lang pictures like *Metropolis* and *Things to Come*, which was directed by William Cameron Menzies. On the first James Bond film, *Dr. No*, I used a lot of electronic computers and mixed metal with marble and wood finishes, which fascinated me as a designer. That's why I came up with these new materials. I felt the subject matter gave me the opportunity to reflect the age we were living in.

When you designed Dr. No, *you were creating the unique futuristic look that would become the hallmark of the Bond series. Where did the ideas for the Bond visual style come from?*

I suppose it was my imagination. Also, I was working with director Terence Young, who had known me for a considerable time before. Although I had never worked for him, he respected me as a designer and left me very much to my own devices. *Dr. No* was a very low-budget picture. We started on locations in Jamaica. I couldn't stay there all of the time, because I had to prepare the studio sets and we had a tight schedule. Before I left Jamaica, I had some basic meetings with Terence. We discussed plans and where the entrances and exits were going to be laid out, but not the concept of the picture. The two producers were also in Jamaica. Then I came back to England and started designing. I had nobody to tell me what or what not to do. So when they came back, it was quite frightening because I had about five stages at Pinewood filled with sets, and I thought, "They might think I'm mad, or they might fire me." I must say Terence appeared to be very impressed and supportive. Of course, once I won the battle with Terence, the producers, Harry Saltzman and Cubby Broccoli, both followed suit.

Dr. No's apartment was the first of many spectacular villains' lairs you have designed on the Bond films. What was the origin of that design concept?

Dr. No's underground apartment stimulated a lot of thought and ideas from everybody. Somebody said, "This big villain has all of this antique furniture and a big aquarium. Maybe he should have some art treasure that has recently disappeared." Someone came up with the idea of the Goya painting of the Duke of Wellington, which had been stolen from the National Gallery. Literally within forty-eight hours, I had to reproduce the stolen Goya painting. I think that started the tongue-in-cheek concept of the Bond pictures, and it became more and more important as we made these films.

What research did you do to design the Fort Knox set for Goldfinger?

Up to a point, we had unbelievable cooperation because of Albert Broccoli's Washington contacts and the fact that the Kennedys loved the Ian Fleming books. I was allowed to fly over Fort Knox in a helicopter to look at the outside, which was incredible—nobody thought I would get permission. Everywhere around Fort Knox there were these strange loud speakers blaring out, "You are now entering a restricted area."

That was quite dicey because on the roof of Fort Knox there were people with machine guns; it was really frightening. Of course, nobody allowed me inside. As you know, the President is not allowed inside of the place.

Is there any documentation on the interior of Fort Knox?

None, and if there was I wouldn't have looked at it. I was pleased again about having to invent a reality for the audience which I thought was more right, more visually acceptable, but one which was obviously theatrical. I knew that the gold vaults in the Bank of England were very low. They're a series of tunnels really; I didn't think that was interesting. Gold is never stacked very high because it is so heavy, but what if you could stack gold up to forty foot in height! That long, tall elevator going up and down could never have worked in reality. I did a complete replica of the exterior of Fort Knox; however, the interior was a complete invention. The amazing thing was the number of letters United Artists received when the film was released: "How were you allowed inside Fort Knox?" So people accepted it completely.

What was the size of the room where Goldfinger has the big meeting with all of the crime lords? That set looked just enormous on film.

We called it the rumpus room. That was quite a big set; it must have been something like a hundred feet by sixty feet.

That room had many mechanical features like wall and floor panels that moved electronically. Were they executed mechanically, or were they moved by stagehands?

It was partly mechanical and partly done by stagehands.

Do you get involved in the actual construction of this kind of special effect, or do you have a team of specialists to accomplish this?

I know enough about it to know it can be made to work, but I leave it to the construction coordinator or the special effects team to work out the details.

Were you responsible for designing the cars, boats, aircraft, and all those spectacular gadgets in the Bond films?

Yes, I came up with the concept and did the sketches, but I never knew how to make them work. I eventually developed a superb team of collaborators. I had very good special effects men, starting off with Johnny Stears and eventually Derek Meddings. They were wizards at making all of those gadgets work. It's fantastic when you can try way-out things, because nothing is impossible; it also encourages you. In principle, everything was possible. On *Thunderball*, we found this old used Hydrofoil somewhere in Puerto Rico and then designed a yacht around it which could do fifty or sixty knots. Aside from a powerboat, there wasn't a boat which had that sort of speed. I designed the other half of the yacht on a Catamaran principle. Both halves were independent and joined by two one-inch slip bolts on either side. It was done by Allied Marine 3M in Miami, and the naval people said, "Ahhh, it will never work." It worked like a dream. We thought we might get the most terrible problems with it; we never had a problem with it, whereas a simple little thing you think isn't going to give you any problem, you may lose two or three days of shooting. So that was exciting on the Bonds. You found people all over the world, somebody who knew how to make it work for you, including the little gyrocopter on *You Only Live Twice*. I was listening to a radio program while shaving, and there was Wing Commander Wallace, who had invented it. So I rang him up and he came to visit me at Pinewood Studios, and then I redesigned it to suit the action. I came up with the idea of making it as a kit in crocodile leather cases. That is the most exciting thing.

Did you keep files on new technological inventions? How did you keep abreast of what new developments were available?

No, I was never much into reading science fiction magazines, but the producers, Cubby Broccoli and Harry Saltzman, were both very good at following through on all of that. Cubby had a great friend, Colonel Charlie Rushon, a retired American colonel, who used to keep very much abreast of inventions and new equipment like the jetpack, for instance. He used to ring me up and say, "You have to see this."

The majority of the studio work on the Bond films has been done at Pinewood Studios. When you work at a large studio, how do you decide where on the studio floor each set is going to be built?

It's a planning exercise. You know that you require x number of stages, and then it's a logistics exercise because some of these stages may have to be filled up three times. So relative to the schedule, you have to work out your stage plans and construction schedule. Let's say you start off on a big stage with a big set which you need more time to prepare, and then you go onto other stages. You strike the big set and rebuild it with three or four other sets.

Is this planning done after you know what all your sets are going to be?

Not necessarily, because you never really have time. Ideally speaking, yes, but the conditions were never ideal. The Bonds were almost nightmares. You had to have a great back-up team to do them. We were sometimes shooting two or three units at different locations, thousands of miles apart. Maybe we were shooting in South America in the jungles of Brazil, and the second unit was shooting in Miami, Florida, and the main unit was shooting in Venice, Italy. Now, all these units had to be supervised; they had to have sets and props. There were big logistics problems, but I had good people with me and so we did it.

Many of your sets have ceilings. Not all designers put ceilings on their sets. Is this something about which you have firm convictions?

Yes, the eye always takes in the ceiling, so why shouldn't the camera take in the ceiling. In the early days, we were all brought up with no ceilings and lighting from the gantries around the set. I had used ceilings before, but on *Dr. Strangelove* Stanley Kubrick said to me, "Nail the bloody ceilings down. I don't want the cameraman to light from the top. I want to use source lighting." So I did that, and I have used ceilings ever since.

As proof of what a convincing job you did in designing the war room for Dr. Strangelove, *I've heard that when Ronald Reagan was elected President, he asked to see the war room.*

Yes, somebody told me that. That's an absolutely true story. I said, "You must be joking." They said, "No."

I understand originally you had a completely different design for that set, and at the last minute, Kubrick changed his mind.

Yes. I was sort of doodling and he would say, "Gee Ken, it's great, great!" So you think you're in business, right? Being rather organized in my way of thinking, I then want to put staff on it to do the working drawings, models, and so on. We'd been working on this for three or four weeks, and then one morning he said, "You know Ken, I need at least sixty or seventy extras for that second level up there, and they have to be sitting around all the time. It could be costly, and what are they going to do? Come up with something else." It threw me completely.

So the original design had a second level?

Yes, it was completely different. It was more like an amphitheater. The second level was like a control room with glassed-in windows looking down. Once I started calming down, my mind started ticking again, thank God. Stanley used to come in when I was drawing, and he was practically standing behind me. Then this triangular concept evolved, and he liked it. Of course, with him being an intellectual, you have to justify everything you do. I had the answer when he said, "Yes, it's all very well with the triangle. What material do you think you're going to do it in?" and I said, "Concrete, like a bomb shelter." So that's how it evolved. I had a circle in the center for a circular table, and he said, "Could you cover that table in green baize?" Now, it's a black-and white picture. I said, "Sure." He said, "It should be like a poker table; there's the President, the generals, and the Russian ambassador playing a game of poker for the fate of the world."

The lighting of the war room set was dramatically effective. What was Kubrick's involvement with the cinematography of these sequences?

Stanley does it; he's a brilliant cameraman. He wanted only source lighting. I had designed a circular light fitting that could be suspended. We sat in my office and experimented with varying types of photofloods. I would sit in the chair, and he'd put up a photoflood at a certain distance to see how much light would fall on my face. The lighting of all the personnel around the table was done through that circular light fitting.

Did you design the cockpit in the plane that carried the bomb?

Yes. We had no cooperation at all from the military; it was considered an anti-American picture. It was so amazing that through technical flight magazines like *Janes* we could get all the information we wanted. So we had all of it at our fingertips and then copied the B-52. The only thing we were not sure about was that little box, the CRM, the fail-safe device. I came up with an idea, and during the shooting we invited some Air Force personnel to visit the set. They went white when they saw that CRM, so it must have been pretty close. I got a memo from Stanley that said, "You better find out where you got your research from because we could be investigated." Basically, it was all from technical data in magazines.

How did you make the car fly in Chitty Chitty Bang Bang?

That car nearly turned out to be my Waterloo. I had a concept of a boat body loosely based on some of the very old Rolls-Royces and Bugattis. I found it easy to make a sketch, but then to build it from scratch! When we built the mockups, I kept changing it before I felt I had it right. I was driving everyone crazy, including myself. Fortunately, we had a deal with Ford and some racing people who built the chassis and the engine, but then that same car had to be a Hovercraft and finally had to fly. Then there was the airship. I never thought of building a full-sized airship. One day, two men who were both balloonists walked into my office and said, "Ken, you design the airship and we'll build it." I said, "You must be joking." "Oh no, no, no. Come up with a design." It was a children's film, so I based this airship on the shape of a sausage and on a French airship from the turn of the century called the La Baudier. They saw the drawing and I said, "Well, give me an estimate." They said, "We'll use a Volkswagen engine, and the whole thing will be about ten thousand pounds." I said, "Well, a model costs six thousand pounds." So I talked to Albert Broccoli, the producer, who said, "If they can build it and guarantee it will fly, then let's do it." So these two had lots of women sewing at the old airship hangar at Cardington. Then we put the gondola on. We were going to fill the airship with hydrogen, which was much cheaper than helium, but thank God we didn't. United Artists insisted that we put helium in it for safety reasons. The first day of shooting, we had five cameras set up outside of London in the beautiful countryside. These two guys are flying it, and the thing takes one dive. They had no idea how to fly that thing. They were balloonists; they didn't know how to use a throttle. So it crashed several times, and I was having a nervous breakdown. Eventually I volunteered to fly it myself, and United Artists and Broccoli said, "Under no circumstances. We can't insure you for this." We kept changing ballasts, increasing certain surfaces, and so on.

One day, the airship was flying over these country lanes in England. I was in my E-type Jaguar, following the flight through cows and fields.

Suddenly it crashed into a lot of high tension wires. Fortunately, nobody was hurt, but United Artists was being sued by irate farmers. All their electricity cut off, and they couldn't milk their cows. Every time it flew, we had to fill it with helium again, which cost another three thousand pounds. It was a disaster. So finally I called on experts from all over the world to find out what was wrong. These experts were in their eighties and nineties; they had built Zeppelins for Germany and France. They talked to me, and everyone had a different opinion on how to make this thing more stable, more airworthy. Finally an old French professor comes up to me and says, "Monsieur Adam, I must tell you something. The La Baudier never flew." I said, "Now he tells me!" But finally we got what we needed.

What was the principal challenge in designing Barry Lyndon?

It was a completely different challenge. I had been used to designing and creating my sort of reality in a studio. Here we were using stately homes and actual places. Part of the picture took place in Germany, but we never went to Germany. Stanley refused to go until the bitter end, so we had to find continental buildings in Ireland. Eventually toward the end of the picture, he sent the second unit to Potsdam and East Berlin to get some of the superb atmosphere of Germany in castles and streets of that period. The painstaking process of reproducing paintings of the period was a different challenge for me.

What painters were you and Kubrick inspired by during your research?

Of course we used the English painters like Gainsborough and Reynolds, but we used also French painters like Watteau and Italians like Zoffany. We used the Polish artist Chadowiecki for some of the continental scenes.

The film depicts the period so realistically, it almost makes the viewer feel transported back in time.

Yes, and that's what Stanley tried to do. He wanted to do it almost like a documentary of the period, but when we started researching and preparing the film, he knew very little about the period. Eventually, he got to know more and more, but we got into terrible arguments because he was more attracted to Victorian interiors than to the stark, more formal eighteenth-century interiors. We used to photograph every location and come back and analyze the photographs, and he would say, "I like that wallpaper," and I would say, "Stanley, you can't use that wallpaper; that's Victorian." Of course, in the end he knew more about that period than I or probably anybody else because of the amount of research he did about the living conditions of the people: the lice in their wigs, the toothbrushes they used, condoms. We went through everything to find out how those people lived. Right from the start, Stanley was insistent that the costumes should not be costumes but should be clothes. So we bought a lot of real eighteenth-century clothes, which one could still find in England. We found that they were all too small, because people were obviously smaller two hundred years ago. We set up our own factory at Radlett, opened up these clothes, and made the new clothes in exactly the same patterns as the old clothes. The thing was to get the actors to wear them properly, to get used to them and walk properly in them. I think we succeeded pretty well.

Sleuth *is a two-character film, but the house the Laurence Olivier character lives in almost becomes a third character. Can you talk about how the house was designed and developed?*

I had a meeting with the director, Joseph Mankiewicz, and he said, "I want this place to be like the third actor in the film, and I want it theatrical. The whole thing should be like a game. They're playing a game, and the set should reflect that in some way." We knew I would not be able to find such a place in reality. I had a concept in my mind which was a type of baronial hall in a medieval manor house. So I went all over southern England and the Midlands to look at possible exteriors and eventually came up with a place near Dorchester at Athelhampton. Joe liked the exterior. I flew to New York and showed him all my sketches and designs, and he went along with all of it. The interiors were built in the studio. I built the main entrance and the oriel window in the studio to match the exterior of the location house.

How did you conceptualize the restaurant in The Freshman?

The restaurant was very difficult, because it was a place which only functioned once, and it was never properly described in the script. I eventually came up with the idea of a temporary structure, like a tent inside a barn. On the outside it looks like a barn; on the inside is a very elegant restaurant. The next problem became how to make the kitchen interesting. My first instinct was a kitchen is a kitchen; you have maybe four ranges together. Then I started scribbling around, and somehow these two circles materialized on either side of where our Komodo Dragon was supposedly being carved up. So that gave me the idea, "Wouldn't it be interesting to make those two circles surgical lamps like in an operation room." I rang up the director, Andy Bergman, in New York, and he was very funny. He said, "Well, you're even more *meshugana* than I am." He was always very cautious about my doing too much to a very funny situation, and then he eventually agreed with me.

In The Freshman *Marlon Brando plays a character who has a strong resemblance to Don Corleone in* The Godfather. *The social club where he has his office is very different looking than the office in* The Godfather, *but it still gives the feeling that this is a very powerful man to be respected. How does the design help to create this illusion?*

In the back of the set behind Brando, I forced the perspective. Like a theatrical set, I lowered the ceiling and raised the floor up to make him look even bigger. I came up with the idea of putting him against a window. Now what kind of window? It was an industrial window, which you find everywhere in New York. The texture on the walls was really incredible. We papered the walls, repapered them, then painted them, and peeled them off. The ceilings and the wainscotting was that tinned material that is so New York. It was to give *The Godfather* atmosphere to it, but in fact it wasn't anything that we had seen in *The Godfather* except in terms of the lighting.

What do you consider your most important tool as a production designer?

The sketch is the all-important tool of the designer. A black-and-white sketch helps me to get what the Italians call chiaroscuro—light and shade. It also gives me a sculptural element of three dimensions. From there I might go into more elaborate sketches, working drawings, or models.

When I first came to Hollywood, every major studio had illustrators, and the art director or production designer was not allowed to do his own sketching—it had to be done through an illustrator. Well, I could never work that way. There are brilliant illustrators around, and I've used illustrators, but first I have to do my concept. The only way I can translate or show my concept is through a sketch. It is that initial concept which is the most important thing. I start off with a tiny thumbnail sketch, and though I may elaborate later on, it is that thumbnail sketch which gives me all of my masses, feeling, and design for a particular set or scene.

Can one be a production designer without possessing drawing skills?

I think it is possible, but it is not advisable and not likely. Certainly in my case, it's the lines which give me the design. I always start off with a sketch, however small, however rough it might be. I think it is advisable for anybody who wants to be a production designer to be able to freehand sketch, to have an architectural understanding of space, and then learn all the tricks of the trade—which lately, unfortunately, seem to be forgotten. In the last fifteen years, I have had difficulty in finding collaborators, assistants, and staff. They don't know what a camera angle is; they don't know what a forced perspective is. In many cases, they have very little cultural preparation. When I was invited by the union in New York to join them in 1970, they waived an examination which they normally give because they knew my work. You had to paint a stage backing, design a stage set, design a film set, and show a standard of proficiency. I don't think you have that sort of standard any longer, and it's important because design is so important—whether it's film, theater, or opera. You are handed a script or outline, a piece of paper, and you have to translate it to visual terms. The fact that the cameraman eventually uses his own creativity to embellish it is fine, but you have to give him something to photograph. The majority of films are now made on location—they are no longer made in studios—and so the function of the production designer has changed. Very often people who call themselves production designers get away with what I call murder. So what has happened is the director of photography has taken on much more importance and gets three times as much money as a production designer. In the sixties, I was on par with the top cameramen. The director of photography has more to do now. With many directors, he's got to stage the action. So they say to themselves, "Well, if we've got to stage the action and do all of that, we want a lot more money." I don't blame them for that.

The Bond films were futuristic in their presentation of contemporary periods. Have you ever worked on a project that took place far in the future?

Yes, I was involved in the original *Star Trek* film when it was to be directed by Philip Kaufman. I worked on it for three months, then Paramount called it off and revived it about a year and a half later. By that time, we were both working on other things. That was really science fiction and way-out. I had a lot of headaches. I didn't find it difficult to dream up a different planet environment or even what this earth might look like in a thousand years from now. What I found almost impossible to design was extraterrestrial beings or forms of life without the whole thing looking ridiculous. You have to start by getting scientists to tell you about the forms of life or what the chemical composition is before you can design anything, because if you start sketching things out, they always look ridiculous with three eyes or one leg. I talked a lot to Kubrick, and he said, "Forget it." They tried it on *2001*, and they gave it up. You can call in the most brilliant designer—nobody can project that.

Where do you think the profession of production design is heading?

I feel there has been a decline in production design over a number of years. Fortunately, I think it's coming back—even if in a very limited form—with people doing these cartoon films like *Batman* and *Dick Tracy*. I would hope there is more of a return to the studio environment, because it's completely creative for the designer—like when you design an opera or when you design a play. You've got to be creative. Along with the right director, the designer can give the public something they have never seen before. That's what we're supposed to be doing.

4

Richard Sylbert

Richard Sylbert spent the first ten years of his career growing with the vital beginnings of the New York film community. He swiftly developed a dynamic style and a strong sense of craft and has gone on to become one of Hollywood's most influential production designers.

Richard Sylbert has the ability to inform the meanings of a film by synthesizing architecture, color, and textures in his design. *Chinatown* communicates the drought facing Los Angeles through a controlled color palette. The pack-rat existence of George and Martha is defined in the clutter of their faculty house in *Who's Afraid of Virgina Woolf?* The reality of a tormented concentration camp survivor envelops him in a prison of cages in *The Pawnbroker*, and a crime stopper of the Sunday supplement comics comes alive through the primary colors and Expressionistic cityscape of *Dick Tracy*.

Richard Sylbert has been nominated for an Academy Award for best art direction–set decoration four times on *Chinatown, Shampoo, Reds,* and *The Cotton Club*. He is the recipient of two Oscars for his work on *Who's Afraid of Virgina Woolf?* and *Dick Tracy*.

Sylbert has worked with many notable directors: Elia Kazan, Martin Ritt, Sidney Lumet, John Frankenheimer, Robert Rossen, Mike Nichols, Roman Polanski, Warren Beatty, Brian De Palma, and Francis Ford Coppola.

Throughout his long career, Richard Sylbert has designed many seminal films. *The Manchurian Candidate, The Graduate,* and *Shampoo* were responsible for influencing the look of contemporary movies in their approach to the overall composition of a film.

Richard Sylbert continues to inspire his peers, merging art with content, by bringing his intellectual and technical command of the craft to every film he designs.

1956 *Crowded Paradise*
     Baby Doll
     A Face in the Crowd
1957 *Edge of the City*
1958 *Wind Across the Everglades*
1960 *The Fugitive Kind*
     Murder, Inc.
1961 *Splendor in the Grass*
1962 *A Walk on the Wild Side*
     The Manchurian Candidate
     Long Day's Journey into Night
1963 *All the Way Home*
1964 *Lilith*
1965 *How to Murder Your Wife*
     The Pawnbroker
     What's New, Pussycat?
1966 *Who's Afraid of Virginia Woolf?***
     Grand Prix
1967 *The Graduate*
1968 *Rosemary's Baby*
1970 *Catch-22*
1971 *Carnal Knowledge*
1972 *Fat City*
     The Heartbreak Kid
1973 *Day of the Dolphin*
1974 *Chinatown**
1975 *Shampoo**
     The Fortune
1979 *Players*
1981 *Reds**
1982 *Partners*
     Frances
1983 *Breathless*
1984 *The Cotton Club**
1986 *Under the Cherry Moon*

1988 *Shoot to Kill*
      Tequila Sunrise
1990 *Dick Tracy***
      Bonfire of the Vanities
1991 *Mobsters*
1992 *Ruby Cairo*

*Academy Award nomination for best achievement in art direction–set decoration.

**Academy Award for best achievement in art direction–set decoration.

What is your method for designing films?
   I have a way of thinking about how you do it. I have a way of doing it, and that makes whatever I do different from anybody else. I've always tried to make something out of what on the surface doesn't appear to be quite so interesting. On the surface, *Chinatown* is just a genre movie about a detective in Los Angeles. On the surface, *Baby Doll* is a Southern comedy. On the surface, *Shampoo* is about a bunch of people with a lot of money in Beverly Hills. Those problems are interesting. It is your assumption about life that makes what you see yours, because you're looking for it. You have this assumption about life from experience. You start with a script, a story somebody wrote. It takes place at a certain time. You read it and you start to write a list. I write lists of requirements for pictures before I start. Here's what you say for *Chinatown*: It's a drought. There will be no clouds in the sky, because if there are clouds in the sky, it could rain. It's in L.A., every building will be Spanish and white. The reason they're white is because it's hotter that way. Every building that Gittes visits will be above his eye level, because it's harder to go uphill than down. Every color will be related, from the white to the color of burnt grass to the color of a shadow on the deepest end. Every door in certain official buildings will be opaque glass, because it looks like frozen water and you can't quite tell what's behind it; it's mysterious. You go on and on and on detailing this idea. Except for the first time you see him, the man who dies is looking down; he's doomed. You don't see any green unless you know it's a statement. So the lawn in the Mulwray house is the greenest thing in the picture, and the orange grove where Gittes goes to look for some information has water. You even design the sets to echo each other. You take the plan of the Water and Power Department, which is an authority, and you work out the plan for the police morgue so that there's a familiar ring to what people do, how they feel, what the colors are. You just continue doing this.
   We make a movie about something specific, and we don't do that movie twice. The needs of the film are what's important. I've always been interested in taste as judgment. Joseph Conrad said, "Taste is the

solidification of your knowledge about any given thing at that time." When you think about a movie in the broadest sense—where it's shot, the locations, the big scene, the small scene, about how people live— you're saying, "I want this in the movie, not that." It's completely selective; it's problem solving, which is the major thing we all do. You solve problems with your taste. What happens is the result that I am always looking for. It's the result that I was taught to look for by William Cameron Menzies, who directed the first film I ever designed when I was twenty-two years old. Menzies did storyboards and illustrations. I didn't do storyboards; nobody did in New York. We were talking to people like Kazan and Lumet: Who's going to do a storyboard? What, are you joking? Not only wouldn't they look at it, they weren't interested in it. They would stand on a set and they rehearsed like people rehearsed. They would work out the problem, and they said, "Ah, that's the best shot at this moment." Here's what Menzies taught me. He wanted control. He used to say to me, "Sam Wood never knew where to put the camera, so I told him." I wanted control, but Elia Kazan knows where to put the camera. I had to take the Menzies idea of controlling each shot into controlling ideas. It is the discipline in saying every sequence in this picture will be related to the next one, and that is going to mean something. The end result will be a kind of wholeness that Menzies got his way; I get it my way. This movie doesn't look like any other movie. You can't do what I did in *Chinatown* to another movie; you won't get there. You cannot use any ideas in *Dick Tracy* for anything but *Dick Tracy*. That's how specific *Dick Tracy* is. That's why it's so original to look at. You know the structure before you start shooting. Then if some location falls out after months of negotiation, you know precisely what you need to replace it. So you have to know what you are looking for. Everything you do in life depends on what you're looking for.

After you have developed the design ideas, what role does the technical craft of production design play in executing them?

The technical parts are pervasive in everything that you look at. How do I get this thing I want to get? Even the smallest detail, like the surface of a wall texture, is part of everything. It's part of movies. I have always been a thorough believer in being the best technician you can possibly be. I studied fine arts in a very fine school. That meant architecture, sculpture, the history of art, and the chemistry of paint. I'll tell you who the great technicians are: Mozart is one of them, Beethoven's one of them, Picasso was one of them in a very modern way, and Rembrandt, of course. The cameraman Vittorio Storaro is a great technician. He's the best I know of. The more you know, the more you know. The more you know, the more you're going to know; and the more you know, the more you can make problems that only you can solve. That's what you do.

How did you get your start as a production designer in New York?

When I was twenty-two I was doing a series in black and white at Fox for twenty-six weeks. It was the first series that had ever been done there. I had a brilliant crew that I trained. We got together and did this every week. I didn't know anything about movies. There was nobody to learn from. I never saw anybody make a movie. I had to teach myself. We developed techniques.

William Cameron Menzies came into town and asked me to do two half-hour film pilots for *Fu Manchu*, which he was going to direct. We were in the Bronx, and we went to lunch in a bar on the corner and Richard Day was there. He was the art director of *A Streetcar Named Desire* who Kazan had brought to New York to do *On the Waterfront*. He was a wonderful man. I was twenty-two years old—I had lunch with Dick Day and Bill Menzies. Then I got a picture to design, *Crowded Paradise*, a wonderful movie with Hume Cronyn and Nancy Kelly. They kept running out of money. It took three cameramen and a year and a half to complete. The third cameraman was Boris Kaufman. The sets were all there on the stage. I took my crew and went to Bermuda to do a series so I could learn to build outside. Nobody went outside; for twenty-six weeks of *Inner Sanctum*, we never made a shot outside. I'd been in Bermuda for a year designing and building a village; that's something you couldn't do in New York. I had all my people. We came back and started a historical series with Raymond Massey. I get a call from Kazan, who says to me, "Two friends of mine told me about you." I said, "Who are your friends?" He said, "Hume Cronyn and Boris Kaufman." I said, "That's nice." He said, "You want to come see me?" I said, "Sure." I went up to his office on 44th Street above the Astor Theater. It was a great little dump. It had a great big black safe in one room. It was wonderful, so unpretentious. He said, "I'm pulling out of California. I'm going to stay in New York; I'm going to start making movies here. I have one more commitment. Take the script home and read it." It was *Baby Doll*. I came back the next day, and he said, "Draw something for me." I drew this slightly leaning classical Ionic column on a porch with an old rocking chair, some junk, and a tube of squeezed-up ointment. Kazan said, "What kind of ointment is that?" I said, "I don't know, Gadge, what kind of ointment is that?" He said, "It's pile ointment, I'll see you in Mississippi."

Splendor in the Grass is a story that takes place in the Midwest. How were you able to make it in New York?

Kazan said, "We're going to do it in color, and we're going to do it here in New York." You can do Kansas in Long Island potato fields.

There's no problem; they're flat. We did a huge color movie for $1,800,000, including the cast! We built it all in the studio—the family's place, the nightclubs—everything was built in the studio. We went to Long Island, Staten Island, the falls were up near Croton. I found a place in Riverdale for the exterior of the institution; it was a beautiful old building. I also used the Riverdale School for the fight scene outside the country club. Kazan never went back to Hollywood. Gadge is the most important person that I ever met; Warren Beatty will tell you the same thing. If Kazan had not decided to write novels, which is what he did for the next twenty years, we would have had a fabulous industry in New York. I had the best ten years you could ever get from 1953, when I did *Crowded Paradise*, to 1963, when I did *The Pawnbroker*. Of twelve pictures that were done in New York, I must have designed ten of them. I had a great ten years. We used to make those movies in thirty-five or forty days. We just got up in the morning and did those pictures; it's much harder to do a movie today.

In The Manchurian Candidate *the brainwashing scenes interchangeably take place on two sets, an amphitheater where the event is actually happening and a ladies garden party, which is the hallucinatory point of view of the prisoners. How were these sets built to interact with each other?*

I made the amphitheater very shallow, where everybody was completely stacked up, but right up in front. Then I built the solarium of the hotel for the garden party. I put both sets on real railroad tracks. You could actually pan around 360 degrees. When you came around, you could switch to the other background; then you could go around and have the first background. That was done so that in one turn you could change sets without cutting the camera.

In back of the men being brainwashed in the amphitheater are poster-size photo blow-ups of Stalin and Mao. What part did these posters play in your design concept?

I put up those photographs for two reasons. That part of the world is about posters and proselytizing. Also, we knew we were going to kill these men. We could splash blood on the posters and wouldn't have to show somebody getting the hit.

What locations did you use for The Pawnbroker?

I remembered that when I was in the infantry in Fort Dix there was an abandoned camp. We used that for the concentration camp. I found an empty store on 125th Street, which had the El, and we made the front of the pawnshop. The whole interior of the pawnshop was built in the studio. Sidney Lumet was easy to talk to about the way we laid it out, because we came from the same period of live television, where you plan everything.

What was the challenge of designing The Pawnbroker *in black and white?*

It's very hard to do texture in black and white, because you've got to get separation and you can't get it by changing colors. So the surfaces of a wall or any texture you can get become extremely important. *The Pawnbroker* is a very good example of texture—peeling paint, shiny greasy walls, and all of those things that kick light around and make shadows, a pattern of some kind.

What location was used for the college campus exteriors in Who's Afraid of Virgina Woolf?

We went to Smith. Gloria Steinem was a friend of Mike Nichols. She was the one who said, "You've got to get Dick Sylbert to do this picture." She was the one who had suggested Smith. There were other choices. When I did *Carnal Knowledge*, Amherst was the choice I made because it was much more colonial and dignified. Smith was perfect because the campus was so small. The old faculty house with the fabulous lawn and the huge tree was wonderful. That was a great tree for the swing, which was part of a very important scene. If you needed a tree, that was the tree. What Smith contributed was the opening tone of the place. The entire house and the entire front porch was all built in the studio.

What was the concept behind the design of the interior of George and Martha's house?

I did a lot of theatrical things in there. First of all, it's about pack-rats. It's about intellectuals in an environment in which they have collected postcards, necklaces, and photographs from sabbaticals in Mexico. It's about how much shit can you collect in one house. I decorated that picture entirely by myself, just as I did on *Bonfire of the Vanities*. I scoured everywhere for that stuff, like the old map of Martha's Vineyard. All the books were handpicked by me—*Summerhill*, *The Tin Drum* was behind their heads on the bed. Each one meant something. The furniture was kind of half junk. My normal instinct is to take something away; you don't put something there. This was just the reverse.

Did you dress the set over a period of time?

Oh yes, I did it for weeks and weeks. Wherever you look in that picture there was some kind of texture, like the peeling paint in that big old kitchen. "What a dump!" In the opening scene there are moths around the bulb. I cut some moths out of paper, tied them to monofilament, and blew the paper moths with a fan so you had these things fluttering around the bulb when the door opened. You know how paint used to get stuck in screens, like in that scene where she leans against the screen in the kitchen at the end. The scene that was the most fun for me to solve was George and Martha sitting in the window at the very end when the sun starts to come up. They talk for two or three minutes, and slowly the sun starts to rise behind them. You're in a studio! I took the black-and-white scenic photographic backing that I shot out of the front of the house at Smith, cut holes in it, and backed it with a theatrical scrim to hold it together. All Haskell Wexler had to do was put an arc light behind it on a molivator and slowly raise the arc light. It was a theater shot.

Was there a metaphor in the design concept of The Graduate?

It was the Montagues and the Capulets, except completely reversed— the families like each other. While the Montagues and Capulets were far apart, these families were alike. They had the same house, except it was reversed. It's two houses on the same street that are identical, except one is left to right and one is right to left. It's called keeping up with the Joneses. They were built on the stage. Dustin Hoffman's house is white with black detailing. All the staircases are perfectly straight, and all the openings are all square or rectangular. There is a rectangular pool in the back. Katherine Ross's house is also black and white, but it's all round. There's a round staircase, round arches, round openings, and so on. The only difference is where there is a pool in his house, at the girl's house there is a solarium where the tiger hangs out and Mrs. Robinson is wearing leopard skin.

Where did you locate the church that is the setting for the climax of the film?

In California. It was the perfect church to make the scene. They were concerned about Hollywood. It took us five months to make the deal. All I had to do to that church was build the staircase on the outside to make it look like it went somewhere. If that isn't a Hollywood church, I don't know what is—with a tree growing in it.

What was your approach to designing Carnal Knowledge?

Carnal Knowledge is a perfect example of chamber music; it's a fugue. It's four equal voices talking together over a period of twenty years. We went to Vancouver to do the movie and rented a brand new studio. We built 90 percent of it in the studio, then went to New York for a few days to do the ice skating and Park Avenue. I decided that the college memories of 1948, the Upper West Side in the 1950s, and the Upper East Side in the 1960s each had three distinct colors. There is nothing on the walls in all of that movie except for fixtures. All the doors are in corners, because it's harder if you're cornered. All the windows in all the sets, including the locations, have windows behind them and more windows and more windows and more windows. What you're saying is these lives are just like those lives. The only thing you ever see is another window. We built it in a studio, so I could build all those other windows, and put small people in them so they could walk around. We had Mike Nichols's cook, who was very short, in one of them. That's a wonderfully laid out picture, and it's very interesting to look at because it allows these people to perform; nothing interferes with the music. That picture is production designed. It is all sets except a few locations.

Shampoo *is very reminiscent of Jean Renoir's* Rules of the Game. *Was it an inspiration for* Shampoo?

Sure, we knew we were making a modern version of *Rules of the Game.*

Lattice is a key visual element in the design of Shampoo. *What were you trying to say with it?*

After researching a great deal of my own friends' beauty parlors, I began to think of the salon as the Beverly Hills equivalent of the Garden of Earthly Delights. I started with lattice in the salon—it's quite common in salons—and I kept pushing it all through the picture. It is outside on the deck of Goldie Hawn's place; it is in the wallpaper in the dining rooms. That's the fun for me. The more you can repeat the idea, the better it gets. The Bistro is lattice; the Bistro has always been lattice. I didn't put it there—it was there—but what I went for was the lattice because what you see is what you're looking for. *Shampoo* is an interesting study because it has a lot of thematic ideas that all work very well. In *Shampoo*, the lower down you are visually, the lower down you are. As you watch the movie, the people who are up above are the people who are up above, like Jack Warden's office—they're getting there. Warren's always on the bottom. Goldie is halfway up a hill, and then the girlfriend is further up on Hutton Drive so you can have that shot looking down when the car leaves. So social levels become something you could play with. I couldn't believe it when I found that plateau. I drove up there one day and I said, "Jesus, I can make that shot from here on Beverly Drive, onto Coldwater." *Shampoo* is a series of visual ideas that are very thoroughly connected. Getting thematic variations is like structuring music—that's what holds it all together. That's why themes are echoed and have variations. That's why music is repetitious—because it's part of what holds it together. That's why you have upscales, and suddenly the next thing you know, you're going down. We're talking here about the visual glue. You make people walk uphill for a reason and then downhill for another reason.

What was the visual concept you used to design Reds?

The idea of the picture was very simple. *Reds* is a perfect piece of nineteenth-century music. It is pure romantic symphonic form. It's Elgar. It's written through, meaning that it has four major movements: America, Russia, America, Russia. What I wanted to do was to begin in Greenwich Village with these low-ceilinged buildings and constantly keep the pressure on them in a world where they were large, they were big. All the Village sets were kept down so that Reed and Bryant look big. When we got to Europe, we wanted to make them look small. So as you saw Russia happening, they got smaller and smaller and smaller and smaller. The color was a cinch because the only color that you ever wanted to see was the red flag and the American flag—those were the brown decades. When you saw that red flag with those painted trains— that was it.

Reds *was a huge project. How did you begin to work on it, and what were the logistics involved in the production of the film?*

We had been talking about the film for nine years. The way I work with Warren is he sends me a script and says, "What do you think?" He gave me big pieces of the first script that Trevor Griffiths wrote. It was 325 pages of Marxism—Trevor's a Marxist—not so terrible. By this time, Warren's got something of a script himself, but much of it is step sheets of scenes and it's getting down to size. I was working on the preproduction and did all the building in London during the time Storaro and Warren were off filming the witnesses. I came to New York. Warren was still in California with this incomplete script, but we knew where we were going. We had all the books that had been written about John Reed and the step sheet. At that point, there were some very good scenes. I went and found John Reed's house in Croton-on-Hudson on a snowy day. I knew it was the house. I put a note in the mailbox. I get a call from a guy in the Garment District who said, "You're right, it's his house. You want to come see it?" I went out there—that's how I began to feel what I wanted to do for the way they lived in Croton. What I did was not a copy of that house, by any means, but I knew what I wanted to do. Then I found a series of photographs. One photograph was of Jessie Tarbox Beals, the first female news photographer, in 1903. A researcher who works for me located Alexander Alland, who was a collector of the photographers Jacob Riis and Jessie Tarbox Beals. So I drove up to his place in Mount Kisco, New York, and for two thousand dollars I bought twenty-five never-seen prints by Jessie Tarbox Beals. They were interiors of Greenwich Village in 1920 from twenty-five eight-by-ten glass negatives. It's the best collection you've ever seen in your life—it's The Village. Then I went into Greenwich Village, and I looked at Patchin Place where John Reed and Louise Bryant lived. I finally settled on Grove Court because the street is in two directions. So I knew from the exterior of the Grove Street house how I wanted to do their apartment in the Village.

Then I went to Provincetown. I called the local historian and he showed me this wonderful museum in which there is a huge model of the Provincetown Playhouse, and I met some of the people who were still alive. I met some of the witnesses. I walked into the house of this old, old man who was totally charming. His mother and father were very famous in the left-wing movements of the period. He lived with cats. Coffee cups with coffee in them were everywhere, there were spider webs on the coffee cups, the wallpaper was peeling off. I couldn't believe it. I told Warren, and they went to film him right away. He's the one who sang that song, "You Can't Come and Play in My Yard." We needed a place for what we would call Provincetown. I was walking down the street in the area where Eugene O'Neill lived. I'm standing in front of this house, and I see a legal notice tacked to the gate. It seemed odd to see this. The door opens and a woman comes out. I knew then whose

house I was standing in front of: I was standing in front of Norman
Mailer's house and the woman was Beverly Bentley, who was in court
with him over the house. She was a very dear friend of mine. So we
had dinner and I looked carefully. She helped me a lot, not only at
Norman's house but at houses nearby, until I had accumulated information I wanted for the places we were going to use as both John and
Louise's house and the theater. So that took care of that part of the
picture. All the research was unbelievable.

*What locations were used for the scenes that take place in Russia? Was there
an attempt to get permission to shoot there?*

Warren Beatty, Diane Keaton, Vittorio Storaro, Simon Relph, and I
went to Russia. Warren had been writing them letters for five years,
and the bureaucracy behaved as if it was yesterday. We sat in Moscow
with these guys for days. Here's the way the conversations went: "Warren, Warren, we think it's very, very progressive, you making this picture of John Reed, but Warren, we have to see a script." He said, "I'm
not going to show you a script." "But Warren, then it's impossible to
do." "No, no, no, I don't think it's impossible." You'd go to lunch;
Warren's toasts were always wonderful. He would say, "Here's to bureaucracy," or "Here's to the Bolshevik takeover," not the revolution
because we were getting more and more pissed off. This takes days.
After a long time Warren said, "Here's what we'll do: you guys shoot
it—your crew, your cameras, your people. Diane and I will walk across
Red Square from the Metropole to the National Hotel so you see Red
Square. That's all we want." "I'm afraid, Warren, that this. . . ."

They were very good about the research that I wanted for the hotel
rooms. We went to Leningrad, and I did all the research that I wanted
to do. We crossed the border from Leningrad to Helsinki. I looked at
Helsinki, and I said, "It's going to work perfectly." I found everything
I needed, like the square for the riots. Helsinki was Russian until 1870.
The same architects that designed Leningrad designed Helsinki.

How many sets were built for Reds?

This was a huge movie; we're talking about 150 sets and locations.
We filled Twickenham Studios in England with the whole first part of
the picture. Luckily, we shot the picture in continuity. The whole studio
was loaded with sets, and we went off to the English countryside in
Birmingham. I found these wonderful places for the Socialist meetings.
We were on a train when I noticed two old English barns, which I made
into the communication center when Louise comes to visit him and
they're bombarded. Meanwhile, there was a group working in Spain. I
had been to Madrid, Segovia, Granada, and Seville. We moved to Finland to do all of the trolley car marches. While I was in Finland, I was
designing the sets for all the hotels in Moscow where Emma Goldman
lived in Russia; those were all being built in the studio. I got all that

information. We exploited Helsinki beautifully. We get back to Twickenham in England for the second time. We shoot those sets, then we
go to Spain to shoot all of the locations in Spain: the ship, the train
interior, and the hospital corridors where he dies. He dies in the studio,
which was being built at the big studio at EMI because Twickenham
wasn't big enough. The agit-prop train was worked on in Madrid. I built
Smolny in Spain. I built the famous Third International meeting in a
warehouse in Spain from the photographs I took in Smolny. They
wouldn't allow me to take pictures in the hallways. I had this little camera
under my coat, but they did let me shoot in the room itself. It was a
beautiful room: it was Georgian. It was neo-classical; it was exactly the
same on either side. So is the hearing room in Washington, which we
also built in Spain. It's the same except for the windows. If it's the same
on the ends, all you need is half of them because you can turn the people
around. What we would do with these huge rooms is to build half and
then just turn everybody around.

After we finished shooting all the sets in England, then we came to
America. We had stopped many times for script and to build, it just
went on forever. We came to America; four months went by and we
still didn't finish the movie. Six months went by. I was doing *Frances* at
Zoetrope; Storaro was in town doing *One from the Heart*. Then we did
the Mexican jail, the publisher's office, and the American jail. This is
December of the following year. We go to the Village and shoot all those
places I had set up two years before. I got a double-decker bus to hide
what was wrong with the Flatiron building. It was shot on a Sunday
morning, and it's a great shot. It's the Steichen photograph, except it's
alive. We went back to Spain to do exterior shots of the train, and then
the picture was over. It took two years to get the picture done. It just
took an enormous amount of time.

What research did you do to design Harlem's legendary night club for The
Cotton Club?

I laid out the club by talking to the men and women who used to
dance there and from some pictures that I found. I knew roughly what
it was like. There was one wall I couldn't figure out. I kept asking these
people, "Were there windows on the 142nd Street side?" and they said,
"No, no, no, no." I finally got wonderful stuff; it took months and
months. My researcher here in Los Angeles found a complete set of
Cotton Club pictures taken by MGM in 1931. MGM was going to do a
movie about the Cotton Club. I had gotten pretty close. Of course, there
were windows there. They kept the dancers in the back; there was a
staircase with twenty-seven steps up into the room. I learned from all
the dancers they were stacked on top of each other; they had no bathroom; they had to pee in coffee cups. The kitchen had a Chinese chef.
The Cotton Club was on the second floor; it was over a motion picture

house. The girls used to go to the movies in the afternoon. I found an empty lot in Harlem that had a theater next to it. I built that whole street: the front of the club, the marquee, and all the shops around the corner and across the other corner. One crew worked to get that done, and then this huge crew was in the studio to build the club. The costumes cost three and a half million dollars, and the sets cost nine million dollars.

Did you use a visual metaphor to design the film?

When you laid that picture out, you had to do it with a tone in mind. "There's a cabin in the cotton"—that was the point of the Cotton Club. It was Whitey's window on the South—that was the meaning of it. That's a terrific metaphor for a club. The black family apartment and the white family apartment were literally built over the same staircase. The two apartments were the two halves of the world. It had to ring a bell. They had to make an echo so that you could feel something.

The world for Dick Tracy *was totally created on the soundstage. How did the visual style of the film develop?*

Warren Beatty and I are very close friends; we've done seven movies together. I am always hired before anybody else. We just talked about what we could possibly do. We knew we had to paint mattes for this whole world. You don't want to take a guy with a yellow raincoat and a yellow hat being followed by somebody with a flat head, and take him out to Chicago. You're never going to get there. Most of *Dick Tracy* takes place at night. The night was very important. We knew we needed the Expressionistic 1938 feeling that would convey the moon and the stars and the darkness. We needed a generic quality. You couldn't say, "That's a Ford" or "That's New York," because you would spoil everything. If a guy is eating a can of food, it says *Chili* on it and it's red. Even the money only has a dollar sign on it. This is totally generic: These are not buildings, these are icons of buildings. You start slowly getting into it. For the shack outside the city, I made over fifteen conceptual drawings to begin to understand this world that I was dealing with. I looked at German Expressionist paintings and Dick Tracy Sunday supplements. We had lots of books on cities; that's where you begin to form the city. There are wonderful books on photography. There are great studies of all the bridges in America. We had big research on bridges, New York, Chicago. We had wonderful photographers that took pictures all during the period of the 1930s and 1940s. Slowly you build this world of your own. The whole picture was shot on the back lot; we painted it. All the sets were in the studio. I had nine stages—it's a totally handmade movie.

You have designed so many visually distinctive films. What do you look for in a project?

In the last ten years, I've done a lot of pictures that take a lot of guts; they're courageous. Even if they're a mistake, they're about trying something, going for something. If you lose, you lose big; you win, you win big. Occasionally, when you get exhausted from those pictures, you do nice little things. *Tequila Sunrise* is a nice movie. It's relaxing to do. I always wanted to design an Italian restaurant and a beach house. So those things help you. Then you've got to go for these giants. I don't want safe movies. I don't want safe directors. I don't want people who are running scared. Warren Beatty has got nothing but courage. Mike Nichols had a lot of courage. I did the fifties with Kazan, Marty Ritt, Lumet, and Frankenheimer—the street people. I did the sixties with Mike, Roman, Elaine May, and Warren. I did the seventies with Warren, Mike, Huston, and Warren again. The eighties are done. I like new directors because there's a future there, not only for them, but there's something for me to think about. Directors count. Scripts don't count because you can fix the script; you can't fix the director. If the director is really good, he's not going to do a bad script if there is any possible way he can avoid it, so that's your best bet. My job is to look for directors.

5

Richard MacDonald

British born Richard MacDonald began his career as a painter who learned his craft by passionately studying the art of drawing. He was a senior lecturer at an art school in England when he encountered director Joseph Losey during a chance meeting that led to an extraordinary collaboration spanning over twenty years and producing a harvest of films.

This prolific relationship began when Losey, an American expatriate living in London, asked MacDonald to do drawings for a film he was planning. For thirteen years, MacDonald worked intimately with the director preplanning and overseeing the design of his films but was uncredited because he was not in the union. During this period MacDonald designed many films for Losey, including *The Sleeping Tiger*, *Time Without Pity*, *The Gypsy and the Gentleman*, *Blind Date*, and *The Criminal*.

After entering the British union, MacDonald's name began appearing on many of Losey's iconoclastic films: *Eve*, *King and Country*, *Modesty Blaise*, *Secret Ceremony*, *Boom*, *The Assassination of Trotsky*, *Galileo*, and *The Romantic Englishwoman*. One of their crowning achievements is the 1964 classic *The Servant*, a film in which the design plays a significant role in creating the claustrophobic atmosphere so necessary for the dramatic role reversal of Harold Pinter's characters.

MacDonald and Losey predesigned each film even before a script was completed. MacDonald drew and designed each set, providing the director with the essential means to conceptualize his vision. MacDonald's participation on Losey's films continued through the shooting process and often included the design of the titles.

Losey found a kindred spirit in MacDonald, a man who shared the director's highly developed intellectual and artistic notions. They would discuss and debate painting, architecture, and conceptual ideas for hours on end during the critical period in which the visual look of a film was conceived.

MacDonald has brought his visual imagination to the work of other pictorially stimulating directors. He was the production designer for John Boorman's underrated sequel to *The Exorcist*, *Exorcist II: The Heretic*, a film filled with exotic imagery and a futuristic prescience. He also designed *Altered States* for the wildly eccentric Ken Russell, with whom he helped create the vivid hallucinatory visions that are the motor of the film. MacDonald also has had extensive creative relationships with the director John Schlesinger as the production designer of *Far from the Madding Crowd*, *Marathon Man*, and *Day of the Locust* and with Norman Jewison on *Jesus Christ Superstar*, . . . *And Justice for All*, and *F.I.S.T.*

Richard MacDonald brings a long tradition of art and architectural history to all of his work, heightened by his unrestrained imagination. His affinity for such materials as wood and stone and a highly developed sense of color, shape, and texture enrich the fabric of a film's overall design.

After his experience on over thirty films, MacDonald still returns to what he believes are the greatest powers of the designer, the ability to see and to draw.

1962 *Eve*

1964 *The Servant*

1965 *King and Country*

1966 *Modesty Blaise*

1967 *Far from the Madding Crowd*

1968 *Secret Ceremony*
      Boom!

1971 *A Severed Head*
      Bloomfield

1972 *The Assassination of Trotsky*

1973 *Jesus Christ Superstar*

1975 *Galileo*
      The Romantic Englishwoman
      The Day of the Locust

1976 *Marathon Man*

1977 *Exorcist II: The Heretic*

1978 *F.I.S.T.*

1979 *The Rose*

. . . And Justice for All

1980   *Altered States*

1982   *Cannery Row*

1983   *Something Wicked This Way Comes*

1984   *Electric Dreams*

         Teachers

         Supergirl

1985   *Plenty*

1986   *Space Camp*

1988   *Coming to America*

1990   *The Russia House*

1991   *The Addams Family*

1992   *Jennifer Eight*

How did you become a production designer?

I met the film director Joseph Losey when Senator Joseph McCarthy threw him out of the United States. He had done *The Boy with Green Hair* in Italy and arrived in England. There was a little French club in Saint James London; it's long gone, but it was a splendid place. There were a great many odd film people, writers, musicians, and all sorts of others in the arts—really quite an interesting gang. I was a member of this place, and Joe came in. At the time, I was teaching painting at the Camberwell School of Art. I was sort of senior lecturer. Losey wanted some drawings made, and a film director who knew me and knew Joe said to him, "Oh, go and talk to Richard. He can do your drawings, he can draw." I didn't know anything about films and sets. A lot of friends of mine did cartoon and model animation films, and I knew their problems. I often did drawings for people, and that was what Joe wanted. That's how I got connected with films. It was my own film school. Joe was a real filmmaker. It was the privilege of teaching yourself, which I've been doing ever since.

Can you give an example of a visual metaphor you and Losey used to design a film?

His metaphor for *The Servant* was that the house was a snail. It had a spiral staircase that went through three stories. It all sort of went convoluting into the kitchen. It's an entity, so everything fits together like a clock. There isn't a wrong camera move. We used to discuss and draw out camera moves. The cameraman, Gianni di Venanzo, was absolutely marvelous. He could shoot through a crack in the door and give you a landscape.

You designed many black-and-white films for Losey. How do you know how the colors are going to translate in black and white?

You know the intensity and how certain reds will go just black—blacker than black. You can get another black which will be lovely, like a velvet black. There's one shot Joe and di Venanzo did in *Eve* with Jeanne Moreau and Stanley Baker. It was shot out on the island of Torcello. We started on the moon rising over a far house across the island, and we went around and across the lagoon and came right around to the Tower of Torcello, and there was the sun setting behind it. It went around and came down onto the beach of the island where Jeanne Moreau and Stanley were sitting. She was dressed in black velvet. It came out so intense because of the little bit of light on the water from the sunset. Suddenly, you saw this black figure sitting there. It's the most beautiful shot; you'd never get that in color. Color has taken away all that depth of focus, all that quality. In black and white, you could use two velvets and could see the way that the nap on one worked against the nap on the other. You could get the feel of it. You could see the density of the material.

Now with color, it's like dropping the whole lot and saying, "Let's see how it comes out." I've seen disasters happen. If you know about color, it's simple, but if you don't know, it sounds utterly complicated. Yellow has a very small band in which it remains yellow; then it goes off. Tonally, it can only be a nice bright yellow in a very small range, and then it goes very bright. As soon as it gets darker, it goes brown, and then it goes grungy. Brown and red have a tremendous range. They retain their color as they get lighter and lighter. They retain their color as they get darker and darker. When you get into the bluer reds, they tend to go to blue, then to purple or to violet. My favorite way of painting a wall is to paint it with a cold gray or a cold brown—a sort of raw umber—and then spatter a warm color over it. The camera can't make up its mind, because it can't quite decide what it's going to do with this cool color and warm color. So it gives the wall a marvelous sort of feeling and a tremendous intensity. You can do it on any color wall. On *The Addams Family*, I painted a wall which actually vibrated. It was painted with a very light ochre-yellowy color and over the top of it a very light lavender blue. This produces a gray which is absolutely vibrant. It looks like a gray, but when the light comes across, it will change and become alive. It was put on one of these encrusted papers which has a textured pattern on it. You can rub the other color on over it so that it's beautifully alive; the color's absolutely alive. It's only knowing about color.

In Day of the Locust *there is a scene where a large movie set collapses during the filming of a Hollywood epic. Were you involved in working out the mechanics of this special effect?*

Oh yes, this was before special effects specialists arrived; you had to do all those things. We worked that out so it fell down perfectly.

How was it done?

It was done on a series of collapsing sections. It was all held up by cables which were let go, and the stunt men just fell forward onto cardboard boxes underneath them. It took four days to shoot it. Now, special effects are all done with vacuums, pipes, and hydraulics. In those days, they were all done with pieces of string, and they worked. In a way, they had a human element to them which gave them sudden life.

The meditation tanks used in Altered States *actually existed in the sixties. Did you use real meditation tanks for the film, or did you design them?*

Yes, we used the real thing, but we invented the transparent one for the time we can see William Hurt inside. We built that just for the look of it.

Where was the tank room shot?

That was a set. We built all those pipes and things. Then we found a basement of a big hotel that had all these pipes and corridors and found places to connect them up.

Were you involved in working out the hallucination sequences in Altered States?

Yes, I went and shot a lot of them in Oxford Scientific. They do microphotography of things like bursting stars. They have high-speed cameras that will photograph many thousands of frames a second. It's extraordinary; they photograph down holes and look at mice breeding. They're charming people, mad as hatters. They did the orange sun with a halo around it, which suddenly goes off into star fields, and you got a sense of space.

Altered States *has many sequences with extraordinary imagery. How did you accomplish the sequence when the William Hurt character hallucinates that he is swallowing himself?*

We built a model of the face and built a rig for the camera to travel down. We built a whirlpool. You got the idea of actually swallowing yourself; going down and out the other end. It produced quite an interesting film sequence. Ken Russell and I built all sorts of elaborate things. We had a grand time building.

The autistic center in Exorcist II: The Heretic *is an incredible set. It is a seemingly endless series of interconnecting rooms with glass walls. How was this done?*

They were six-sided modules that were all locked onto each other. The ceiling was also six-sided. There were sheets of Mylar stretched on frames, which reflect with no distortion. Those were put all around the studio walls facing the modules. That's what gave it that endless feeling; they just went on reflecting forever. John Boorman was trying to give it a sense of science.

The therapist, played by Louise Fletcher, was able to dim the lights so that all of the modules went black, except the one where she was about to hypnotize Regan, played by Linda Blair. What was the concept behind that?

That's how you'd get into the past, by dimming it out.

In Exorcist II, *there is a visual metaphor which links the canyons of New York City's skyscrapers with the canyons of Africa. Where were the African canyon sequences shot?*

Most of those canyons in Africa I cut myself out of polystyrene in Ireland in Bray Studios. You can cut polystyrene with a hot wire and make marvelous rocks.

Where did you create the spectacular outdoor terrace for Regan's New York apartment, which overlooked the skyline? Was a matte painting used for the background?

We built that on the roof at the Warner Communications building. That skyline is real; that's the balcony there. We built a back wall entrance into the bedroom, so that we could put the bed right on the edge. We tried to get a shot looking right over the top of her head down into the canyon. It's sort of maximum vertigo.

How did you create the mirrored effect of the New York skyline in the interior of the apartment?

In the background, we lit a great big photomural of the New York skyline. The louvers of the window were Mylar, so they reflected the view of the skyline, which split up. John Boorman's a great bloke for inventing; you can work with him on things.

You have worked on many films that express futuristic visions; do you have any theories about how to design the fantastic?

I believe in the biggest fantasies, but unless they're based in some sort of real knowledge, you can't take off. You can't build fantasies unless you really know what you're doing.

Did you use real courtrooms for . . . And Justice for All? *They have a very distinctive style to them.*

Those were real courtrooms. We dressed some of them just to bring out the portraits of the judges. That is really one of the things which Joe Losey taught me. He loved to build in the character of the people into the furniture—where they'd been, what they were. It's second nature to me now to see a house and almost see the relatives of the owners. When you look at other people's houses, your eye puts that in.

How much of The Russia House *was shot in Russia?*

We shot all of the exteriors in Russia. The only interiors that were shot there were inside the writers colony. All the other interiors were done in good old late Victorian hotels and other public buildings in London. I found that it was very easy to match our interiors for Russia in London; you just dressed them for Russia, and no one knew the difference.

Why do the interiors match so well? Were British architects involved in Russian architecture?

Yes, British architects went to Russia. For a certain period they are exactly the same. The Russians commissioned artists to paint walls and to refurbish their palaces.

What was your design concept for The Addams Family?

I said to the director, Barry Sonnenfeld, "To me, they're royals; you've got to make them eccentric and exclusive. The only way you can get away with it in film is to make them absolutely content with their eccentricity. I'm not going to dress their house with newspapers and magazines like any ordinary house; that's not their act at all. They're interested in themselves and their goings-on. The furniture is old; they don't mind that it's falling to pieces." I put Rennie Mackintosh chairs in the dining room. People think they're modern, but they're not. These chairs have the perfect Addams look. I've built a dining table to go with them, because I couldn't find one. Set in with heavy Victorian furniture, it's quite interesting.

You have worked with many directors who are highly sophisticated and inventive on a visual level. Does your relationship with them help to give the film a pictorial richness?

That's part of the language which I think is lost on people who are inadequately developed technically. That's why Joe Losey was such fun to work with—the same with Ken Russell and John Boorman—they know. You can make references to things which are hidden in all our pasts. You can drag them up, and people will recognize them. It makes the film richer for them. It's not just a piece of trellis or something; it belongs to some particular architecture.

Do you think it's necessary to be able to draw to be a production designer?

To me, someone who can't draw isn't a designer, they're a chooser, unless they can actually see something in their mind and draw. The Addams house was drawn. It's an involved house. You draw it and build it. We built everything that was in the drawing on a land fill; there was nothing. It took two hundred loads of earth to build the cemetery. We built a road and hill. I drew the plan for the whole house, and it was built with very few alterations. I really don't understand how someone who can't draw would do that. I know costume designers who do the same thing. I'm amazed how people get away with it.

Do you consider space one of the major tools you have as a production designer?

Yes. I design for space and how you feel it—making things so you actually feel the space. You use it to shape things. I shaped the set I built for the exterior of the Addams house. You take a piece of land, and you shape it the way you want it, so it absolutely works from certain points of view. The roads work in this direction, in that direction. You think like that in your head. A few years ago, I went to a computer demonstration. This producer said, "You must see this. We feed in the plan of your set, and now you can see it from any angle you want." I said, "How did you think I made that plan? I looked at it from all these angles in my mind; I don't need a computer to do that." It would be a nuisance to me when you do the alteration of it. When you alter it, everything else alters, so everything's got to be in your mind, otherwise you're not free to do it. I can do it in any way, because I know it in my mind. I can bend the whole thing together and push it off in any direction. You can flatten the walls and increase the size of a room. It's a tactile sense. You actually feel fabrics, you feel rooms, you feel space. It is that sense of relationship which makes the quality of things.

Do you think it's important for a production designer to understand perspective? How is it used to create dramatic effects?

Yes, you bloody well know it! You've got to know how to distort it and how to actually play with the damn thing. I build all my sets in perspective. There isn't a straight wall. I do it all the time. I've just done it on a school we had to use for *The Addams Family*. I put in lots of arches down both corridors and made them diminish slightly in size. It gives you more depth. The story is so episodic it needs something to hold it together, a sort of atmosphere. You've got to give them a house to live in which is so secure that whichever part you are in, you know you're in the same house. You can see everything from anywhere. From the door in *The Addams Family* house interior, you can literally see the whole length of the house through the picture gallery, through where the organ is right through to the library. The rooms all lead into each other. You can see the staircase from both sides of two rooms. I put in pocket doors, which slide into the walls in all of the rooms. You can shut them off; you can pull a door out of the wall. It's a sort of catacomb. It's an idea of how you can work out space with a unit of views.

Do you have a good visual memory?

I've trained it. It used to be part of the business of drawing. Memory drawing was one of the subjects of the old drawing exam given by the board of education. They would describe a still life object or an activity, and you had to draw it from memory. The great thing about Joseph Losey was that he also had the same visual memory of things and atmospheres. So that made him an interesting bloke to work with, because we would have conversations about a scene, and you'd find that you had built the room, the house, and everything around the conversation.

Do you think films will continue to be shot in the studio, or do you think the current trend of shooting the majority of most films on location will put an end to this tradition?

Most of what I've done here in Hollywood is built on the stage. I don't know how much longer that will continue. I think it will. They've either shot every location, or they can't go someplace because it's too expensive. So if they want to do something, then they're back to building on the stage.

What is the best way to train a production designer?

I think the best training for a production designer is to spend the first thirty or forty years of your life as a dilettante really seeing things, examining things, enjoying things. By then you've got enough experience. I mean traveling and drawing what you see and not just photographing. You can photograph things—I do lots—but you've still got to draw things. You've got to do a drawing for every ten photographs. Painting makes you see; you look at things. It makes you remember things, because you sit and look at something and draw it, and it's in your head forever to use. You take a photograph of something, and you think you've got it. You haven't got it unless you look at it. Most people looking at photographs only recognize it because it's Auntie May and the children somewhere, but they wouldn't know St. Peter's from St. Paul's if it wasn't for Auntie May and the children. People don't focus on things until it's actually something that means something to them, like Auntie May. If you can draw, you've got an eye. My pieces of paper are endless descriptions of communications. They look like hieroglyphics to some people, but they exactly describe the chairs, the lamp, and the table. They describe how things work. It's a language. If you aren't absolutely able in your mind to pick a up bus, turn it upside down, and chuck it over a cliff with it revolving as it goes down, then you're not really what I'd call a competent draftsman. If you look at any of the masters, like Leonardo, they could draw anything in any sort of way. Look at Goya's bulls. He didn't have a camera, he looked. He could see a bull. It was drawn from life, looking at bulls. It's something which is gone with the camera. If you draw well, you can see anything and put it where it is; you feel the space. A drawing is a living thing.

6

Paul Sylbert

The worlds of music, painting, philosophy, and poetry envelop the metaphors Paul Sylbert has created to root a fertile design that extends beyond time and place, deep into the essence of a film. The ability to merge metaphors with filmic content is supported by over four decades of experience and technical expertise that create reality out of the lyricism of ideas.

Paul Sylbert entered the film business in New York in the 1950s. He and his brother, Richard, were the art directors on two films for director Elia Kazan, *Baby Doll* and *A Face in the Crowd*. In 1957, Paul Sylbert was the art director for Alfred Hitchcock's *The Wrong Man*.

Sylbert has designed and directed for the theater, opera, and television. In 1971, he directed *The Steagle* and later wrote about the experience in *Final Cut*, an insightful look into the corporate world of Hollywood filmmaking.

Paul Sylbert has collaborated with many fine directors, including Sidney Lumet, Robert Benton, Stuart Rosenberg, Milos Forman, Warren Beatty, Paul Schrader, Brian De Palma, Michael Apted, and Mike Nichols. He has designed such acclaimed films as *One Flew over the Cuckoo's Nest*, *Kramer vs. Kramer*, and *Heaven Can Wait*, for which he was the recipient of an Academy Award for best art direction–set decoration.

His most recent projects are *Rush* for Richard and Lili Zanuck, and the adaptation of Pat Conroy's *The Prince of Tides* directed by Barbra Streisand, for which he was nominated for an Academy Award.

1953 *Roogie's Bump*
1956 *Baby Doll* (associate art director, with Richard Sylbert)

1957 *A Face in the Crowd* (with Richard Sylbert)
      The Wrong Man
1969 *The Riot*
1972 *Bad Company*
1975 *The Drowning Pool*
      One Flew Over the Cuckoo's Nest
1976 *Mikey and Nicky*
1978 *Heaven Can Wait***
1979 *Hardcore*
      Kramer vs. Kramer
1980 *Resurrection*
1981 *Wolfen*
      Blow Out
1983 *Without a Trace*
      Gorky Park
1984 *The Pope of Greenwich Village*
      Firstborn
1985 *The Journey of Natty Gann*
1987 *Ishtar*
      Nadine
      The Pick-Up Artist
1988 *Biloxi Blues*
      Fresh Horses
1990 *Career Opportunities*
1991 *The Prince of Tides**
      Rush

*Academy Award nomination for best achievement in art direction–set decoration.

** Academy Award for best achievement in art direction–set decoration.

What is your starting point for designing a film?

Where does a designer begin? I begin with the script. I read a script and get a reader's response to it. Then, as I go through it, I begin to see it in terms of design. For *Rush*, I got a call from the Zanucks after I'd read the script, and they said, "We've just come back from Austin, Texas. We were told it is a very good place to make movies, and we know you've worked there." I said, in effect, "You're in the wrong town; this movie has nothing to do with Austin. For this movie, you have to be on the coast."

This is what I concluded after reading the script. It's a story of two cops, a young girl and her partner, an older cop, a narcotics officer who's a junkie. It was a story about two things that are naturally repellant like oil and water: you mix them and they do not mix, they try to stay separate. That's the essential conflict. Cops and narcotics have that exact condition. When a cop becomes a druggy, that's exactly like mixing oil and water. So I said, "You have to be somewhere near oil and somewhere near water, like the Houston area." As to the story's movement, he's a sacrificial figure, the sufferer who suffers. It's a passion play; it's the story of the descent. It's a descent into hell for both of them. Oil installations look like the mouth of hell with flames belching out. Where does oil come from? The bowels of the earth. All the hell images were right there! From the beach in Galveston to Pasadena, we had all the installations and all the water we ever wanted. The strongest elements were the co-mingling of things that ordinarily repel each other—oil and water, drugs and cops. I wanted railroad tracks in that picture, too. Everything is shipped by rail; you're always around railroad tracks. What do the words "tracks" and "lines" connote to you? They're the same words you use with cocaine, so I wanted shiny tracks and lines in the imagery.

The colors of the film were entirely controlled by several photographs I took. I went out to a gas station after a rain and photographed oil and water. When a little water drips into oil and the light strikes it right— 28 degrees, the same angle as a rainbow—you get the rainbow. It's like a prism breaking up light; you get the complete color range of the spectrum. The base is a very dark brown and a deep blue-black—earthy tones. I gave a set of photographs to the director, the set decorator, and the costume designer. The period of the film was 1975; all those oil colors are seventies colors, they're psychedelic rainbows. Oil colors have a metallic aspect—they look like peacock hurl, which is another thing I gave to the costume designer and the director. So the whole basis of the color of the film is this suggestion of oil and water; the colors unify it wonderfully.

The controlling images were things that both repel and attract and don't mix without wonderful patterns. The patterns in oil are wonderful. All the wallpapers you see are basically old seventies metallic wallpapers that have been glazed over with oily asphaltum to tone them a little bit. If you wanted to paint a van from that period, you looked at the book of the guy you found in town who used to do vans in the seventies and who still has pictures of them. There they were, the metallic colors: the browns, golds, and the blues. Everything has this metallic quality, every-thing is reflective. Remember the vinyl clothing in that period? Every-thing has that shininess, all to suggest this impossible situation, the attempt to mingle oil and water and the whole descent into hell. When you do a picture on location, it helps to be in the right place.

It seems as if it would be impossible to design a movie without having a conceptual idea of how to do it.

I don't think you could do it well. Ideas or concepts are basic; it's like the relationship between theory and practice. One doesn't exist without the other. They're constantly interacting, but you can't make yourself a prisoner of this kind of thing anymore than you can reach for symbols. It's a jumping off point, and like a good boxer you've got to stay flexible, you've got to know when to bob and weave. There are times where you're going to have to make a shift. You have to stay loose, because reality constantly makes demands on you that you also have to deal with.

Using the Lowenstein apartment you designed for The Prince of Tides, *can you give examples of how defining the characters led to the design of the set?*

I make up a list. I always make a long list based on character with the help of my wife, who's my assistant. The idea is to create a suitable fiction. Those things I write about characters and the dramatic situation are really a designer's version of the movie. You have to begin with the specifics. Who is Lowenstein's husband? After reading the script, I had in mind a man with Herbert Von Karajan's style and ego. He was a fiddle player rather than a conductor, but a musician is a musician, especially a world renowned soloist.

I grew up in that world; my uncle worked for Sol Hurok. I wanted to create an apartment which was not *hers*. The office was hers. He is not going to tell her how to do her office, but he is a man who dominates her—the apartment reflects him. The apartment was done as a reflection of this man's ego. Now who is this man? We made a long list of adjectives that represented this man: European, international, cosmopolitan, polished, elegant, powerful, fascistic, talented, domineering. Then opposite to the column are all the materials and styles that would match this list. The Lowenstein apartment in New York has black marble floors, because everything has to reflect and fragment. The scene is about a marriage breaking up. The dining room is solid black mirror. The rest of the apartment is black and white. The entire East Side skyline is reflected through the windows. When you're looking in the room, you could be outside. Everything reflects: the marble, the glass, the mirrored room. The idea behind it was maximum drama, fragmented lives, maximum contrast, glamour, and illusion—is this real or only a reflection? Is this marriage real or a trick of perception? It had a kind of richness, too, which was intimidating. The library is made of African Movinga; it's the most exquisite wood you've ever seen—rich and tigerish—which is what I wanted because he is so predatory. On the wall is an original Rosa Bonheur, a sketch for *The Horse Fair*—also powerful animals. I wanted the apartment to be neo-classical, Napoleonic—Lowenstein is a little Biedermeier dictator. It is all inset lighting, dramatic spotlighting, and there are wonderful exotic flowers just here and there, a suitable collection of art, but very few pieces. I used a copy of Kaspar David Friedrich's Roman ruins. The standby painter did it in his spare time. That's a beautiful copy, marvelous job, crackle, everything. Kasper David Friedrich is a nineteenth-century artist who has a great romantic-mystical flavor which even the coldest violinist would claim to have. Also he did ruins, which are a neo-classical motif. I also used Friedrich drawings and Dutch drawings. Jeroen Krabbe, who played the part, is a Dutch actor. Kasper David Friedrich is also good for the really in-people. I wanted to connect Lowenstein's world with the world of the artistic *haute-monde* and money. Every one of those adjectives on the list was in it. An idea has to get into the work or it is nothing. Nobody ever saw those pieces of paper. Barbra Streisand never saw them. I do it for myself. People who have seen the film got all these ideas without them being said. Barbra didn't see that apartment finished until a few days before we shot it, but she liked it a lot.

Do you think it's important to have a broad range of knowledge about the world to be a good production designer?

Stanislavsky's first requirement for his school was that the students had done something else. He preferred engineers, failed medical students—he didn't care what they did, as long as they knew something about the world and had some other discipline. The more disciplines you have as a designer, the better off you are. I studied art very young and music at the late age of forty. I knew music as a listener and opera designer, but not from the note, and I didn't know how to play an instrument. I took up the classical guitar, and the help that has given me in structuring a film is enormous. Music moves through motive and modulation. I tried to do that same thing with color. *Blow Out* was based on a tonic triad. Red, white, and blue were my C chord. The killer was a superpatriot. Patriotic gore—that's what it's all about. It's done in Philadelphia, which was the Bicentennial city. They still had the red, white, and blue Bicentennial walks in the street when I got there. I thought, "This is going to be red, white, and blue and three secondary colors, yellow, black, and green." The first scene in the picture has no red, white, and blue, no black, yellow, or green, but it has fuchsia, chartreuse, and all the colors in the previous De Palma film, *Dressed to Kill*. What you don't realize is that's not the movie, that it's the movie within the movie. Then there's a cut, and you've got two guys sitting in a screening room. The screening room is red, white, blue, and black, and you don't even notice it, and it builds from there.

Music is ambiguous. The whole diatonic structure is ambiguous. You may not know what key it's written in until you're a page or two into it. That's the same thing I tried to do. You don't feel it at first, but there is red, white, black, and blue—even his tie. Screening rooms are black;

you take it for granted. His office has bright blue walls on which you'll find a target that's red, white, and blue. It begins to come together little by little, until the scene at the end with the fireworks and that whole world of the Bicentennial celebration is all red, white, and blue. It built up through the entire film. It never made anybody uncomfortable. It worked so well in the city of Philadelphia because it never pushed the reality away, it was just an underpinning for a political, patriotic melodrama, and it was an opportunity to really use music to structure a whole film.

Where was One Flew Over the Cuckoo's Nest *shot?*

At an empty ward, at a real institution in Eugene, Oregon, left over from a period in the sixties when there was a movement to make them look other than like institutions. All the wards were decorated and painted pretty colors. They were done like Grandma's kitchen with little curtains on the windows. Once I had a conversation with Milos Forman, I understood that he wanted an earlier feeling. I went to earlier institutions to get some idea of what it had been like before. Those colors they had in Oregon would not have worked at all for the film. You needed to set faces and bodies against something much more neutral. I made it the off-white color an egg would get if it were heated. It's an ecru, a mother's old linen, because the mother image was very strong in that film—Big Nurse and her suffocating maternalism. Their white costumes are seen against the off-white, so the faces stand out strongly. Some of the most effective shots were those faces, especially at the end, when the Indian goes through the window and there are close-ups of actors with their heads swiveling suddenly, and all the madness is right there. I had to make a ward in which you could shoot continually without seeing any lights. The lights were built into it. It created an environment for these people that would work no matter what you were doing day or night.

In what year was the film supposed to take place?

The film was meant to be in the sixties, roughly. It shouldn't have indicated any very specific world. It was in part its own world as all madhouses are, but it was essentially a real place in a real time. It felt Kafkaesque. When Orson Welles did *The Trial*, he made a terrible mistake, which was to make that world Kafkaesque in the completely wrong sense. Kafka must be played in a real world; that's the contrast. Anybody who's read Kafka knows that he reads like Dickens. Everything was perfectly real; what was happening was unreal. Kafka's favorite writer was Dickens. A man becomes a cockroach in a real world. If he becomes a cockroach in a fantastic world, it ceases to be fantastic.

How did you find the mansion for Heaven Can Wait? *The credits state the film was shot at Filoli Center.*

The studio rule was you couldn't be more than thirty miles away. I flew in a helicopter and took pictures of every house within thirty miles, and the right one wasn't there. On my desk, I had a picture of Filoli from *Architectural Digest* with an article about it going up for sale for $2 million, and it was empty. All it showed were the gardens and a little glimpse of the house. I said to myself, "I can't see enough of the house, but the gardens are wonderful. I'd like to have great grounds." Filoli is an acronym; it was made up from two letters from the words *fight, love*, and *live*. A man by the name of Bourne, who was a great robber baron, had the house built in 1928 on 750 acres on a bluff. The San Andreas fault runs right through the house. It was taken over by the Roth family. Lurlene Roth closed the house when her husband died, kept the gardens open, took 250 acres, and made it the Filoli Institution. The gardens were open to the public a certain number of days a week.

One day, Warren Beatty went to a party and somebody talked to him about Filoli. He said, "You know anything about Filoli?" I said, "Yes, I have a picture of it on my desk, but, Warren, that's not thirty miles away. That's in Woodside, California." He said, "Go anyway." I made an appointment to see a man who was running the organization and walked through it. The pool house was a mess, the pool was cracked up, but for the most part, the gardens and the exterior of the house were pretty well kept up. The interior was empty and gloomy; thirty years of coal oil was on those walls. Lurlene Roth wouldn't change a thing. I said, "Warren, we can't use it unless I can paint and redecorate the whole place." I headed for the San Francisco Museum. I usually go to the local museums, because I love to look at pictures. I saw Roth's name on the board in the museum. I talked to the conservatory department and asked if I could take a young conservator to Filoli and show them the original color of the hallway. They agreed to it on the condition that Mrs. Roth's secretary be there. I was an art student, I had studied the chemistry of paint, I knew what was under that shit. The conservator took a little swab and removed all the grime behind the molding of the little closet at the turn of the stair. He showed the secretary this lovely dove, putty color. She said, "Okay, you can paint it that color." So I repainted the whole lower floor, except one room that had linen walls, which I would have had to strip. We didn't need it. I was able to redo the dining room, the lower living room, library, the marble floors in that wonderful garden house, the pool area, and completely decorate the house. The ballroom, which we made into a gym, had wall murals of Ireland by an Italian painter Bourne brought from Italy to paint Erin for him—he was homesick. The lower floors and the exterior were all used. The whole upper floor was redesigned and built on the stage; it felt just like the rest of the house. When the set was done, I got a note from Warren saying I had gone $250,000 over on the dressing alone. They had no idea what they were in for with a house that size decorated for the richest man in the world.

The wallpaper, bedspread, and pillows in Dyan Cannon's bedroom all have a similar pattern. What was the concept behind this?

The idea of her bedroom was a joke: there is a print, on top of print, on top of print. There was a story about the apartment of an assistant to Diana Vreeland, the fashion mavin. Her apartment had *tchotchekalas* on all the tables and all these printed fabrics. Her children had come home from school one day, and mother was wearing her Gucci gown, sitting on her Gucci couch, among her Gucci pillows. The kids looked all over and never found her until she moved, then they realized she was in the room. I said, "That's the kind of bedroom I want." I was sending up the rich and the way they lived.

Ultimately, was it still cheaper to use Filoli rather than building the entire set on the stage?

In the fourteen months we worked on the picture, six months was spent making models before we even got to Filoli. I made a double-decker model of a set based on Hugh Heffner's place. Any one of the models would have cost well over a million bucks to build. Filoli cost us maybe half the price of one of those sets, dressing and all.

How did you create the illusion that the way station in Heaven Can Wait *was up in the clouds between earth and heaven?*

I thought, "We are not in heaven, we are not on earth, we are somewhere in between. It needs a shadowless world; the light is all around us. How do I do that?" My assistant, who had been in the Navy, did a little research. He found a Navy grid of steel strips used for decking. It was narrow, about an inch and a quarter deep, with spaces about an inch wide, which pass 85 percent of the light and can still carry the weight. We covered the decking with muslin soaked in water. We use muslin in the theater all the time; you can light through it. It was lit from underneath, and arcs were used all around a white cyclorama to lose the horizon. We had two big buckets of dry ice at the corners of the stage; we tilted them and the froth poured out. We hired Bob McDonald, the same special effects man who had done the original *Here Comes Mr. Jordan*, who said, "You need to maintain a temperature of 64 degrees on the average for it to lay down." The froth would just stay there, because we'd kept it cool enough. It was a world without shadows.

What was the concept behind the idea of the plane that was used to transport people to heaven from the way station?

It was modeled on the Concorde. The idea was a big bird putting people under her arms. The whole idea was to make it motherly. Even the runway is my version of an umbilical cord. What I did was to find the fuselage of an old DC-6. I brought it onto the stage and the rest was built onto it with plywood. It didn't have to fly, thank you, but it was really the big bird. What are the pearly gates? Pearlescent paint; it was all painted with pearlescent paint. The key painter came up with that. The dark suits the people in line wore just made it right. The whole idea for heaven was Brooks Brothers, a well-established firm; that's why they're all dressed up like that. Against the white, it was whimsical and never threatening.

In Kramer vs. Kramer, *Dustin Hoffman plays an advertising man. How did you decide what his apartment should look like, and how does the design help to define his profession?*

In the middle sixties, I spent a few years in the advertising business with a commercial firm; I know this world. The director Bob Benton came out of advertising, too, but earlier. The big issue was the apartment Kramer lived in and where his neighborhood was. Bob had that world in 1962, and he wanted to use a big, sprawling apartment like a West Side apartment. I know exactly where Ted Kramer lives, I know his grocery, I know what subway stop he gets off, I know the bars he goes to. I went right to Third Avenue and photographed six buildings between 61st Street and 71st Street. I found two buildings that I really liked. I brought the pictures and a floor plan from a little efficiency apartment back to Bob. All I had to do was to adjust doorways and move things a little bit to let the camera see. I said, "It's got to be a new apartment. It's got to be efficient. It's got to be basically white. It's got to be in an area where all these guys live." Bob gives in.

To decorate the dining room, I went to Conran's. Advertising art directors love the attention grabbers—boys and their toys. If you say, Kramer wants to be George Lois, but he could only afford one thing a little like George Lois, there's a Foulon print which he gets from a store on 57th Street. Kramer couldn't afford a piece of modern sculpture, but he gets some bizarre looking cactus and puts it on a pedestal, and it worked. I also believed that they'd get an antique rug from an aunt or a piece of furniture from her mother. That was the right place. You felt that this guy wanted to be somewhere, he wanted to be bigger than this. That apartment had a lot to do with why you felt comfortable in that movie, why you felt convinced in that movie. You saw his attempt to cook. Can you imagine that scene being in anything but that confined little efficiency kitchen between the dining room and the hallway? It was made for that.

The nook is a very important part of the apartment. It is where many of the most critical scenes dealing with Hoffman's relationship with his son take place. One of the most expressive things about it is the uncluttered simplicity of the back wall which frames the two of them.

I've done three pictures with the cinematographer Nestor Almendros; he is wonderful. Nestor said it better than anybody. "If the production designer doesn't put it out there, we can't create it, we can only light it." That's it. DPs can't create character, they can only create mood. They can't create objects. They can't create the environment. They can't tell you what these people like or dislike, or what they want to live with or who they want to be. They can only light it. The test of a good cameraman is a man who can light a wall without a picture on it. A good cameraman takes pictures off and bad ones put them on. We had family photographs in the hallway, and for certain shots Nestor actually removed them just to keep the clarity of the head. Gordon Willis knows how to light that way. Storaro won't hang a picture where it doesn't need one. Hacks hang pictures; they want to busy up the wall because they don't know how to deal with it.

Why were there two phones on the desk in the office of Ted's lawyer, played by Howard Duff?

We shot it in the office of Sidney Cohen, who is the model for the lawyer. Sidney Cohen was a famous lawyer who got the first guys off the blacklist in New York. The two phones, the cane, and all the pictures on the wall are from Sidney Cohen. He was Bob Benton's lawyer and mine.

Hardcore *presented two very different worlds. The first is the Calvinism of Grand Rapids, Michigan, and the second is the world of pornography. What concepts did you use to create and contrast these two?*

It goes from Rembrandt to hell in one move. The delft stuff and all that Dutch world in the house in Grand Rapids was great for those uptight people. The contrast between Grand Rapids and the porno world was between Calvinism and hell.

You used a wide color palette in designing the porno world.

There's a wide range of colors and the whole idea was to have a broad palette. The narrowness of the palette of the Grand Rapids scenes—the brown tones and the blue delft and the wood—was a reflection of the spirit of Calvinism. I kept the palette narrow in Grand Rapids so that once I got into this new world, I was suddenly free to do anything. The idea was to free the palette. I was allowed to go red, white, pink, orange, black, powder blue in the motel rooms and whorehouses. The wildness was a color version of the anarchy that went on in that other world.

Wolfen *has a very unique vision of New York. How much of the film was shot on location?*

All the major interiors are sets. Vincent Canby thought that church was there, and he is a New Yorker. That was an empty lot in the South Bronx. We built that church from the ground up for a million dollars.

In the opening of Wolfen, *Vandermeer, a multimillionaire, is murdered along with his wife while walking in Lower Manhattan. Later we see the opulent penthouse where they lived. What did you design into these scenes to interpret the character of Vandermeer?*

Those silhouettes of the Dutch windmill in the opening are because of his name, Vandermeer. We took the idea of the Dutch background. The Dutch were the first settlers in New York, the first Governor of New York. We didn't have the money for a real tall Dutch mill, which is what the director wanted. In the research we came across a little sepia sketch probably done in the sixteenth century of a Dutch horizontal mill, and we built a Dutch horizontal mill with sails. It worked well because there are the spooky shadows of the people against the white canvas sails. The idea for the penthouse was to make Vandermeer, Rockefeller. Rockefeller has a contemporary museum. It wanted modern art. I had a sculptor do that fake Lachaise that falls over. I also wanted gold objects. The furniture was Italian leather; it was very new then. The architectural inspiration was Alvar Aalto's work. The apartment was white and brushed steel; it was like a bird cage. You could see the whole of New York Bay.

How was that view created?

We made two translights of the entire New York Bay, one for night and one for day. They were 120 feet surrounding that apartment.

There is a room in Wolfen *that is filled with high-tech surveillance equipment. Were you involved in setting up the equipment for the surveillance room, and what atmosphere were you trying to communicate through your design?*

The set decorator and I set up all of the high-tech equipment. It was projected through the back or fed in electronically. After the set stopped, there was another twenty feet to the wall all lined up with banks of projectors and equipment feeding that information in. I didn't fake it; there are no little trace lights going up and down for no reason. It was exactly what you would have in a place like that. I hate that stuff that looks like Saturday afternoon serials where everything has to flash, move, and twit. The surveillance headquarters had to be convincing, because those big executive places exist. Mine was split cinder blocks; it was New Brutalist bunker. The idea was the two levels where they had to be able to look down. They even look down at their own people. It was that kind of chain through the whole movie. Everyone is always looking down: in the surveillance room they look down, in the penthouse they live looking down, you look down from the church. You're always being watched. Then there is the contrast between the rich and poor done with both form and color. The movie is about who's watching you; it's both surveillance of terrorists and surveillance of the public— surveillance by the wolves of the world.

How did you create the house in Firstborn? *What was done to the location house you used?*

I took the kitchen apart and we rebuilt it, then we built a complete duplicate of the entire set on the stage. The scale is the same. The exterior yard was also on the stage. The yard was not translights, it was painted.

Some of the yard was shot on the real location, but you also had to see the outdoors from inside the house. It's mixed in together, a good match. We used black and white mounted photo murals tinted with oil paints.

How do you match the lighting between a studio exterior and a practical one?

I only shoot a backing on an overcast day or after a rain, when there is no directional light. There are no shadows on the backing, so the objects that you put in front of it get the light and convince you that the light is coming from that direction. *Firstborn* was one of those jobs where you do it well and nobody's going to sing about it, but it had the right world. The Teri Garr character had a nice little secure "dream" house, and then someone invades it. Her bedroom is very childish. The idea there was very important—that she never grew up. She was still romantic in a girlie sense and that was nearly her undoing. The kids could see better than she could.

How did you create the view of the backyard from the apartment in Without a Trace?

It was a miniature. That whole apartment was a set. The backyard you saw when you looked out the back windows was completely built to scale. It was based on my backyard on 64th Street. I reduced it from thirty yards to thirty feet. When you do those jobs, the idea is really simple; you're making proportion do the work of perspective. There is no perspective in it, because the camera constantly has to move. All you can do is keep the perpendiculars and reduce the scale. You use mathematical formulas and try to work things quite accurately for the camera because the camera doesn't lie.

How is the formula determined to get the correct scale?

There's a scene in *The Wrong Man* where a prison guard slides open a little slot in the door of a cell, and you see Henry Fonda inside the cell pacing up and back. The guard says, "Come on out, Mr. Balestrero." Then he opens the door and Fonda leaves. That row in the Tombs was built on a stage in Hollywood. Hitchcock said, "I have to use an 18mm lens in order to see inside this slot, but you know what a distortion an 18mm lens creates. How big do I have to make the cell to make it look like a six-by-nine cell through an 18mm lens?" He said no one had been able to solve this sort of problem for him. Well, the formula was very simple. My assistant and I sat down and in an hour had the answer. The reason they call a 50mm lens a normal lens is because objects remain in perspective approximately as they do with your eye. So 50 becomes the constant; therefore it's a ratio of 18 to 50, roughly 3 to 1, which means looking at a cell 3' 9" deep through an 18mm lens is exactly what a 9' cell would look like through a 50mm lens. Lens over distance times 50mm over x—it's high school algebra. But because 3' 9" is so restricting I made it 4' 6" and Henry took little steps. You'd swear he was in a 9' cell. These problems are the fun part. Hitchcock loved to fool with them.

That's the fun of this business; it isn't all fancy sketches and swatching. Film is sleight of hand, and that's why Welles loved magic. What was Melies? A magician. The campfire scene at night in *Bad Company* was done on a sloped floor in a gym in Kansas. We do this all the time in movies. Movie magic is illusion, not fakery. There's a technical side that's very important. You are not making movies if you are just going out and uncapping a lens. You have no control. It's fine for documentaries, but a film should be an object which you create, like any other art.

If a film is an adaptation of a novel, like The Prince of Tides, *do you read the book as part of your research?*

Yes, the novel helps you. A lot of detail that gets dropped from the script is in the novel. There are details you find that are useful, little descriptive things about the way people live. You also get a sense of the setting. It's always worth reading.

Do you like to be directed the way a good director works with an actor by talking about feelings and metaphors?

Yes, images, metaphors. Any director who gives an actor a line reading doesn't know his job. Kazan would say, "Ever see two dogs walking down either side of a street ready to fight?" And without confining them at all, those two actors knew exactly what to do. When directors work like that with you, it's wonderful. It only stifles creativity to tell a designer in too specific terms what or how to do their job.

How does a production designer turn poetic ideas into reality on the screen?

I read books, diaries, letters, all kinds of things for any period picture— that's a must. There's always architectural research. Architectural research is absolutely necessary; you can't invent that. If you're doing a fantasy, you still need it. A fantasy is like a bird: it has a lightness, it has to fly, but a bird couldn't fly without the reality of the resistance of the air. If it doesn't have a connection to anything, it is likely not to be any good. You've always got to start with something real and shape it to suit the needs of a particular script. You cannot impose a style on a film. It must grow out of a vision arising from the script and a knowledge of how to form the various scenes into a whole, and it should, like the film itself, have its own movement. Style in film results from every part of it, and those parts must cohere, and they must be directed at some effective result. Design is not self-expression. It is an expressive use of objects, forms, and colors in the service of the script.

7

Albert Brenner

Albert Brenner was born and raised in Brooklyn, New York, and studied scenic design for the theater. While he was designing for the theater, he began to work in live television during the golden age of television for both the CBS and ABC networks. Brenner was involved with many classic shows from the era, including *Car 54, Where Are You?* and *The Phil Silvers Show*.

After his experiences in theater and television, Brenner segued to feature films as an assistant to Richard Sylbert. Brenner worked with Richard Sylbert on *The Pawnbroker* and with production designer Harry Horner on *The Hustler*, which won an Oscar for black-and-white art direction–set decoration.

During the late 1960s, when many young television directors were moving to the West Coast to begin careers in features, Brenner also made the journey and quickly developed a solid reputation as a Hollywood production designer.

Albert Brenner's career has been filled with a cornucopia of motion picture styles and genres. He has designed many comedies, including *The Sunshine Boys*, *Silent Movie*, and *California Suite*, Westerns like *Monte Walsh* and *The Legend of the Lone Ranger*, thrillers such as *Coma* and *Bullitt*, the science fiction films *Capricorn One* and *2010*, plus numerous dramas, including *Scarecrow*, *The Morning After*, and *Backdraft*.

Brenner has worked with directors Arthur Penn, Jerry Schatzberg, Mel Brooks, Herbert Ross, Michael Crichton, Peter Hyams, Sidney Lumet, Ron Howard, and Garry Marshall.

Albert Brenner's work as a production designer has been nominated for an Academy Award five times on *The Sunshine Boys*, *The Turning Point*, *California Suite*, *2010*, and *Beaches*.

The hospital in *Coma* and the hotel lobbies and suites for *California Suite* and *Pretty Woman* are just a few examples of Albert Brenner's artistry. These studio-constructed sets highlight the production designer's ability to weave reality out of movie magic.

1967 *Point Blank*
1968 *Bullitt*
1970 *Monte Walsh*
1971 *Summer of '42*
1972 *The Other*
1973 *Scarecrow*
1974 *Zandy's Bride*
1975 *The Sunshine Boys**
      Master Gunfighter
      Peeper
1976 *The Missouri Breaks*
      Silent Movie
1977 *The Goodbye Girl*
      *The Turning Point**
1978 *Capricorn One*
      *California Suite**
      Coma
1980 *Hero at Large*
      Divine Madness
1981 *Only When I Laugh*
      The Legend of the Lone Ranger
1982 *I Ought to Be in Pictures*
1983 *Max Dugan Returns*
      Two of a Kind
1984 *Unfaithfully Yours*
      *2010**
1985 *Sweet Dreams*
1986 *Running Scared*
      The Morning After
1987 *Monster Squad*
1988 *The Presidio*
      *Beaches**

1990 *3000*

  Pretty Woman

1991 *Backdraft*

  Frankie and Johnny

1992 *Mr. Saturday Night*

* Academy Award nomination for best achievement in art direction–set decoration.

How did you become a designer?

I studied scenic design for the theater at a time when live television was blossoming in New York. I worked as an assistant to a theatrical designer who was going into television, so I went along with him. I worked with the CBS and ABC networks in those live television days. It was fast, right on the spot, energetic, and it was creative. You got to do shows. You were in the pool, they would assign something to you and you worked. I worked on the first Bilko and *Car 54, Where Are You?* series, and I did television films as well.

How did you become a production designer in feature films?

Dick Sylbert and his brother Paul were the two main motion picture people in New York. Every time a show came in, Dick and his brother Paul would be the ones who would get it. One time Paul was not available, and I asked Dick if I could be his assistant. I told him I would give up being a designer in television to be an assistant to him in film, and he said yes. That's basically what got me started in feature films. It was one of those things where you just put one step in front of another—people get to know you, and they give you a shot at it. Then you have to carry on from there.

Early in your career, you worked on The Hustler *with production designer Harry Horner. Where were the pool sequences shot?*

The entire film was done in New York. We used Ames pool hall, which was on Broadway. The sets were built in the old Fox Studio, which was on 53rd and 54th Street and Tenth Avenue. The space was so small there was never enough room to build a pool hall that had more than one table in it, because a pool table is nine by five to begin with, and you need a five-foot perimeter all around it for the stick. Roughly, you're looking at an area of about twenty feet in length by fifteen feet wide for one table, and then you have to put in another table and another table. Harry designed half a table that we could always just get into the frame so you would see the corner. We got away with it successfully. There are a lot of people who still love the film and never notice that, except for Ames, the pool halls only have one table in them. That was an interesting job. Harry's a marvelous designer.

You have designed many comedies. Are they different to design than dramatic films?

Yes, absolutely. I find comedy is difficult to design. As Mel Brooks says, "Comedy is a serious business." The straight line has to be given, and then the punch line has to be given. In *The Sunshine Boys*, the punch line comes as George Burns exits the room. The room couldn't be longer than his walk from where they were standing to the point where he reaches the door to say his punch line and then goes out the door. So you had to calculate. It wouldn't have worked if it were too short or too long—it had to be just right. I did that again in *The Goodbye Girl*. There's a scene where it is Richard Dreyfuss's first night in the apartment, and he has come in and taken over. He's in his bedroom, and Marsha Mason goes to bed in her room with her daughter. She begins to hear a guitar being played and she's furious. She gets out of bed, goes out of the bedroom and down the hall, fuming and delivering dialogue at the same time about how she's going to throw this guy out. She finishes her dialogue at the time she reaches the door of his bedroom and knocks. I laid out the location of those two rooms based on how long it would take her to get out of bed, walk, come out of the room, go down the hall, and stop right in front of his door as she finishes her dialogue. Then I went to the director, Herbert Ross, and said, "This is what I've done, and this is why I've done it. What do you think?" Herbert said, "Well, let me see." He went onto the stage with me, and he paced off the same distance as I did. Of course, being the director and having the final word he said, "Move it over about a foot."

In The Sunshine Boys *Walter Matthau lived in an Upper West Side New York apartment that was bursting at the seams with all sorts of wonderful memorabilia from his career as an entertainer. How did that design evolve?*

The set decorator, Marvin March, and I talked a lot about that memorabilia. The director, Herbert Ross, had a lot of input on that as well. We started with the fact that the Matthau character was a big star at one point, and he is reduced to this two-room apartment in the Ansonia Hotel in New York City. He's taken all of his furniture, his boxes, all of his memorabilia, and everything that he had in his five- or six-room suite when he was a star and has crammed it into this small space, because he's not going to give up anything. I mean he hasn't given up the Christmas cards that he's gotten for five or six years; they're in a box somewhere. Everything was once in a bigger space. That was the idea for the decorating of the apartment.

You used the actual exterior of the Ansonia Hotel. In designing the studio set for the interior, what architectural elements did you have to adhere to in order for the exterior and the interior to work together?

The layout for the interior space was a decision easily made by looking at the exterior of the Hotel Ansonia. It has round turret towers in the corners: you have the opportunity to make one of those rooms circular. You're certainly going to believe it by looking at the outside of the building, but the shape and division of the interior space has nothing to do with reality. There are two ways into the bathroom, there are three doors into the kitchen. Where have you ever seen anything like that?

Why did you design all of those entrances and exits inside the apartment?

It allows the director the fluidity of moving his people anywhere he wants to make the scene play. Look at the scene where Richard Benjamin comes in and brings Matthau his lunch. They're sitting there talking, and he tells him about the show he's going to put them into, and Walter says, "With Lewis? No, if it's with Lewis, you haven't got me!" And he gets up and starts walking. It's not just these two men sitting at a table or standing around. Matthau goes from one room to another, out one door into another, all the time followed by Richard Benjamin. There are two back doors to the bathroom, three to the kitchen. You go to the director and point them out. Whether he uses them or not is up to him, but at least you have given your contribution.

Several of the Neil Simon projects you have designed were adaptations of the original Broadway plays. Do you find the theatrical design of the original production helpful to you when you are designing the film?

No, I don't, because you can get influenced by what they did on the stage. What I find helpful about the stage is the mechanics. Since theater is what I studied, I've used a lot of stage mechanics, such as turntables, rolling stock, and sets that fly. I bring that to this industry whenever I can. It's one of the tools I use.

In Coma, *there is an enormous room where scores of comatose bodies are suspended. Where did the concept come from, and how was it accomplished?*

The concept of the room followed the writer's description of a functioning warehouse to store these people. We knew from the script that they would have their bodily functions taken care of and there would be ultraviolet light. The shape of the room came about because I was looking for locations outside of Boston and I drove past a grim-looking building and said, "That's the one we have to use!" It is a Xerox Company building, and that's the one we actually used for the exterior. We had ten real bodies on slings, and the rest of them were dummies that hung in the room we had built. We had tables that were operated with truck jacks. We would lay the person on the table and jack them up to the height of the slings that were then put on their wrists, legs, and under their buttocks. When they said, "Roll it," ten guys would press the buttons, and the hydraulic jacks would go down. They'd rush off with the tables and start filming, because you could only stay up there in that position for a minute or two. When they yelled, "Cut," out came this army of tables. They got underneath the people, jacked them up again so they could rest until they were ready to make the next shot.

The majority of Coma *takes place in a hospital. Were any of the scenes shot in actual hospital rooms?*

No, we built them. We were trying to use Massachusetts General for the exterior of the hospital, but they were very upset with us because they didn't want it known that it was even possible to do any of that story. I sneaked into the hospital with a friend for reference material. I put on a gown and everything. I had a camera hidden under my coat and went around taking pictures, because they didn't want us in there at all.

The sets you built for the hospital interiors look very realistic. Did you have to cheat reality in any way to serve the story you were telling?

If you remember, Genevieve Bujold escapes from the operating room by climbing up into the drop ceiling. No operating room in the world has that. All the ceilings in operating rooms are solid, because it has to be antiseptic. A drop ceiling could cause dirt and dust, but we needed it for the story, so it was a cheat. I don't think anybody cares.

Did you get cooperation from NASA to design the spacecraft and command facilities depicted in Capricorn One?

NASA lent us a mock-up of a spacecraft and allowed us to cut it up so we could have more ports in it. They also gave us some equipment that we used and permission to use their insignia. They helped us a lot.

In the film, the astronauts are forced to deceive the public by faking a landing on Mars, which is staged in a television studio. Where did you build that set, and what research did you do to conceive it?

The Mars set was built on a stage at an abandoned airfield in California City. Luckily we knew from information which came to us at the time from the space probe that Mars had a blue sky. We hadn't known that; we presumed it was black like around every other planet, but it wasn't, it was blue.

What were you trying to accomplish in designing the spaceship in 2010?

I thought, "We have a great opportunity here in designing this spacecraft, because in space you're weightless. You can move laterally, vertically, you can move in all kinds of directions." I would say, "Oh, here's a terrific idea. Let's put in a fire pole, so if you want to get from one level or section of the spacecraft to another, you can simply float out by grabbing the pole and going hand over hand." But what happened was you were moving from one box to another box, like going from the living room to the kitchen. It got so complicated I couldn't figure a way out. Finally I went to the director, Peter Hyams, and said, "I'm having trouble figuring this thing out." He was instrumental in actually getting me off the dime about the design. He said, "Why don't you start with what you do best, a New York apartment. Think in those terms and then let's retrofit it with space paraphernalia." So I started thinking in my normal terms: "What am I going to do? What does the camera see? How is the camera going to see in all directions?" In *2010* there is a general assembly room where you can look in any direction and see down into another space. The camera can go out to the flight deck, to the sleeping bay, to the other base—all radiating from one point. The interior of the ship, was one basic connecting set. It was a hub. You were always able to see down those long hallways; you didn't turn a corner and disappear. That helped to solve my problem, and it also brought me back to what I normally do, which is to allow the camera to see a maximum amount.

What was the concept behind the set decoration of the spaceship set in 2010?

It was supposed to be operational. We are talking about a time when a spacecraft is big enough to have a colony on board. There was a greater amount of space, and you had to fill it with technical equipment. In its time, *2001* was innovative, nobody had ever seen anything like it before. But looking at the film now, you can imagine that an interior designer did that movie. It had padded walls and tufting going for it. Our space-ship in *2010* was a tug boat, a workhorse—it was a machine to do work. It wasn't designed by an interior designer, it was designed by engineers. Then other people would come along and say, "Wait a minute, where can I put the galley? Where can I put the beds or the hammocks?" Wherever there's space, you put it in. So it was just chock-a-block with all oddments and bits and pieces that looked like they were functional, but for us were really just decorative.

What other sets were used for the spaceship interior?

The pod bay was another location because that was a long vertical room. The exterior of the spacecraft had a long shape coming off the lower end at the bottom, which was where they clamped onto the original Discovery ship when they found it. We used that shape as the interior of the pod bay, where we kept all the pods to travel with. The pods were all hanging in racks. Since it was such a tall set, we had to move it off to somewhere else on the stage. But because of the cut— which is the greatest invention in motion pictures—there is no way you can tell that set was not attached to the other set. The flight deck was somewhere else. We had the entire flight deck put on gimbals so we could rotate it. When the ship accelerates at the end of the film and everything gets thrown back against the walls, we simply inverted the set with everybody in it, and everything fell, including the stunt men— that's how that was accomplished.

What is a gimbal?

It's a device used in ships to cradle an object and make it steady, although the surface below it is moving. It's sort of like a gyro. We built the set into a box, which was then capable of being pivoted in any direction.

All production designers have to deal with practical light sources for interior sets. On 2010, was it more complicated because you were dealing strictly with artificial light and not daylight?

That's true, it was a little bit complicated, because Peter wanted to light with the available sources that we put in the spaceship as opposed to bringing in heavy equipment to light it. It worked halfway between. He still had to enhance what we did because the light level was so low in the ship, but as a cinematographer, he's capable of doing that.

In The Morning After *the feeling of Los Angeles is achieved primarily through the color scheme. How did you arrive at that pastel palette that was used?*

The director, Sidney Lumet, said to me, "I think of Los Angeles as a tube of Necco Wafers." That was the starting off point. Once we had that idea, then I began to break it down and make a location list of where Jane Fonda walks. Why not have her walk down this particular street with this bright red wall? Why not have the cab stop at a place where the wall is just big, pure, and yellow? Then I searched for the locations and found them. Sidney is one of those people who doesn't mind packing the truck up and moving to another location to get what he wants. So once all of the locations were established, shown to him, and he agreed to do it, there was no question that's what we would do.

Where were the hotel lobby and suite for Pretty Woman *shot?*

The hotel lobby was built and the hotel suite was built. A lot of people don't know that. If the audience comes out humming the scenery, you're in serious trouble. The trick is to do it so well that nobody knows. When they don't know, you've succeeded, yet that's the terrible part of it because nobody can come along and say, "Hey you did a nice job," because they just think it was there and we went and shot it.

Was the design of the hotel lobby in Pretty Woman *based on a specific hotel?*

Yes, it's based on the Beverly Wilshire, because Julia Roberts goes down Rodeo Drive and the proximity of that hotel to Rodeo Drive was the key factor. We built our own lobby and then played the exterior of the Beverly Wilshire Hotel. In *California Suite* we were supposed to be at the Beverly Hills Hotel, but that was built also. The exterior to the hotel was built right outside the stage door. The entrance to the hotel was built right on the stage door. So you drove up and walked through the hotel entrance, which was literally the stage door, and you were in the lobby of the hotel.

Why didn't you use the real hotels?

Who in a real hotel would let you come in there for weeks at a time with all of your equipment, stop their business, and reroute things so that you could use their lobby? Nobody's going to do that, so it is almost a foregone conclusion that you're going to have to build the lobby.

Did you re-create the lobby of the actual Beverly Hills Hotel for California Suite?

Oh no, I never do that. None of it was a detailed copy; it was an impression of the hotel. I left out a lot of the shops and things that were unimportant. When you looked at it, as long as you got the impression this was the Beverly Hills Hotel, that was good enough. You learn an awful lot from this business. When I designed the hotel suites in *California Suite* and *Pretty Woman*, I found out no hotel in this country decorates the rooms or suites. They're all painted white or off-white, because they don't want you picking up the phone when the hotel is filled and saying, "Get me out of this room. I can't stand the wallpaper." So all of them are just white. Possibly they will put wallpaper or decorations in the bathroom or the entryway, but the suites themselves are painted a neutral kind of a color, and they keep the furniture bland as well. When we did *Pretty Woman*, we wanted to impress, so it's decorated unlike anything would ever be. When the cheat is necessary, you go ahead and make it, but make it err on the side of believability rather than on disbelievability.

What were the biggest challenges in designing the fire fighting sequences in Backdraft?

They're real fires, and the biggest problem was take 2.

What did you do for take 2?

A lot of times we were able to save much of the stuff that we were burning. Many other times the scene was going so well they just let the thing burn instead of saying cut. In that case, the decorator, Garrett Lewis, went insane. We had a dress factory that burns, and he had to get thousands of bolts of fabric that had to burn. Well, the budget on that was enormous. They would say, "You can't have that much money. You've got to get something for less money." So Garrett went out, bought these remnants of fabric, and cut the bolts in half so you could only see the faces of them to try and double the amount of fabric. However, he bought the cheapest fabric you could buy. Now that ended up being polyester, and some manmade fibers are toxic. They don't burn, they melt into a large lump. We didn't know this going into it. What was thought to be a money saving device turned out not to be, because now we had to go back and buy only cotton fabric, which they didn't want to pay for at the start of the film and was far more expensive. It was a big job; it was a harrowing job. We did very well with it. There were a lot of things that we developed. Everything's built out of wood, and we had to flame-proof or flame-retard it so that it didn't burn quickly. We'd mixed things into the paint to try and slow down the course of the fire. We had lots of tricks we had to do. Ron Howard, who directed the film, wanted the fire to have a brain much like the shark in *Jaws*; he wanted it to be able to outthink the firemen. In one case, he wanted to have the fire come across the ceiling and down the wall to block the exit and stop the firemen from getting out the door. Well, fire won't do that, you can't make it go down the wall, so we built the set upside down.

The old Fred Astaire trick.

Right, so the fire went across the floor and up the wall. Then you inverted that, and it looked like it was coming across the ceiling and down. The effects department spent a long time trying to develop fire that did things, fire that changed its color, changed its shape, which is very hard to do. At one point, we had garden sprinklers sprinkling out alcohol or diesel fuel, and we ignited it so that the flame would be spinning around. It wasn't an easy job. The fires are real, those guys are really in it, but we had a great time. It was a great deal of fun.

In the climax of Backdraft, *there is a scene where William Baldwin runs across the roof of a building that is on fire. How was this accomplished?*

We built the rooftop on the top of a parking structure, so when we looked out, we could see the buildings around us at eye level. We interlaced the boards on the roof the way you would interlace your fingers, and they're hinged on the back end. Because they were hinged, they would just fall down into a hole. The special effects team would put them up carefully and put a slide underneath the boards—which you could not see—so they would not fall. When the slide was removed, the boards would fall. The faster you removed the slide, the faster the boards would collapse. So now our stunt man would run just ahead of the slide. Attached to the back end of the slide were huge gas jets of propane to throw the fire up. The floor would collapse under you, and the flames would come up. It was a sensational effect. After Ron Howard yelled cut, we would turn off the valves, pick up the boards again, put the slide back underneath it, and go for take 2.

After Baldwin successfully makes it to the end of the roof, he goes over the parapet and begins to descend. As he is doing this, the windows on the floor below him blow out, and he is forced to crash through a window that leads to the elevator shaft. How were you able to have him fall through the shaft while it was filling up with water below, with flames coming at him from above?

I built three sides of an elevator shaft. The top of it also was built in perspective, so it looked like it went up for ages. We lowered it into a swimming pool in order to make it look like the water was rising in it. If it wanted to, the camera could stay on the deck of the swimming pool just above the water level and you could see the water rising, because the back of the shaft is going down and all the elements that are on the back wall are slowly sinking into the water. It's movie magic.

You've designed several Westerns. Have you done a lot of research about what those Western towns looked liked historically?

I've done about five of them. A kid from Brooklyn designing Westerns—that's funny. You always do research. These towns weren't all built out of old unpainted timber that was rotting and falling apart. They were going towns, but the perception for most audiences today is that they were old and weather-beaten. The problem with Western towns in movies is that they are all isolated; there's never any money to build a house in the distance or the road going down, so all of the towns are just simple little islands stuck wherever they are. Not everybody is in the town; somebody lives just outside of the town. A lot of times, designers will try to put in buildings under construction somewhere in the town because it gives them more space to work with.

You have had extended relationships with set decorators Marvin March and Garrett Lewis. What is the relationship like between the production designer and the set decorator?

I knew Marvin early on in New York. He was a carpenter before he became a decorator. We have a good rapport, as I do with all the decorators I've worked with. Garrett Lewis and I have worked together on several films. I don't consider the art department as I; the art department is we. It's me, the art director or the assistant that I have, and the decorator. We sit around and chat it out—we talk about what we want to accomplish, the colors we want to get. We keep a continuity of everything going all the time. Marvin March and I have worked that way a long time. Garrett Lewis and I have worked that way a long time. Marvin and I and Garrett and I have been nominated for films. There should be a tight-knit thing between the decorator and the designer. You have to; you can't separate it. It's one and you have to be able to work together.

What is the dividing line between the set decorator and the property master's responsibilities?

The prop master does the working props, the everyday things that are handled on the stage by the actors. That doesn't mean he goes out and gets them by himself; he answers to the art department. Garrett or Kathe Klopp, who is the decorator on *Frankie and Johnny*, will say to the prop master, "We're going to decorate the diner with this china, these cups, and these glasses. I will get them for you. You need glassware or things the actors are going to handle; we'll get them and give them to you." The little things like the eye glasses somebody wears or a wristwatch or the plate of food—that's the prop master's job. He will take care of that, but what he hands the actors for the most part is decided by the art department.

So the set decorator's domain is furniture and other major furnishings for the interior.

Yes, furniture, wall coverings, the floor, draperies, and all that sort of thing. There are many times when I change the floor plan of the set because the decorator will come along and say, "You know I've found this terrific piece of furniture. It's great, it will work like a charm in here, except that you've got to give me six inches or a foot more of wall because I haven't got enough space to put it in." We'll alter it, we'll make the change, because ultimately what we're trying to do is get the best possible product made. How can you stand there and say, "No, I will not change that six inches!" That's stupid.

Do you consider costume design part of the art department? How do you work with the costume designer?

The wardrobe is part of the art department. The wardrobe comes on a bit later so we've established the color concept. We've talked it over with the director, and he's agreed with it. When the costume designer comes in, we say, "We're working within this parameter of color." They say fine, take samples, and do their thing within those colors. You don't tell them what kind of costumes to design.

How do you work with the director of photography?

The DP comes on late, because he earns so much money nobody wants to have him in the early preproduction period. What I try to do is get together with the cinematographer when he comes on. Hopefully, I know him and we've worked before. If not, I try to find out what colors he particularly hates, so we don't hold up the company because he says, "I'm not going to shoot it." On *Frankie and Johnny* I'm working with Dante Spinotti, who is a marvelous cinematographer. We've worked with him before on *Beaches* and there's a rapport. I go to him and I talk about the color. He talks about the layering of color on the film, so that we design things to work out best for the film. On *Frankie and Johnny* there is a love sequence at the end in which Frankie's apartment should have a glow. It's all happiness at the very end of the film, though in the earlier parts of the film, and in Frankie's life in general, the space she lives in is rather cold and you're not impressed by it. It's just rather dull. Now you want to make that room glow at the end of the film without putting in a new set of furniture and a new paint job on the walls because nothing has changed, it's only a week that has gone by. By working with color and color gels with the cinematographer, we worked out a system. If Dante puts slightly blue gels on his lights, the apartment will appear to be bluish and cold in color. If he puts violet or lavender colored gels on his lights, the walls change and radiate a warmth. Carefully selecting the color does that. That was a collaboration. I went to him and said, "This is what I would like to do. Let's see if I can find a color." Then we ran a test on some colors and ended up saying, "Okay, this is the one that will do it for us."

What was the biggest design challenge in Frankie and Johnny?

There are six or seven bedroom sets, and they're all small pops—it's for a montage situation. I'm trying to show an entire life in one five-second segment in a bedroom, which easily can be two walls, a bed, and a dresser. You can do that five times and change the color or the wallpaper, and you'll have five or six bedrooms just like that, but that doesn't say anything about the character who lives there. So I have designed these little sets to say immediately the kind of person who lives in that space and make it more than simply two walls in a bedroom. They're just an assortment of wall surfaces placed strategically. When you place the camera where I say you should place it, you will see a living room, a hallway, a children's room all in one clip. When you stand back and look at it, it's nothing but a few odds and ends with some furniture in front of it. It only works for the camera, which is important. The camera has only one eye.

What is your philosophy in working with the director of a film?

It's the director's film, and the first thing you do after reading the script is to discuss it with the director—find out the visual concept of the film he's trying to make. If you can either enhance that or come up with another suggestion or a different outlook for him, then you suggest those things. He may take them or he may reject them, but I can't simply read the script and do what it says: "This is a bedroom." Two walls is a bore. I can't do that. I have to make it interesting for me as well as doing what the script says. I know writers feel that what they've written is all important, but four pages of dialogue of two people sitting in an automobile and you'll go to sleep in the film. You've got to take it out somewhere and do something. Now, if you can think of something where the director might break up that sequence, you suggest it. He may come to you and say, "Hey, these four pages in the automobile are not going to be here by the time we shoot this. I'm going to move it somewhere else, so come up with something." You're always trying to get an emotional feeling out of the audience by what you do on the film. The music does that, the lighting does that, the camera work does that. To try to get a mood or a feeling is essential in a motion picture.

Is there anything you haven't done as a production designer?

I haven't done a musical, which I would love to do, but I think I've done everything else. I've done Westerns, I've done horror films, I've done science fiction, I've done a lot of comedies. I've been very, very lucky in this business. The business has been good to me. I've worked continuously ever since I got into it. I just work.

8

Mel Bourne

Mel Bourne studied to be a chemical engineer at Purdue University with the intention of entering the wire and cable business. Upon graduation he served in World War II. After the war, his plans changed when he redirected his career interests to the theater. An apprenticeship with the Paper Mill Playhouse in New Jersey led him to Yale University's School of Drama. After graduating Yale, he worked in the theater and assisted the legendary theatrical designer Robert Edmond Jones.

Bourne made a transition from theater to live television during the golden era, and was the designer of programs as diverse as *Howdy Doody*, *The Hallmark Hall of Fame*, *The Goldbergs*, and *The Goodyear-Philco Playhouse*.

In 1976, after many years of working in commercials, Woody Allen gave Mel Bourne the opportunity to design *Annie Hall*, a breakthrough film for the director that launched Bourne's career as a production designer in feature films.

Mel Bourne and Woody Allen collaborated on seven films in which the design was central to making each project visually distinctive. The environments in the quirky romantic comedy *Annie Hall* succinctly delineate cultural differences between East and West Coast lifestyles. The austere world of *Interiors* is created by imagery reminiscent of the great Flemish painters and provides the ideal setting for the emotionally crippled characters who inhabit it. Bourne's work on the film was nominated for an Academy Award for art direction–set decoration. The glittering splendor in which New York is lovingly displayed in *Manhattan* presents a black-and-white tone poem celebrating the city. *Stardust Memories* uses the cinematic worlds of Ingmar Bergman and Federico Fellini to create the milieu of a contemporary film director encased by his fame. *A Midsummer Night's Sex Comedy* constructs a past that reflects our present.

Zelig concocts a documentary reality, and *Broadway Danny Rose* revisits the heyday of show business on Times Square with the famed Carnegie Deli as the center of its universe.

In addition to Woody Allen, Bourne has worked with many visually inventive directors, including Robert Benton, Adrian Lyne, Michael Mann, and Terry Gilliam, and was the production designer of the original pilot for the groundbreaking television series *Miami Vice*, produced by Michael Mann and directed by Thomas Carter.

Bourne has defined the diverse locales of New York in *Annie Hall*, *Manhattan*, *Fatal Attraction*, *Still of the Night*, and *The Fisher King*, for which he earned an Oscar nomination, but is equally adroit in rendering the neon night world of Chicago in *Thief* and the farmland beauty of the American Midwest in *The Natural*, a film for which he also received an Academy Award nomination.

Mel Bourne's understated decor and firm command of architectural space provide an artistic clarity and serve to anchor the emotional center of a film.

1977 *Annie Hall*

1978 *Interiors**

　　　Nunzio

　　　The Greek Tycoon (art director, with production designer Michael Stringer and art directors Gene Gurlitz and Tony Reading)

1979 *Manhattan*

1980 *Stardust Memories*

　　　Windows

1981 *Thief*

1982 *Still of the Night*

　　　A Midsummer Night's Sex Comedy

1983 *Zelig*

1984 *Broadway Danny Rose*

　　　*The Natural**

1986 *FX*

　　　Manhunter

1987 *Fatal Attraction*

1988 *Cocktail*

1989 *Rude Awakening*

1990 *Reversal of Fortune*

1991 *The Fisher King**

1992 *Man Trouble*

　　　Indecent Proposal

* Academy Award nomination for best achievement in art direction–set decoration.

How did you become a production designer?

I dabbled in painting and sculpting at an early age. I went to Purdue University, graduated as a chemical engineer, and hated every minute of it. I went right from college into the service. While I was convalescing in Washington after the war, I thought life was too short to be in the wire and cable business, which was what I was supposed to be doing when I got out of school. I decided to try something that I really might enjoy for the rest of my life. I loved the theater. I applied for work at the Paper Mill Playhouse in New Jersey, where they were doing professional productions of operettas with New York people. I worked there as an apprentice scenic artist and an apprentice prop man at night. My day started at eight in the morning, finished up at eleven-thirty at night, and I loved every minute of it. I decided this seemed like something I might really want to do. I applied to Yale and studied in the department of drama. When I got out, I worked in the theater. I was assistant to a lot of wonderful designers, but the man who was my patron saint was Robert Edmond Jones. I worked with him until the end of his life. From the theater, I slowly got into TV, which back in those days was live. Then I did commercials for years. As far as doing features was concerned, I couldn't get arrested. I felt one day I would get to do a picture; I didn't know when. Woody Allen was the only person at the time who had the guts to try anybody new. He opened the door and gave me a chance to work with him on *Annie Hall*. He's a talented, creative kind of a guy, and that's how I got into this.

You have worked in the theater, television, commercials, and feature films. What was it like to make the transitions between those mediums?

In theater, your tools are your imagination. You don't have to be as realistic as you are in TV or in film, so the parameters are much larger. When TV was live, you used a lot of the same basic thinking as theater. The physical end of TV today is much closer to film than it is to theater. The transition from TV to film was not difficult, because I had the good fortune to get great, great experience doing commercials. I've done sets for commercials that are almost as large as anything I've ever done in a film production. I worked in commercials for years, so I had a chance to experiment, to fail, to try things you never could in some other areas.

How would you define the production designer's job?

The production designer not only contributes to the visual end of a production, they must also deal with the producer on the nuts and bolts—the financial end of a film. A portion of the production designer's responsibility is a knowledge of budgets, scheduling, and how things work logistically on a film. We all go into production design because of the creative end, which is obviously more fun and less wearing on the gut, but the production designer is the bridge between the financial end and creative end.

What makes you decide to do a project?

I care about the script, and I care about who directs that script. I don't do a movie because it's going to give me an Academy Award nomination.

What do you look for in a script when you read it for the first time?

When I read a script, it's the same as when I go to a movie. I don't read it in terms of what the challenge is scenically or visually, or whether the clothes are going to be spectacular. When I start out, there is a response on an emotional level. I just read a script the way I'd read any fun kind of story, because that's why I'm in this business—it's supposed to be fun.

What are some of the reasons why you would pass on a project?

There are many reasons to pass on a given project. If the property is not moving, evocative, or entertaining, I'll pass on it. I have no need for that; I've worked too hard. Second would be whether I could make the kind of contribution I would like in some congenial way. If you can't work with people you think you are going to be able to work with, mostly the director, then forget it—it's torturous. Logistics have a lot to do with it. If a picture's being done in a swamp in the Philippines, you have to think twice whether you want to put in four months in a swamp in the Philippines. The director of photography is very important to me. I have given reasons to directors who respect my opinion for not wanting to work with a specific DP. These instances didn't have to do with personalities but quality—with what I thought a DP should contribute to the total picture in dealing with the director and the designer. There are many DPs who dismiss anybody below the director, but the best ones don't.

The director, the production designer, and the director of photography are really a triangle, aren't they?

They certainly are. The director has the vision, and you are interpreting his vision. The DP is putting it on film, and you are both contributing to the visual style of the film; it is an incredibly intense and personal relationship. We're in one of the most collaborative arts, and the production designer is one of those collaborators. The production designer is a close collaborator with the DP to supply the director with a feel, a look, a rhythm. The director is the guiding spirit; everything should come from the director. A production designer has got to have an input on the total visual end of the film. A designer and the DP should be working on the same wavelength, which comes from the director.

What crew members do you hire at the point you become the production designer on a film?

It depends on the size and scope of the film. If there are a great number of different locations with a lot of building, then you need to hire a very strong assistant who is your right hand—the art director. The set decorator works directly under you, because that person has to be very much in tune with your style. They bring in samples and pictures so you can eliminate furniture, urns, vases, and statues that you find inappropriate and uninteresting. Then you hire an eager-beaver type who wants to be in film and is attracted to the art department to act as an art department coordinator. This is a position with all the leg work— getting coffee, doing research, writing letters, finding new materials, going to library picture collections. If you need more help, you get draftsmen and set designers who do additional drafting. The location manager and location scouts are very much a part of the art department. A lot of times, the production manager wants to have control of the location manager so they can say, "Look, don't say anything to Mel, but go out and find six places within two blocks of each other, so if we can't shoot at one place, we can shoot at another." My concern is to hold the money down, too, but my first concern is to get it to look right. I may be the only designer who has contract approval of the location manager. I make the choice, because it's such an integral part of the work we do. Now that more and more pictures are being done on practical locations, it's extremely important that you get what you're looking for.

Do you hire or suggest who should be hired as property master?

I hire the property master in conjunction with the director, because he has to work with the director so much more than he has to work with me directly.

What are some specific areas you have researched for films you designed?

On *Reversal of Fortune* we got into a whole study of some of the families that live up in Newport—the scale, the money. I keep notebooks on each film on that kind of information. For the baseball material on *The Natural*, I had a woman working for me who was a whiz at getting research and making wonderful arrangements with baseball equipment manufacturers to get research and props from them. She became very friendly with people in Cooperstown and got a lot of information for the production. There's a carnival in the Midwest at the beginning of the movie when Hobbs pitches against the Whammer. It's supposed to be 1919. I had to build a carnival from scratch in a field. So what do you do? You do research having to do with carnivals at the time. Where do you get the equipment? You have to find out where to get all those wonderful things that were given away at carnivals in 1920. All of this has to be researched and worked on. I went up to an outfit in Toronto which sends carnivals all over the world. They had a ferris wheel from 1910 in working order. I went through all of their stock. I have a book on psychiatry at the turn of the century for *Zelig*. I went into a whole study of what hospitals were like back then. It's such a wonderful thing to be able to uncover this material. You go to libraries, picture collections, and photo morgues. I would never have come to this in a million years if I were in the wire and cable business. It's a wonderful, wonderful field that I'm in. I love it, because you're exposed to such diverse lives and environments.

Do you maintain personal files on locations?

Yes, I have a room filled floor to ceiling with files of all kinds of outrageous things. I have loft files from *FX*. I have photographs of 250 lofts from *Fatal Attraction* alone. I have probably the finest collection of photographs of baseball stadiums in the Western Hemisphere from *The Natural*. I have files on bars, saloons, supper clubs, period bars, restaurants, good upper-style Chinese restaurants, lower-style Chinese restaurants. I have thirty, forty firehouses. They might change over the years, but the research value is great.

Who takes the photographs?

The original photographs are taken by scouts or myself. They bring them back, and I say, "Let's look at this." I go, and if I feel it's interesting, I then bring the director.

How do you work with a location scout? Let's say you need a firehouse for a location. What information do you give the scout?

First of all, they read the script. Then I pass on the information that I want. For example, I tell them, "I don't want a contemporary firehouse; I want a firehouse that has a lot of old oak trim. I want the old kind of quintessential firehouse that has tile walls. Go out and find it."

How do they proceed to find the location?

They might call up the fire department and get a listing of all of the firehouses and when they were built. It's just like doing research in college. You've got to do a tremendous amount of leg work, and if you don't do it, it shows immediately, but it's fun and interesting.

What is the next step after the locations are found?

After your scouts come back with locations that look promising, you go out with the director. The decisions on locations are usually gone over by the director and the designer and, secondarily, the producer and the DP. It's really a meeting of the minds. Generally, if the director likes it, that's it, it's a buy.

Do you use sketches to communicate to the director what the sets should look like?

I start to doodle away in working out whatever sets may have to be built. I do a lot of the drafting myself having come from an engineering background. Certainly, coming out of the theater, I had to know how to draw scenery, not just sketches but working drawings.

Annie Hall *was your first feature as a production designer. What was the genesis for the design of Alvy's parents' house in* Annie Hall?

Originally, the father was a taxicab driver and they lived in the Flatbush section of Brooklyn, which is where Woody came from in real life. We found a house in Flatbush that Woody wasn't thrilled with, but he was going to go with it. Woody has an expression which I love: "If we had to start shooting tomorrow, we'd go with it, but let's keep looking." He doesn't want to settle, he wants to keep searching, striving for better and better. I didn't know Woody at all. I was in awe and tentative with him at the beginning, but on our way out to Coney Island to look at other locations, I said, "I know you like Fellini—I want to show you something that out-Fellini's anything Fellini has ever done." So we got to the Cyclone roller coaster and I said, "There's a seventy-three-year old lady and her three-hundred-pound son living in this apartment built into the Cyclone." He was bowled over and said, "Can we get in there to look?" We went in, and there was this woman with a pacemaker and her son who was hitting the wall wherever he went because he was so big and heavy. It turned Woody on so much that he said, "This is where Alvy grew up. We're going to use this!" So he went home and rewrote the head of the script. I had to build the roller coaster outside the windows of the apartment in the studio, so you could see it during the interior scenes with his parents. That's what I would call collaboration. That's what a designer should contribute to a production. The more creative people like Woody, Adrian Lyne, Terry Gilliam, or Thomas Carter are all wide-open to suggestion.

Was the scene in which we see both Annie and Alvy at their respective analysts' offices accomplished using spilt screen technique?

That split room was built on a stage and shot live. Half was Diane's with white walls and the Abstract Expressionist paintings, and half was Woody's with paneled walls with deep colors and the Egyptian motif in the pictures. There was a dividing wall which came to a point. Those were cliches of the two different kinds of analysts.

The house in Interiors *has a beautiful yet oppressive look to it in terms of how it was decorated. What was the concept behind this?*

It all came from Woody's conception of Eve, the mother played by Geraldine Page. She is a decorator. She decorated all of the spaces.

How was the house chosen, and what was done to it to capture Eve's personality?

One reason we chose that house was its relationship to the beach in front of the house. It was the right proximity from the windows down to the beach, and there was a great view of the house from the water. It was a wonderful house to begin with, but what the people had up on the walls was very different from what we needed. With Eve, everything was so subtle it was almost to the point of being subliminal. Woody would go over little things with me that nobody would even think of. We reglazed all of the windows because the glass wasn't absolutely clear and we could not get perfect reflections. There are major scenes, like the one with Diane Keaton standing up against the glass looking down at the beach toward Geraldine Page. We spent so much time and effort on things that nobody saw. There was a perfectly straight line of putty on every window, because that's what Eve would have done. We scraped every window in that house to make sure there was no extra putty showing. A major portion of our work was done out there while I was still ripping down and rebuilding walls in that house.

I felt that muted clay beige color was a wonderful color for Eve and was wonderful for flesh tones. It was subtle to me. Even though we used a lot of artificial light, I wanted to see it during the day. I mixed a lot of colors and went out to the house, and put it on three-foot-by-three-foot wall sections and looked at it at different times of day. I painted the window walls along the beach a lighter shade than the other walls in the house to lose the shadows and to achieve a look of uniformity. I decided I would add a little more green. I added a touch more raw umber. You can't do these kinds of things with a lot of other people, they don't care, they don't appreciate it. You can do that with creative visual directors; it had to do with the total movie.

The look of the house is very reminiscent of a Flemish painting.

I would certainly say the light quality would be more toward Vermeer or Dutch and Flemish painting than anything else. You can't in any way disregard the cinematographer, Gordon Willis, who I think is a real artist. *Interiors* would have been nothing without Gordon. I worked with Gordon in commercials when he was an assistant cameraman, so we knew and respected each other. What I did was supply a background for Gordon and Woody on which to shoot. This was an example of three people totally working together. If someone else had shot that movie, it might have looked like the most ordinary thing in the world, because if you take apart the elements of that movie, they were not evocative of great visual responses. It was just what Gordon did with a blank wall, with a shaft of light, with someone's face in shadow in a given space.

What was the primary design concept behind Manhattan?

We all had a very strong idea of what Woody was trying to get to. As opposed to many directors who want to make New York look like the most miserable place in the world, in *Manhattan*, Woody wanted to make New York look like a sparkling gem. He wanted it to be exciting, rich, and full. There are visual elements that were worked out by Gordon Willis and Woody, and in a minor way by me, to make New York look as wonderful as it could.

What was your involvement in the creation of the opening montage of New York City?

We went all over and picked places. Woody wanted us to achieve that quality of glamour: the wonderful, velvety rich blacks, the sparkling, crystal light of a beautiful chandelier, the flare of lights off signs. Then we decided whether changes had to be made in the wattage of bulbs under canopies and in the lighting. So wherever we could, we tried to just goose it along a little, possibly covering a light that was intruding by just putting black in front of it to leave another light as the focus.

Several of the films you have designed for Woody Allen were photographed in black and white. What are the challenges of designing in black and white? How do you know how the values will translate?

I worked at NBC from TV's infancy—the golden years. We worked in a gray scale. Scenery was not painted in color, so I was used to working in black and white. You go ahead and think in terms of what you would do if it were in color. I use a panchromatic filter to see the value difference of those colors and what I'm going to get in black and white. If they are too close in value, I'll change it so I can get what I want. Possibly I'll accentuate a highlight, a shadow, or a wall behind somebody. This is totally on my own, not having to do with what the DP is going to do.

How does Woody Allen's method of reshooting affect the production designer?

In many cases I have been off on other films, and I either get the art director who worked for me to follow through if he's available or I have to call in somebody else to whom I give the drawings and specs and they look at the footage. The first time we shot what we called "the white room" in *Zelig*, where Mia Farrow analyzed him, it was built on a small stage uptown. I pulled a carpet out of the bedroom in my apartment, because I couldn't find what I wanted anywhere else. The carpet is kind of light, and I felt it was right. We had used the set twice, shooting it, going away and letting it stand, then reshooting. When it came time to strike it, I said to the production manager, "You think we should hold this?" because Woody had some questions about what he was going to do with the scene. The production manager said, "No, he's got all he needs." We scrapped the set; everything was taken down. About a month and a half later, I was working on another picture, but it was around New York; I was available. The next thing I know Woody is going to do reshoots of "the white room" in two weeks. It was a simple room to do, but it was just the idea. We rebuilt the set. I pulled my bedroom carpet out again and brought it down to the set. This time I said to the production manager, "Don't you think we should hold onto the set?" He said, "Yeah, I guess we better." I ended up going back and forth with my carpet. That set was reshot eight different times.

Was more than one of the eight shooting sessions used in the completed film?

Definitely, maybe two or three. With Gordon Willis, you *can* do the same lighting. I wouldn't guarantee it with some others that I've worked with, but with a Gordon, he knew what he did with the light because it wasn't coming from forty-three different directions.

Thief has a very strong visual style. How did the design concept of the film come about?

I didn't know the director, Michael Mann, at all. I got a call from him asking me if I would read the script for a picture he was doing. I saw elements in that script that I really liked so much for a variety of reasons. Mike comes from Chicago and I grew up in Chicago, so this was a kind of emotional tie to begin with. He asked me to come out to L.A. We were in a tiny little office at Paramount. He was smoking cigars at the time. There was an air conditioner in the window, and he turned the damn air conditioner off because we couldn't hear each other. It was such a tiny little cubicle, and here he was blowing this cigar smoke. On the way out to L.A., I was thinking about the film. There was a light quality in Chicago I remembered growing up as a kid that was an emotional response about Chicago that never left me. I thought about that, and I discussed it with the cigar smoke blowing in my face, and it set off a total point of view for Mike. I didn't have to say another word. He didn't know me from Adam and I didn't know him except for the cigar, but the minute I mentioned the wet, acidy kind of light that comes from the street and the neon in Chicago, which to me was the essence of how the space should be filled almost at all times, he liked it. Mike is very into all of the elements of a film.

I had a lot of input on the clothes. We sat down and talked and had a clear picture of what the James Caan character looked like, what he wore. It was the start of what ended up in *Miami Vice*. Even though he is very strong-willed, Mike really let me make a contribution. We had water all over the place, because it just seemed to help the rhythm and the emotional response to what you saw. I constantly reminded him of areas where we could do that without intruding upon what he wanted to get out of the script. Every bit of it was a collaborative kind of effort. We had a brand-new cameraman, Don Thorin, who never shot a feature before—a very nice guy who didn't have any ego problems. He really listened to what Mike wanted and, fortunately, to the little contributory areas that I got involved with. *Thief* was a picture really coming from one source—Michael Mann.

The interior of the bar in Thief *was very evocative. Whether it was day or night, and most of the scenes are in the day, it always looked like night.*

Absolutely. You go into any bar in any town—New York, Los Angeles, especially Chicago—and it doesn't matter whether it's day or night, whether it's snowing or it's 110 degrees and sunny outside. We wanted that dreary, gritty, night look as a juxtaposition to the wet, neony exteriors. The whole thing had that night glint off of beer glasses.

Thief *has several incredible safe-cracking sequences which contain surgical-like shots detailing the process. What research did you do on safe-cracking?*

We did so much research. Basically, this story was taken from John Santucci, a reformed jewel thief. He helped us and told us scientifically, down to specific tools, how safes were broken into. Dennis Farina, who was in the film, was on the Chicago police force at the time. Now, of course, he's a wonderful actor. He was a friend of Santucci's and had pulled him in a number of times. So you got knowledge from people who really knew what the hell was going on. We did tests of the torches that were devised by jewel thieves and metallurgical engineers to break through metal. Every little element was gone over—fuse boxes, different security systems. With Mike you went step by step trying to find out specifically how we were going to do it, what was going to photograph, what would get across to an audience, because it doesn't mean beans if it doesn't get through to an audience.

What location did you use for the big safe-cracking scene towards the end of the film?

That jewelry store at the end was all built at Zoetrope Studios in L.A. The walls of the safe were real. There were layers and layers of metal and asbestos in the walls. That paid off, because you really get the smell of that arc and you get the feel of the mass of that metal. We had to work with the L.A. police force and the fire department to make sure that the studio wasn't going to go up in flames.

In Still of the Night, *Roy Scheider is a recently divorced psychiatrist who has just moved into his own apartment. That must be an interesting design problem, because the apartment he shared with his wife was probably decorated by her or at least partly by her. How do you arrive at what his new space should look like?*

I had left a relationship at about that time, so I was well aware of some strange things that you end up with. You wonder why you would take this and not that. There was a sense of it being unfinished. We didn't want it to look like it was totally decorated by any means. He might even have been there three months, but there were still pictures on the floor waiting to be put on walls. At that point, his life was not well ordered on a personal basis. So that's what we were trying to achieve.

What was your approach to designing Scheider's office?

The director, Bob Benton, wanted it to be the kind of analytical psychiatrist's office that so many of us had been to in and around New York—a nondescript space with that fifties Swedish Modern furniture. In designing it, everything was fine, except I couldn't find a good analyst's chaise. I saw it in my mind, but I couldn't find the damn thing. I drew one up with a teak frame, and the carpenters built it. It was exactly what Bob wanted. It's now in my bedroom and is not used for any analytical sessions. It's a piece of scenery, but I still like it.

What research did you do in order to design the sequences which take place in the auction house?

We did a lot of research at the old Sotheby's about how the operation works. I went to the homes of women who worked for Sotheby's to see how they lived.

Where were the auction house scenes shot?

That whole complex, the backstage of the auditorium, the office, and all the antiques in storage were built on two stages. We copied a lot directly from Sotheby's. For instance, the auctioneer's stand that we made was nothing but a copy of the one at Sotheby's. They asked if they could have it, so they are still using the one from the movie. That was a big set. We had a lot of very authentic pieces to come up with. We had a Duane Hanson piece of sculpture that scares the hell out of you. We made a Rosebud sled for the film. I got photographs to make sure ours was going to be very authentic. It's hanging up in the warehouse. We had so much that you couldn't see, but the actors saw it and felt it.

In designing and dressing a set, how much do you provide specifically for the actors to help their performances?

I don't do it specifically for actors unless it is something they really feel will help them emotionally with their role. That comes out of my stage background. It's so collaborative; you have to work together. I like to feel I'm supplying an environment for an actor in which they feel totally within the character. When Glenn Close put in her first day of acting on *Fatal Attraction*, she searched me out at the end of the day. I was so pleased when she threw her arms around me and said, "Mel, that place is the quintessential place that Alex would have."

Where did you create Alex's loft for Fatal Attraction?

I had long discussions with the director, Adrian Lyne, and many with Glenn about what kind of woman Alex was. We had already seen some of the clothes she was going to wear. Our location department came up with over 250 lofts. Most were thrown out, but others Adrian and I would go to look at. For one reason or another he would say, "This isn't right." We ended up with one that Adrian thought we could work with if I built a couple of walls but the landlord wouldn't let us, so we continued to look. It was getting very tight. Adrian felt it had to be in the meat district. Finally we came across this roach-ridden, rat-infested hovel over in the meat district that had eight-foot ceilings. We walked into this place and I thought, "Dismiss this place with these ceilings." I just saw all kinds of problems. Adrian got excited. He said, "Look at those metal shutters on the windows. Look out the windows. Look at the meat across the street!" Forget about shooting, forget everything. He had a response to that space that was right for him. With a creative person you go along with that. The producer, Stanley Jaffe, was with us and he said, "Let's get out of here." I said to Adrian, "What is there about this place you really find so appealing? There's no room." Adrian pulled me out in the hallway and said, "Mel, everything's been so terrific, but you're dragging your feet on this thing." I said, "Adrian, we showed you 250 goddamn lofts. I'll do whatever you want to do. I could give you elements that we've seen in other lofts in that space; I'm just being the devil's advocate here. You've got to shoot in eight-foot ceilings in the middle of summer, not me. I'm thinking of our DP and your space." He said, "Don't worry about it." Eventually, it was fumigated; I ripped every wall out of this space. I had dumpsters there for a week emptying out. We took down the ceiling that was there and raised everything up a little bit.

After the shooting and editing was completed, it was decided there should be a new ending for Fatal Attraction. *Market research had determined audiences wanted to see the two women fight it out. What did you have to design for the new ending?*

The layout we used for the house in the suburbs didn't lend itself to the way the new ending was written. There was nothing up on the second floor. There was a little room where we built our bathroom. Consequently, I had to build a second floor that was going to work with what we shot before. We had to build the staircase and the hall to match. We used four different bathtubs to get that end scene to work the way Adrian wanted it. The first was the standard old foot tub that was sitting in the bathroom we built. I had to build another tub because of the fight with Michael Douglas reaching in the water. I had to find three tubs that were exactly the same with round edging so that I could cut off the back of one and the front of another, elongate them, put the two of them together, raise it three foot, six inches in the air, cut away the bottom of the tub, and weld a steel tank to the bottom. We put the cameraman below Glenn Close in the water, shooting towards the ceiling to see Michael Douglas reaching over and burying her in the water. Glenn Close had to leave to do some other movie. We shot it in two different places. We were shooting some other exteriors up in suburbia, so we went to a church and set up another tub that was all glass, so that when Michael Douglas sticks his hands down, we're shooting at her, and we see her eyeballs and everything under the water. All of that was intercut very well by Michael Kahn, Peter Berger, and Adrian, who I think is wonderful.

The architecture of the prison where Hannibal Lecter is incarcerated in Manhunter *is just extraordinary. What was the design strategy?*

I knew from discussions with Michael Mann that we wanted to be almost on the cutting edge of sci-fi. We knew the exterior and the hallways of the prison had to go with the gloss white cell that I built. Outside of Durham, North Carolina, there is a pharmaceutical outfit called Burroughs Wellcome. It has a very Brutalist Provocative architecture. The minute I saw it I wanted to use it as an exterior and for the hallway of Lecter's cell. They wouldn't let us shoot the exterior or their whole public hallway. It was fantastic, but we couldn't talk them into it, so we had to look for another place. We couldn't find anything for the exterior, and we were scouting all over. We spent a lot of time in Atlanta. I had heard about the Rich Museum but had never been there. I was an admirer of Richard Meier's architecture. I went to the Rich Museum, and it just looked great. I brought Mike back to look at it, and we ended up using the Rich Museum as the exterior of Lecter's jail.

The most striking design element in the film is the home of the serial killer.

Yes, Dolarhyde's house was one of the fun things of my career. We actually looked at a couple of houses to try to use as practical locations. One was on the Mississippi River outside of St. Louis, which was where that house was supposed to have been. Logistically, we just felt we could do better around Wilmington, North Carolina, which was our base of operation, but we never could find a house. So Mike said, "You better go ahead and draw something up." I said to him, "I'm going to make it look like a kind of a crazy, 1930s radio," which was just an extension of saying, "I'm doing it in the style of an architect I admire, William Lescaze." Mike said, "You can go as far as you want." So I did a lot of research on Lescaze and architects of the 1930s and went ahead and designed Dolarhyde's house. I kept making changes before we started building. At the end of every day, we'd have a meeting and Charles McCarry, my set designer, would write on the drawings, "Today's version of Dolarhyde's house." I enjoyed every minute of it. It was built in a swamp right on the Cape Fear River in North Carolina. We had to have two men with shotguns to kill the snakes and the gators while we were putting in the pilings to put in a foundation. It was all built on pilings. The whole house didn't look that way, but we had to because it was tidal water. We mostly had movable earth going up to the house so the earth would rise and fall with the tide. It was a stylized movie. Denny Farina's FBI office was all white. The things we did were not the norm. Some of the best things I've ever done were in *Manhunter*.

How do you feel about the product placement deals that studios make for feature films?

I have had some unpleasant situations with product placement. I am considered a very difficult person to deal with in a variety of ways, but the intrusion of obvious and inappropriate advertising is something that I will not accept at all. When I'm working on a production, I will give them 150 percent of everything that I have, but where it affects the integrity of the film—forget it. I will not accept that. I never have, and I never will.

Each person who works on a film has tools to work with: writers have words, the cinematographer has light, editors have structure. What is your most important tool?

Space, more than any one element. One could say color, line, a study of materials, but they all have to do with how they're used in space; that comes first to me. So many times you see something enhanced by an expanse of one kind or another. A man riding a horse in the lowest fifth of a full screen frame with the sky above him tells you a story emotionally. It might be a scene from *The Pawnbroker* in upper Manhattan where the camera is following through a series of hanging elements to the little man behind a grimy, gritty cage in a very tiny, constricted space. I like to believe when I work on a movie, I am going to have a spacial environment that will not intrude on the story. In my vision this is the kind of space in which the character should be moving. As long as the audience says it's authentic, that's all I have to do to make my contribution, nothing more.

What is your philosophy as a production designer?

My philosophy is to give the director an emotionally appropriate spacial environment in which an actor can tell a story. I don't want it to intrude; I don't want it to make a statement. I want to be able to help tell a story that a ten-year-old child watching a character on the screen will have an emotional response to. His parent will understand it in another way, but they both will have a chance to do it on their own terms, as you would looking at a painting. I don't want them to be looking at what Mel Bourne perceives a character should live with.

You don't want them to go out singing the sets.

Right. This I learned from Robert Edmond Jones, a man who was revered for his lighting, scenery, and costumes. He said, "The minute you read in the papers how brilliant you are, you better take stock and watch what you're doing, because you don't want to overtake the essence of the project."

What would you like to do that you haven't done?

There are two things that I haven't done. One is a Western and another is a film set in the eleventh, twelfth, thirteenth, or fourteenth century. I'd like to do that. It's easier to do than a contemporary picture, but it's still fun.

Why is a period film easier to design than a contemporary one?

It's all prescribed for you. You take what you want from historical research. It's like going to a wonderful supermarket. You just open up an architecture book and say, "I want that arch, those stairs, those windows, I want that kind of grill," and you put it all together however you want it. It is much more of a challenge to make a contemporary apartment photogenic, to make it work for the character, and be interesting than doing something in period.

Do you feel that production designers are getting the recognition they deserve?

I think they have been getting more and more recognition as time goes on, and I'm happy to see more and more recognition of the total visual package on a movie. It's always flattering to see your name used in some nice context. I enjoy reading that somebody likes my work. As people become more technically knowledgeable about the total film business, they are more apt to be familiar with a designer than with a film editor, for instance, because an editor's work is so much more subtle to the layman, but you can see if something looks pretty to you or not. So it's easier to get the recognition as a designer, and I don't think the designer has to get any more recognition than he's getting. I think a truly dedicated person is interested in working on a good movie, rather than doing a film because it affords an opportunity to display great creative prowess.

9

Tony Walton

Tony Walton's career demonstrates that a designer is a designer. He created the sets and often the costumes for over sixty theatrical productions in England and on Broadway. His theater credits include *The Ginger Man*, *A Funny Thing Happened on the Way to the Forum*, *Golden Boy*, *Pippin*, *Chicago*, *Woman of the Year*, *The Real Thing*, *Hurlyburly*, *I'm Not Rappaport*, *Grand Hotel*, *Six Degrees of Separation*, and *The Will Rogers Follies*. He has been nominated for thirteen Tonys and won the award for best scenic design on *Pippin*, *House of Blue Leaves*, and *Guys and Dolls*. Walton created both the production design and costume design for a majority of the films he has worked on: *A Funny Thing Happened on the Way to the Forum*, *Fahrenheit 451*, *Petulia*, *The Sea Gull*, *Murder on the Orient Express*, *Equus*, *The Wiz*, *Just Tell Me What You Want*, *Deathtrap*, *The Goodbye People*, and *The Glass Menagerie*. Walton received five Academy Award nominations. He was nominated for both art direction and costume design for *The Wiz*, costume design for *Mary Poppins* and *Murder on the Orient Express*, and won an Oscar for art direction on *All That Jazz*. Walton has designed for the opera and the ballet. He has designed elaborate musical revues for Bette Midler and Linda Ronstadt. His television work includes the Diana Ross New York Central Park concert and the award-winning *Free to Be You and Me*. Walton also has designed book illustrations, theater posters, and caricatures.

In theater Walton has had long relationships with directors Mike Nichols, Bob Fosse, Tommy Tune, and Jerry Zaks. In film he has worked with Sidney Lumet on seven films and has had strong collaborations with Richard Lester, Mike Nichols, Paul Newman, Volker Schlöndorff, and Bob Fosse.

From the New York of *Prince of the City* to the time-tripping fantasy of Fosse's *All That Jazz* to the exploded reality of *Death of a Salesman*, Tony Walton's incredibly prolific career is filled with an exciting design sense that serves many mediums and many worlds.

1964 *Mary Poppins*
1966 *A Funny Thing Happened on the Way to the Forum*
      Fahrenheit 451
1968 *Petulia*
      The Sea Gull
1971 *The Boy Friend*
1974 *Murder on the Orient Express*
1977 *Equus*
1978 *The Wiz**
1979 *All That Jazz (with Philip Rosenberg)***
1980 *Just Tell Me What You Want*
1981 *Deathtrap*
      Prince of the City
1983 *Star 80*
1984 *The Goodbye People*
1986 *Death of a Salesman*
      Heartburn
1987 *The Glass Menagerie*
1991 *Regarding Henry*

*Academy Award nomination for best achievement in art direction–set decoration.

**Academy Award for best achievement in art direction–set decoration.

You have designed sets and costumes in both the theater and film. Is it your philosophy that a designer is a designer?
I come from a tradition where as a designer you are responsible for everything visible on the stage, including costumes and make-up. It's a European tradition. So it was quite a surprise when I started to work steadily in New York and discovered that there was a whole other philosophy. At that time, I was trying to be a lighting designer as well, and when I entered the union here, I entered in all three categories but soon realized it was not really possible to work effectively in all three disciplines simultaneously. I always used to do costumes as well as set design. In the Broadway system, it is virtually impossible to do both effectively now. I quite often do both costumes and sets on a film if the situation permits. It's a little easier on a film, because you don't have

to have everything ready on one day. It's spread through the shooting schedule; that's a big help.

Mary Poppins is a children's fantasy created entirely in the studio utilizing both live action photography and animation. What was your involvement in the art department, and how did everyone work together?

I was called production design stylist on the in-house listings. It was just sketching out or painting suggestions of how things should look. Then somebody else might come up with a better suggestion, and the better suggestion almost always won. There was a staff of artists—mostly from the animation territory—who did suggestive mood sketches for sequences. It was thrilling. You could do a little doodle, and it would be rushed off to have models made. My involvement was so naive and totally gleeful; I was so new to it all. I was a kid in a candy store. I designed all the costumes, but on the scenic end I mostly did lots and lots of suggestive sketches of the houses, the park, the gates, and the bank. But Peter Ellenshaw, who was a remarkable matte artist, and other staff artists also did a lot of stylistic sketches. Peter Ellenshaw was the hand of Dick Van Dyke doing the sidewalk drawings. We were all involved in trying to keep that sequence naive. That was actually one of the frustrations of the movie. We were always hoping the whole Jolly Holiday sequence would have the rather primitive chalk-drawn quality of those pavement pictures throughout. In our concept sketches it always did, but it would go through the sausage machine, as it were, and come out looking like backgrounds for *Bambi*.

Was Walt Disney directly involved with the film?

Deeply. We would have little confabs with Walt Disney. He'd approve the sketches, and then they would go down to the animators. He'd say, "Look, it's actually supposed to look this naive. It's not a mistake." They'd all say, "Yes, yes," and then it would gradually find its way back to what they were sure Disney had liked in the past. Disney found himself in a frustrating situation. He was the only game in town of that particular sort, and the people who had great longevity at his studio were perhaps fearful of where they could go if they weren't working there. I was very conscious of his frustration that the work so often came back looking the way they believed he felt comfortable. Quite often he clearly wanted to go further. There were occasions when Disney would stay late at night or come in very early in the morning and go through the artist's trash bins trying to find drawings that were more imaginative amongst the rejects. He would pin those back on the board and say, "Go with that." I believe Disney always had that impulse to try to stretch visually. As far as I was concerned, he was completely accessible. He used to have very frequent staff meetings to go through the storyboards, the plotting, the music, and we were all involved in that. Everybody was encouraged to speak up. I've always been a big mouth, so it was never a problem for me to speak out, but very early on I was encouraged by one of the old guard to cool it. According to him, I wouldn't last long there if I were too outspoken, but truthfully I never got that feeling. I actually enjoyed Walt Disney very much. He was very welcoming and always seemed to be happy to have some kind of dialogue going even in the dailies. Quite often dailies are sort of holier-than-holy for the director. Nobody wants to know or hear if something isn't quite right, but it wasn't like that at all there. Disney was really interested to know everybody's feeling. "Is the hair right?" I mean everything, every detail.

In that sense was Disney ultimately the director of the film?

Oh yes, it was very much his baby. There was a very distinguished director on the film, but the storyboard implied exactly where the camera was supposed to be, and the storyboards were quite strongly adhered to. The film was really 1,000 percent storyboarded; it was very, very meticulously laid out.

Was all of Mary Poppins *shot in the studio?*

Yes, everything. It's such a conscious choice. I think Disney very determinedly wanted to make *Mary Poppins* a somewhat stylized and highly controlled film. *Mary Poppins* was a huge family operation all filtered through Walt Disney, even the way some of the special effects were done. Disney had done little rough technical drawings. They were not very slick, but he had drawn them suggesting what the special effects techniques should be.

What was Richard Lester's concept for what ancient Rome should look like in A Funny Thing Happened on the Way to the Forum? *The result seemed to be a very realistic environment.*

Richard Lester was very interested in the other face of history. We always see this scrubbed and polished version of ancient Rome. There used to be an advertising image for Pearl and Dean which had soaring white Roman columns—a very idealized image of ancient Rome. Lester would say to Syd Cain, the executive art director, and myself, "I want the polar opposite of that."

The color orange is a key design element in the costumes. How did you arrive at that?

Well, it's a range of reds, oranges, and yellow-golds stemming somewhat from the terra cotta of ancient Rome. I had designed the original Broadway production and co-produced it in London, and Dick didn't want the movie to look anything like the stage production. He had loved it, but he just wanted to go a completely different route. So I said, "Why did you come to me then? Why don't you have somebody start completely from scratch?" He said, "I assume you know this theatrical version better than anyone else, so you'll know better than anybody how to make the film different."

Our hope, in addition to trying for the grubby reality of Roman back streets, was to get into the brightly colored quality of its vaudevillian roots. One of the things that appealed to Lester in researching ancient Rome was the use of so much polychrome; even the statues were painted. It's startling when you try to imagine the Acropolis as it was with so many colorfully painted ornaments. I had been aware of this in doing research on the stage show but had gone another route. It was one of the chief points of departure for the film; there were a great variety of colorfully painted surfaces, although we didn't want any of it to look brand-new. The characters played by Zero Mostel and Jack Gilford are both slaves in the same household, so they were tied together by the related colors that really kind of scream out in the context of their house's interior. It was fun to try. I kept thinking that it was incredibly risky, but Dick kept saying, "Oh, don't worry, you can keep all the background people in kind of sludge colors, as long as we get all the principals in jewel colors. I think I'm going to be able to make it work."

You have designed many films for Sidney Lumet. Although he is primarily known as a tough New York street director, the films you have collaborated on represent a wide visual range.

They're such weirdly different films. So far we've worked together seven times, and none of those films are in any way alike.

Lumet also has a theatrical side. You've gotten to see both sides having designed Prince of the City *and many of his theatrical adaptations like* The Sea Gull, Deathtrap, *and* Equus.

All his roots are in the theater. His dad was a great star of the Yiddish theater, and Sidney was a very successful child actor. More often, I've been on his theatrically rooted movies. With the gutsy street side, he's able to take much more advantage of what exists on location rather than calculatedly designing anything. *Prince of the City* is a story of conscience. He wanted to start out as if it were one of his street movies with a lot of colorful and random excitement and gradually refine and reduce it so that the audience can get inside the heads of the principal characters. That was both a very calculated design scheme and camera scheme. *Prince of the City* and *Deathtrap* are interesting in terms of Lumet having made them back to back. Although there were hundreds of different locations in *Prince of the City*, many of which actually were sets created in Manhattan's old Custom House, the camera is almost completely static throughout with rapid cuts from sequence to sequence. And because *Deathtrap* was theatrically static and takes place almost in one environment, the camera never stops, it's moving all the time. It would have been fascinating to have made a film of the filming, because you had all these grips and gropes continually moving massive parts of the set and the lighting equipment in the course of the shot. The camera was circling and weaving. Huge pieces like the central fireplace and the staircase would have to be swung out of the way and then swung back into frame in the course of the shot. It was wonderful to see all these huge guys having to do it delicately and silently during the scene.

Did you use the real Orient Express train for Murder on the Orient Express?

No, in fact it didn't even exist then except for bits and pieces in museums. The old engine was in a shed just outside of Paris. We had to shoot the actual exterior departure of the train in France, because the engine wasn't capable of running on English gauge railroads. The European, Continental, and English gauges are different. It also wasn't thought that the engine could go more than a few miles without the risk of exploding, so we built the Istanbul railroad station in the train shed outside Paris. Then we dressed the train up with wagon-lits logos and so on. Some of the carriages were rather sad and had to be spiffed up quite a bit to be acceptable as Orient Express carriages. All of the interiors and quite a bit of the exterior is actually a studio-constructed train. I've seen the movie once on Channel 13 when Claire Bloom introduced it and said how lucky we were to find the real train, but actually we got bits and pieces of doors, basins, luggage racks, and so on from Belgium, where they were in storage in a railway museum. We used what we could, but re-created a whole lot of it.

What were some of the problems in using the working engine?

We got to the Swiss Alps to do the sequence where the train breaks down in the snow. This place had been selected, because in the history of the world there had never not been snow at this particular time of year. So, of course, we got there and there was no snow.

You can always count on that.

Yes. We sat there for a day or two, and then Sidney said, "I think you're going to have to work this sequence out with models." Actually, I was quite looking forward to going back and creating that. The entire unit was set to return to England the following morning but woke up to find that the God who looks out for filmmakers had delivered an immense snowfall in the night. Sidney has almost always had that kind of weather luck.

How were the train interiors done?

All the interiors of the train were done within the studio. Sidney wanted to avoid too much raised platform work for speed of shooting, but he also, to his great credit, wanted to avoid the slightly unreal overscale version of train corridors and compartments that you usually see in movies. They make it easier to move the camera around, but Sidney wanted the train to feel believable, however romanticized, so we did keep to the true proportions. He thought that in the studio it would be just that much easier to tear things apart and to move the camera. This meant that since the carriage was set so low there was frequently a risk of the camera shooting through the windows and seeing the studio floor or the ground. So in addition to fogging up the windows somewhat, we made huge wraparound cycloramas that were actually very close to the train. They were made of rear projection screen material and painted on with acrylic paint. The cinematographer, Geoffrey Unsworth, and I worked out between us that the rear projection wraparound was painted in a slightly fogged focus to have the appropriate scenic feel of the distant landscape. It would have an unbelievable barrage of lights coming from behind, so that it would be completely translucent and have that kind of very overbright light that you get after a snowfall. So despite the fact that the backing was actually very close to the windows, we avoided that feeling of a dead stop; it would just be luminous. It was so translucent that you had the feeling that it was just light going to the distant horizon.

What was it like to work with Geoffrey Unsworth on Murder on the Orient Express?

Absolutely one of the great gents. Oh, what a treat to work with. Sometimes, particularly in England, you get a small war between the cinematographer, the camera department, and the art department. I've been generally very lucky, but in the English tradition it tends to be a sharp division, and Geoffrey Unsworth was one of the real exceptions in that he wouldn't consider doing anything that would affect the design concept without calling on me or whoever's department was appropriate. He was a great artist. He was wonderful. Sometimes in our fake Istanbul railway station, everything would be all set to go and Sidney would say, "Are you ready, Geoffrey?" and Geoffrey would nod and not say anything. It was always curious to me that he wouldn't speak. Then one time I went down to watch closely what was really going on, and I realized that the reason he wasn't saying anything was because the moment the camera rolled, he opened his mouth and let his cigarette smoke escape across the lens. There was just this little veil of smoke, so that a very slight diffusion would happen. He had all sorts of tricks like that.

In the credits of All That Jazz, *Philip Rosenberg is credited with the production design, and you are credited with the fantasy design. What was the genesis of that relationship?*

It had become complicated for me because the project had a false start. When Bob first approached me, he was going ahead too fast, and I was already right in the thick of *Just Tell Me What You Want* with Sidney Lumet, so I just couldn't do it at the time. *All That Jazz* was originally going to star Richard Dreyfuss. He and Fosse had filmed some tests together and had a falling out. There was a long delay that finally ended up with Roy Scheider taking the part. As a result of this, I was then able to rejoin the production. In the meantime, I had introduced Bob to Phil Rosenberg, who had worked with me in various capacities over the years as a specialist scenic artist, art director, and earlier as a model maker and draftsman in the theater. We have a long, long relationship. I was thrilled it appeared that was going to work out, but Bob was always very peculiar and reticent about starting new creative relationships, so he asked me to come back in. We worked out a collaboration that was perfectly fine for Phil and myself. Our territories as credited are not really representative of what actually happened. Phil was as much involved in the fantasy sequences as I was, though I got credit for them, and I was involved with him in the rest of it and the selections of locations and so forth, but we had to figure a straightforward kind of billing for the credits.

It's remarkable how All That Jazz *manages to keep a consistent visual style when dealing with fantasy and reality in such a time-shifting fashion. How was this accomplished?*

Bob, Phil, and I had already done so much chatting about the style of the film, and it was clear what a very peculiar jigsaw puzzle it was going to be. It was like five separate movies running concurrently. It was evident that I had the feeling that if we didn't have a cinematographer with a very, very clear personal attack, it was possible the film could degenerate into these five concurrent movies rather than one focused film. So I fought very hard for Giuseppe Rotunno. I feel very good about it. Bob was a huge fan of his work, but when we met with him, Bob became very anxious because Rotunno's English was sparse. Bob, quite wrongly to my mind, thought of himself as technically naive and very dependent on the kind of deeply intimate working relationship he had with Unsworth on *Cabaret*. After much prodding by me and his agent, Sam Cohn, Bob finally decided to take the plunge. Rotunno is the kind of artist who addresses himself completely to the needs of the material. He really thinks nonstop about what particular kind of light will affect the mood and the storytelling aspects of every scene.

We all worked very hard on the fragmentation problem of *All That Jazz*. We made a number of copies of a flip-flop book for every sequence, like those children's Jacob's ladder things. It's the equivalent of a pocket storyboard for the film's palette. We made one for every sequence of the movie that showed exactly which story thread was being featured at any given point. We tried to get on paper what the basic palette was for each thread, whether reality, fantasy, hallucination, or whether it was cold or warm or crisp or soft. I quite often do this for movies of any complexity. In this case, we made one for Rotunno, one for the costume designer, Albert Wolsky, and one for props and set dressing, so that all of us would know exactly what part of the visual palette we were in at any given moment, whether it was an Angel of Death sequence or rehearsal or a medically induced hallucination or whatever.

The idea was to be absolutely clear where we were in any one of those strains.

Where was the opening audition scene in the theater shot?

At the Palace Theater.

Did you do anything to the theater?

Almost nothing. I remember thinking when we saw it that the back wall was amazing.

What were those pipes on the back wall?

They were radiators. It was beautiful, and I remember thinking as that scene was being shot, "Jesus, we're going to get credit for this." They're gone now, alas. I just designed *The Will Rogers Follies* for that theater and was sad to see how the back wall has been renovated.

The pattern of the pipes on the back wall was a strong design element.

The way that was shot, of course, is Fosse's design eye. He had a remarkable eye. Fosse and Rotunno made something really beautiful out of that, something not everyone would necessarily see.

Was there any overall concept about the kind of locations that were to be used in All That Jazz?

There are almost no exteriors. You see a little bit of an exterior on a reflection of the taxi window when Joe Gideon's wife and daughter are heading to the hospital. There's one tiny scene after the audition when you see a glimpse of Broadway from the Palace Theater, but you never actually see the sky.

Was that a conscious decision?

It was conscious to the extent that it was pretty much true of Bob's professional life, which was so rigorous. He was very demanding, but he was more demanding of himself than anybody. So it was almost as if the work became the encasing environment. There was never any escape while you were in it.

The film really captures that. It is almost as if Joe Gideon lived in those rehearsal rooms. The design for Gideon's apartment was really perfect for a New York director. Was it at all a spinoff of Fosse's actual apartment?

To some extent, yes. It wasn't a set; it was a found apartment on 67th Street, just down from the Cafe Des Artistes. We took everything out, but it did already have that strange black bedroom, which was Fossesque; of course, that was probably why it spoke to us. Fosse was always saying that he didn't really ever want to nest. The apartment he lived in at the time of *All That Jazz* was kind of a hangover from the previous owner. He just had the things from his career that gradually accumulated there, some of them just leaning there, some stuck somewhat randomly up on the walls. Our location setting for Gideon's apartment did have that feeling, and a lot of the dressing was posters and a few neon signs. The sign that says "Oh Wow" actually did exist in Bob's apartment, as did a neon figure of a dancing man. Most of the work on the apartment set dressing was Phil Rosenberg's. My contribution was helping select the apartment, designing the Joe Gideon posters, and supplying some set models and costume sketches for the set dressing.

What was the concept behind the posters?

They were mostly to somehow suggest Bob Fosse's work, and they showed Gideon's passage from a choreographer to theater director to a film director. The whole poster end of it was enormous fun to do, because you couldn't use anything that was exactly derived from Fosse posters, but it was fun to try and suggest them.

Did you work with Fosse's actual posters, or were they just familiar to you?

I was familiar with them. The producer and co-author, Bob Aurthur, came up with a lot of suggestions for titles, and that was fun, too. We suggested some, and we chose our own cast names for the imagined stars or sometimes scrambled our own names to be in them. Because Joe Gideon would have almost certainly had his caricature done by Hirschfeld, I had the opportunity to do a false Hirschfeld of Roy Scheider. Fosse had been caricatured by Hirschfeld twice, so I did a sort of square root of those caricatures bending them toward the look of Roy Scheider. Hirschfeld puts his daughter Nina's name somewhere in every drawing. My daughter's name being Emma, I put this little Emma squiggle in the bend of Gideon's sleeve, and it's signed, "Waltfeld." All of those things are just fun to do. Nobody ever sees them, but sometimes they're helpful for the actors.

There is a very interesting use of mirror images in All That Jazz.

Some of that was the luck of being simultaneously in theater and film. At the same time, I was actually doing a ballet in San Francisco, and the set used half-mirrored material called Mirrex Mirror Scrim. I showed it to Fosse, and he thought it would be useful for the Jessica Lange sequences so that you couldn't quite tell when she was in front of the mirror or behind it. Sometimes she is not there beside him but seems to be, because she's joined with him in his reflection. In those instances she's actually behind the mirrored material being lit through it. He is in front of it being reflected in it, and she's behind it appearing through it. Later when it was discovered that we wouldn't have any money to shoot any kind of spectacular ending due to Columbia suddenly pulling the plug on the film, Fosse said, "Well, can you think of anything to do with that mirror stuff?" So it was a very inexpensive way of doing that whole last sequence, which was just thrown together to wrap up the incomplete movie. It was heartbreaking in a way, because what we had designed for the original final sequence was kind of wonderful.

What was the original ending?

Originally, it was to have been the opening night of *N.Y. To L.A.*, the production that had been in rehearsal before Gideon's heart attack. We had planned to film it at the Opera House at Purchase. The Opera House owned a gargantuan organ that had been given to Carnegie Hall by Holland, and it turned out to be too big for Carnegie Hall. Rockefeller, who was building this whole Purchase complex, said, "I can take the organ. We'll build a plant for it." So they constructed a building on the side of the Opera House for the organ to be stored in and a little railroad track for it to ride in onto the Opera House stage. It completely filled the proscenium opening. That was an amazing thing to come across. I had designed a New York skyline for the *N.Y. to L.A.* number that exactly paralleled the profile of the organ pipes. It was to have been painted on a scrim that would cross-fade from the New York skyline through to the organ pipes and, with a tremendous chord, was to slide rapidly off stage revealing the Los Angeles palm tree setting behind it.

In addition to this sequence, I had been working for quite a long time on computer adjusted imagery of all the recurring images, the eyedrops cuts and the repeated "It's showtime, folks." These computer adjusted images were supposed to be a segue from the hospital monitor's imagery via some hallucinatory medical imagery to the big opening night showbiz ending in which we were to see the replacement stage director, played by John Lithgow, taking credit for most of Gideon's work and being congratulated by the producers while Gideon is conveniently forgotten. The recurring "It's showtime, folks" images were distorted hallucinations to be overlaid the way that Fillmore East and West had used organic liquid projection in the sixties, but we couldn't even afford the projectionists to project the footage we had already worked up for this sequence. It was very frustrating not to be able to film any of that original final sequence. None of it was filmed. The epilogue with Jessica Lange was shot up in the lighting gallery at Purchase. The black box theater there is where we ended up improvising that whole last concert concept, which was done scenically for virtually nothing. Due to the film being halted, there was a lot of pastework that had to be done, and Bob was able to do much of it through the Jessica Lange segments. They were the last things we shot. In many ways it was fortunate that it came as late as it did, because we were able to use design elements that had been in other parts of the film as a kind of attic of the mind. There was a jumble of artifacts in those scenes. We actually used some of the props and even some of the test pieces that we had done for what would have been the final, much more grandiose musical sequence. We'd done tests of translucent paintings of images of the heart and its ventricles and abstracted imagery of heart operations. So those things were lying about or flying about amidst all that mish-mash of artifacts behind Jessica Lange. It's just all Fosse's skill and sleight of hand that made that work.

What was your design concept in adapting Death of a Salesman *to the screen?*

The hard thing on *Death of a Salesman* was to find a way of doing a play text that was not being translated into any kind of film script or screenplay and to arrive at a hybrid that was not quite a movie and not quite a theater piece but would allow a theater life to survive on screen. It was hard but fascinating, because the script of *Death of a Salesman* is already a strong stylization. All the memories are written as concurrent, but when they made the first movie, they became flashbacks, because that is an acceptable movie convention. That was very upsetting to Arthur Miller, because to him they weren't flashbacks, they're actually concurrent and overlapping memories. Willy Loman is experiencing all these things simultaneously in the course of his breakdown. So it was just fascinating to find ways of doing that. A lot of the physical territory of the movie doubles as various different locations; for example, the scene in the restaurant where Willy takes his sons for an Italian dinner and then goes to the men's room. When he's in the men's room, he hears the voice of the girl. When he comes out, it is actually exactly the same room, except the tables are now gone. There's a bed and things are slightly changed. Some of the walls are moved slightly inward to different relationships, and it becomes the hotel bedroom in which his son catches him in a long-ago flirtation. That kind of segue happens throughout the film, where we used the same elements in different ways to suggest a new environment. It's actually the same environment, just twisted.

Many of the interior spaces in Death of a Salesman *have unconnected walls which have a view of an exterior background.*

Yes, they are all like that, actually. The director, Volker Schlöndorff, was interested in everything being fragmented like Willy's mind. It's sort of like an exploded Norman Rockwell—the ungluing of America. The point of departure was that the writing in filmic terms is very, very poetically heightened and sometimes very dense. So although you can receive much of it on a more or less realistic level, there are times when the language becomes heightened to the extent that it's unacceptable in a realistic environment and some kind of stylization becomes necessary. Part of the "real" story had to work acceptably, but there were times when we needed to be able to lift away from the reality in order for the poetry to survive. We started from the premise that nothing that wasn't specifically mentioned in the original play script could be there. That was an incredible challenge that we only very occasionally didn't adhere to. Usually, in movies you dress things to have something interesting as background for the camera to compose with. In this case we tried to replace conventional set dressing with interesting wall textures and color. We did make one addition not mentioned in the script—the needlepoint American flag on the living room wall, which was used to ironically heighten a specific moment—but everything else is identifiable in some way from the original play.

It almost had a German Expressionistic look to it.

That was probably from Volker Schlöndorff and Michael Ballhaus, who was the cinematographer. They were both initially thinking—because of the original working title of the play, "Inside His Head"—that maybe the house should be a huge skeletal skull. Filmically, that became just impossible to sustain. Then we got to the idea of a Norman Rockwell world blown apart. That was interesting just as a study, because whatever one's feeling about Rockwell as a painter or illustrator, he was an astonishing art director. In his illustrations there's usually a key piece of furniture or a portion of one, and you know from its character that it's the waiting room outside a doctor's office. You somehow know immediately where you are from the tiny but very explicit selections he made. So we tried to take our cue from him. Schlöndorff wanted to be able to see somebody in close-up, framed with the texture of reality so you could believe it, but then be able to slowly pull back if the verbiage was getting too dense or too heightened and show this was not intended to be taken realistically. The camera could even drift over the top of the walls and draw attention to the artificial nature of the set.

What was physically behind the open spaces between the walls?

First of all, there was usually some plumbing element, pipes, or a radiator in the gap, and then behind that there was a complete environment which started out as a distant view of a romantically stylized graveyard behind their earthen backyard where Willy and his sons played ball. During the to and fro of the time frame, their view of the graveyard becomes erratically obliterated by the new buildings that have crowded in on them. This is the root of Willy's despair, so we had a number of flexible buildings with half-mirrored windows that we were able to move around to crowd in more and more and occasionally evaporate when Willy reverts in time in the course of his breakdown. Every place Willy goes to is reachable through the same overscale tile floor grid pattern—even the office. It moves through the black and white tile of their apartment into a checkered red and black for the hotel room and restaurant. Then it goes to a linear graphic grid for his boss's office, but it's always there in some form or other binding everything together. Even the windows of the different environments always duplicate his familiar kitchen window.

Did you look at Jo Mielziner's design for the original Broadway production of The Glass Menagerie *when you were planning the film version directed by Paul Newman?*

Yes, also for *Death of a Salesman* and I showed them to everybody. I love finding out everything that has ever been previously done on a project and then just seeing what boils up. You end up making it your own, and of course, you can't really avoid that because your own short-comings make it yours in some ways, whatever you do, providing you're not indulging in duplication. It's one of the things I occasionally get into arguments with students about whether or not it's important to establish a visual signature even before you leave school so that people know who you are and can identify your work. Many students seem to feel it's important to do this. There are famous stage designers who really have a strong personal style signature, but for my taste it's the last thing you should ever think about. You should be pushing off in every con-ceivable direction you can to heighten your strengths and buttress your weaknesses and learn as much from the masters as you can. Your lim-itations or special strengths will inevitably result in your having your own style anyway.

Do you feel it's necessary to understand the world in which a film takes place in order to design it?

Usually, yes, but sometimes the opposite is true. The fact that you know nothing about it and can view it as if you were a visitor from outer space and are seeing it freshly means you may have to do an incredible amount of research. That can be a real turn on. I don't have a lot of interest in futuristic things or machine-oriented movies. Viscerally, I'm just drawn to things that are more rooted in feelings than in effects, things that have a more human point of departure and I can somehow identify with, and then as soon as I say that I think, "I love the most stylized kind of musical, as well." So maybe I'm talking through my hat. I'm just starting out designing on a theatrical revival of *Guys and Dolls*—it's one of the great treats to get involved in a magical classic like that. I have almost no point of contact with it in my everyday life ex-perience. Damon Runyon's work is truly exotic to me, and I'm loving every moment of trying to make contact with it—so forget everything I just said!

10

Terence Marsh

After completing art college in England, Terence Marsh followed his love for drawing, painting, and motion pictures to Pinewood Studios, where he learned his trade during a six-year stay.

In 1960 he left Pinewood to freelance and worked on *Lawrence of Arabia*. It was on David Lean's masterpiece that he met the director's principal production designer, John Box. Marsh spent the remainder of the decade with Box, learning the designer's high art on *Of Human Bondage, Dr. Zhivago*, which won the Academy Award for art direction–set decoration, *A Man for All Seasons*, and *Oliver!*—the recipient of an Oscar. By decade's end, Box went on to produce *The Looking Glass War* and hired Terence Marsh as production designer.

In addition to David Lean, Terence Marsh has worked with a diverse group of fine directors, including Fred Zinnemann, Sir Carol Reed, John Huston, Richard Lester, Richard Attenborough, Sidney Pollack, Robert Aldrich, Franklin J. Schaffner, Mel Brooks, Gene Wilder, John McTiernan, and Paul Verhoeven.

Marsh's work as a production designer expresses a remarkable range over a wide spectrum of genres: romantic comedy in *A Touch Of Class*, period drama in *Mary, Queen of Scots*, warfare in *A Bridge Too Far*, the Western in *The Frisco Kid*, contemporary drama in *Absence of Malice*, slapstick comedy in *Spaceballs*, the psychological thriller in *Magic*, and period musical in *Oliver!*

For the 1990 box-office smash *The Hunt for Red October*, Marsh designed and built a high-tech interior of an American submarine that was so realistic he was told by the U.S. Navy it foreshadowed how submarines will look in the future. His painstaking attention to detail created an authentic claustrophobic atmosphere that brought a frightening reality to the Tom Clancy thriller.

For over thirty years the work of Terence Marsh has proved that a production designer serves the needs of the film and its director. From the battlefields of World War II to Cuba during the revolution, from David Lean to Mel Brooks, Marsh's mastery has brought just the right look to the diverse screen worlds he has portrayed.

1964 *Of Human Bondage* (art director, with production designer John Box)

1965 *Dr. Zhivago* (art director, with production designer John Box)**

1966 *A Man for All Seasons* (art director, with production designer John Box)

1968 *Oliver!* (art director, with production designer John Box)**

1970 *The Looking Glass War*
     Perfect Friday
     *Scrooge**

1971 *Mary, Queen of Scots*

1973 *A Touch of Class*
     The Mackintosh Man

1974 *Juggernaut*

1975 *The Adventures of Sherlock Holmes' Smarter Brother*

1976 *Royal Flash*

1977 *A Bridge Too Far*
     The World's Greatest Lover

1978 *Magic*

1979 *The Frisco Kid*

1981 *Absence of Malice*
     Sphinx
     Sunday Lovers

1983 *To Be or Not to Be*

1984 *Finders Keepers*

1986 *Haunted Honeymoon*
     Miracles

1987 *Spaceballs*

1989 *Bert Rigby, You're a Fool*

1990 *The Hunt for Red October*
     Havana

1991 *Basic Instinct*

1992 *Damages*

*Academy Award nomination for best achievement in art direction–set decoration.
**Academy Award for best achievement in art direction–set decoration.

How did you become interested in production design?

I was always crazy about painting and drawing, and I was always crazy about the movies. When I used to go to the movies, I would see this title—art director. I had no idea. . . . I used to think, "Art, I love art, and it's in the movies." So I made it my business to find out what they did, and when I finished art college, I was determined to get into the movie industry. Fortunately, at that time, there were still big studios in England which made twenty to twenty-five films a year and that had a permanent staff. There was Shepperton with the Kordas, Rank at Pinewood Studios, and Elstree MGM at Borehamwood. I was very fortunate to get taken on at Rank at Pinewood. I was given a contract and felt terribly important for next to no money, but at least it was a continuity of employment, a marvelous way to learn the trade. They kept regular departments where you were told which movie you were on. When you were winding down on that movie, you were placed on another movie. You were put on all sorts of movies and into other departments—scenic, special effects—to see how they did things, how things went together. I got a thorough grounding, knew the problems the guy in the other department had, and was with good professionals who taught me. They were very firm and strict then; it was much more like joining the Army, but it was good for me. I spent six years and worked on some wonderful pictures with some very good art directors. You can't help having some of their talent rub off on you if you're fortunate enough to be in their proximity. Young people now don't have the opportunity to go to a studio and spend six years, because the business is so freelanced and fragmented.

You worked with the production designer John Box on many films early in your career. What was that experience like?

Oh, wonderful. I think he's one of the greatest. I met John in 1960 when my six-year contract was up, and I left Pinewood to go freelance. That was a big point in my life. The first picture I worked on was *Lawrence of Arabia*. We became firm friends and stayed together right through. There was *Of Human Bondage*, *Dr. Zhivago*, *A Man for All Seasons*, and *Oliver!* After *Oliver!* he became a producer, and I was production designer on his first film as a producer, *The Looking Glass War*. So I spent the whole of the sixties with John. I admire him very much and like him very much. We're still very close, we still stay in touch.

What would you say you learned specifically from John Box?

I learned how to deal with people and how to get my own way in the most charming, most surreptitious manner. John was absolutely great. I was very impressed by the way John handled people. On *Lawrence of Arabia* they particularly needed a very strong person because there were so many problems. At times, there was more than slight friction between Sam Spiegel and David Lean that someone had to deal with, so John was the figure. He's never been given proper credit for this, but basically, he's the one who ramroded *Lawrence* through. David would confide in John. He had a wonderful overview. I learned so much in the way of administration. A lot of production designers are too channeled to their own particular task; the responsibility is monumental. Sometimes I'm guilty of it. I try not to be, but John could always take an overview. He could always step back and see the grand pattern, rather like a general on the battlefield. I learned that from John. John is a designer who always goes for the simple things, which great painters do. "What are we trying to say? What's the statement we're trying to make?" And we'll go for it, rather than someone saying, "Isn't this beautiful? Isn't that beautiful? Let's put that in." He's very direct. John Box was a very fortunate encounter for me.

On A Bridge Too Far *there is a great deal of military equipment. Where did you get it?*

There had been thousands and thousands of gliders made for the invasion of Holland and for D-Day, but we couldn't find one glider in existence. We couldn't even find any drawings of these gliders in the Ministry of War, so we had to start from scratch. We made our own drawings of how we thought the Horsa and Waco gliders would be made, and then we made all these gliders. Then we couldn't get enough tanks, so we made fiberglass ones that sat over a Volkswagen chassis with tracks that went round but didn't quite touch the ground. They were with the real Sherman tanks. When you saw them coming, you couldn't tell which ones were ours. You'd never spot them in the film; they looked marvelous. We had the good ones in front. We got eleven DC-3 airplanes in total, and there were always two or three that were down with engine trouble. So we had to put those aircraft into the sky optically. It was a lot of work, but it was enjoyable. Richard Attenborough is a very good guy to work with who understands everyone's problems. Geoffrey Unsworth was a great cameraman, and somehow, although it was daunting and problematic and a great headache at the time, in retrospect it was pleasurable.

How did you work with the military technical advisers on the film?

We had a colonel who had been at Arnhem as our military adviser. He was a wonderful man, Colonel Waddie. He was very good, but didn't understand some of the crazy things we had to do for the sake of the movie. For instance, we'd want people in a foxhole, but with a view of the city, and he'd say, "This is ridiculous. They wouldn't be on this high ground, they'd be down there in a hole." I'd say, "Yes, but if we were there, all we would see is the sides of the foxhole around them— we could do that in the back garden. We have to see Arnhem from here." "I do understand," he said, "but it is militarily very wrong." There were lots of occasions where militarily we were wrong, but we were wrong with full knowledge, because we were making a point about something else which we had to see in the same frame. He eventually came around to our way of doing it.

Did you base your designs for the strategy and planning rooms on historic photographs?

Yes, the Nazis used to photograph everything. There was a wealth of reference for them and the Allied rooms. We used to adapt them to suit our own purposes. A lot of those planning rooms were on location. It depended on what we could find to use; some were built. Our maps weren't exactly correct militarily, but we were trying to show the audience what state the battle was in at various places.

Were the battle scenes storyboarded?

Oh yes, the battle scenes were storyboarded and were rehearsed quite extensively, particularly that soldier in the tank who comes over the bridge. That was rehearsed and rehearsed. We had a big model of the bridge. It was rather military. People were around this big model of the bridge saying, "The camera will be here, the tank will move to here, he fires, and you'll go to there. You'll photograph that, and you'll be on a long lens from here. Don't start the camera until the tank passes this mark." Everything was planned to the last detail. Richard's very good at that.

Was the big newsroom in Absence of Malice *built in a studio?*

No, that was real. The Miami Herald let us use their newsroom. Sydney Pollack had to pull a lot of strings to get that. We could only use it during their down period, which were strange hours like ten at night until four in the morning. In fact, most of *Absence of Malice* was real. We built within real interiors or redressed real interiors. We built about three sets in a little studio down in Miami. For the warehouse where Paul Newman kept his liquor business, we knocked a couple of holes in a warehouse. This guy had a warehouse and in the back was a wonderful channel with ships, but the warehouse had no openings or windows. So I said, "Would you mind if I bash a couple of big holes in your wall and put a deck outside?" He said, "No, I'd be delighted," which is what we did so we could see out to the ships going by and get some interest in it.

Did you design the ventriloquist puppet that Anthony Hopkins uses in Magic?

Yes, we wanted it to look vaguely like Tony Hopkins so we used Tony as the model. We did various drawings caricaturing Tony's face. I was always calling it the dummy. You mustn't say dummy. Ventriloquists get very mad if you say dummy. It's a ventriloquist figure.

It's clear from the outset that it does resemble Anthony Hopkins, but as the film progresses, it begins to look more and more sinister as he slips further into insanity.

Yes, we changed it. We painted it differently: the eyes got redder and there were lines under the eyes. Either the sketch artist or I would paint the face as we got on, so it became more and more sinister. By the end, we did use a different figure. It's a funny thing, because we had a very good ventriloquist as our adviser on the film who taught Tony. Tony's brilliant at everything and he became very good, but he was using the ventriloquist's own figure, and he got attached to this figure while ours was being made in the same pattern as the one he was using. We used it as the prototype. Some people who were moonlighting from Disney actually made it for me. When we got our own figure to give to Tony and he had to lose George or whoever it was, he didn't want to at all. He said, "No, no, it doesn't feel right, I want George. I don't like this. I can't work this one." And it was quite tricky. We said, "But you've got to use it. This one looks like you, and it's the movie one."

Were there any special effects incorporated in manipulating the figure?

No, Tony did everything.

The setting of Magic *takes place in the Catskill Mountains in upstate New York. Where was the film shot?*

It was shot in northern California.

It really looked like it was shot on location in the Catskills.

Yes, everyone that's seen it has said it looks good. It's a lake we found in northern California. We shot it over Christmas; if we had gone up to the Catskills at that time of year, it would be covered in snow, so we had to do it in California.

Do you try to find principal visual metaphors for the films you design?

Not consciously. I never set out with, "This is what this room is going to look like." First of all, I read what sort of characters there are and what the stage directions call for. Basically, it's the director's film. If I go off on my own and have a different vision than the director, then I'm in trouble, he's in trouble, and the movie is in trouble. A lot of it is in discussion with the director talking about how he wants to shoot it—whether he wants a long walk from this door to there, or if he wants to see that person in full figure with a light behind them. We're a background function all the time, and out of that comes the scale, shape, and the color of the set. It's really how the director wants the actors to appear.

So the design of a film evolves; it doesn't emerge full blown at the outset.

It always evolves with me. I can't speak for other production designers, but I know with me it's always from chats with the director, unless I get some brilliant idea and bounce it off the director. It is basically talking that brings out what eventually is seen on the screen. John McTiernan was terribly useful for me on *The Hunt for Red October*. He was not specifically saying, "I would like this," or "I would like that," but just little things like "Make it small." Most directors and cameramen hate to be in a confined space; they like elbow room. John was wonderful; he wanted the claustrophobic feeling of being on a submarine. We had one set which was Sean Connery's cabin where he murders a man at the beginning of the film. I made the cabin what I thought was tiny, because they are tiny in reality. When you go into these submarines, which I had to do, and see it for real, you wonder how they live like that. I showed the sketches and the plan to John, and he said, "No, make it smaller." I said, "But John, it's only about ten feet now." He said, "No, make it smaller, smaller." That set was incredibly small, but it served the purpose. It looked terribly authentic. Those sets were tiny because of John saying, "Make it small; make it difficult for us, because that's how it is and that's how I want it to look."

How did the high-tech look of the American submarine come about?

We had the task of making the *Dallas* control room look as though it was designed. Every piece of equipment in a real control room in today's nuclear submarine is wonderfully high-tech and millions of dollars apiece, but they're sort of stuck everywhere. It looks like a World War II interior, but it's stuck there for a reason: if anything goes wrong they can get at it, but it's not designed. If the audience were to be shown a real submarine control room like the *Dallas*, they would think, "Oh, they must have got a stock set of a World War II submarine and used it." The audience wouldn't have believed it. John said, "Think of a Boeing 747 cabin, and let's try to make it like that." We made it in these beige and biscuity colors, which are warm and friendly, as opposed to the black and silver and gray of the Russian sub. It still satisfied the U.S. Navy observer who was on the set every day to see that it was authentic. We had to make all the hydrometers and fire controls authentic. All the buttons had to be believable to the Navy, and yet to the audience it had to look high-tech.

The Navy was wonderful to me. I could photograph the most amazing stuff, but certain things were forbidden. When you go onto these nuclear submarines, they cover up certain things with blue plastic covers. It was funny doing things like the depth and speed gauges. If you asked them, "How deep can the submarine go?" they would always say, "Four hundred feet." You'd say, "How fast could it go?" and they would say, "In excess of twenty-five knots." I thought, "Don't kid me, these submarines do far more than that," but I couldn't get it out of them, so I put on the depth gauge that three thousand feet was maximum. On the speed gaugè, I put fifty-five knots per hour. Having no lead, I had to make it up. When we were putting the depth gauges in, the Navy man came and said, "You'll have to change that," and I said, "Why?" He said, "Just change the depth gauge." I said, "But that's only a guess." He said, "Well, the guess is a little too good; I'm afraid you've got to alter that," and they made us alter it. In the end, the Navy brought their design people around our set and they liked it. They said, "Submarines are going to look very similar to this in the future."

What is the source lighting on a submarine?

It's all artificial; part of their generator is fed off into lighting all their lights. At night, they go into blue. Red is battle stations. They have battle lanterns that cast a red glow. All the instruments are lit, all the buttons are lit, so that's one source of light. Then they have fluorescent lights all over the place. We designed our own lighting a little more snazzy than the real stuff.

Are the lighting positions on the sub you built the same in the real subs? Do they have overhead lighting?

Oh yes, they have overhead. They don't have underfloor. We put underfloor as well. That was largely to help the director of photography. We wanted this upward glow. It's funny, on a submarine they change the lighting up top when it's evening so the guys don't have the constant light all the time. So they create the evening.

In the Sidney Pollack film Havana, *there is a depiction of the Cuban Revolution. What location was used for this?*

We couldn't go to the real Havana. The Cubans wanted us, but the Treasury Department wouldn't allow us to spend American dollars in Cuba. Havana is unique. There is no other Caribbean city like Havana; there just isn't. It's a great city, which no other island has. We had to create it. We went to the Dominican Republic because it's so backward. It's like Cuba was in 1958. We had to build everything except the sugar cane fields, which is the reason we chose the Dominican Republic.

Do you think you have a style as a production designer?

At the beginning of every film, there are always the discussions of, "What style is this, high key, low key; do we use filters; is it crisp and clean?" In the end, it is what it is. Basically, a film takes a life of its own; all the personalities bring their agreements or disagreements to it. You can never preplan a course or style of a film. You can try, but it's like a giant amoeba; all the entities form one, and it goes its own way. It's a very strange thing. It's amazing, critics actually read far more into a movie. I've spoken to several directors who've said, "Did you read what this critic said? By cutting to this I was subliminally saying this, that, and the other. That thought never entered my head, but it's good. It sounds like I'm terribly clever." This is a strange business, because every movie is a prototype. There isn't a set pattern of how to make a film. There are no rules. It's not like setting up a jig to make doors or windows. Those are going to be okay, because you've done it before. You're dealing with something new for every film: the subject matter, the group of people that come together, the challenges they face.

Production designers are invariably dealing with something. In *Havana* it was 1958 Cuba with the Mafia, Batista, and the political situation. You have to go into all that research, because there's always someone out to prove you wrong—that a certain leaflet wasn't out in 1958, it didn't come out until January 1959, or something minor. You have to do your homework; you have to immerse yourself in it. The movie before that was about submarines. So if you're going to make a movie that's seen by millions of people—a lot of them U.S. Navy people—it has to be authentic, it has to be believable. If you've never been inside a submarine and you have to create a set within four months with people operating it, you have to do a hell of a lot of work. I think it hits costume designers as well, but production designers more than anyone, which is both exciting and daunting at the same time. This is one of the bonuses for a production designer. You are thrown into worlds you know nothing about. It's a continual education; you find out things.

How important is the amount of preproduction time you are given to prepare a film?

I think the great thing is having the preparation time. Decisions are made for the wrong reason. They say, "Well, we just don't have the prep time, because so and so actor can only work from May to June." Then that's the number of weeks you've got. It doesn't matter that you need the time, the actor's available for that period and that's it. Or, "We must have a Thanksgiving release. Working backwards, we need thirty weeks for postproduction; therefore, you've got to start the day after tomorrow." David Lean is the only one I've worked with who said, "We need to do this properly. We need this time here, this time there, then we'll start rehearsals." A lot of directors are trapped the same as I am: the major actor is available, so you have to start.

Production designers are in a unique situation. The cinematographer shoots the sets you design, and the editor edits the material photographed from that set. You are responsible for creating what almost everyone else who works on a film will work with.

The production designer has to get it there. The editor has his film, it's already been shot, and he works his magic on an entity that has been given to him. The production designer is the only person who presents things in three dimensions that everyone can criticize. Everyone has their own opinion: "Well, I wouldn't have chosen that color," or "No, I would never have that sort of answering machine." Everything is up for criticism by everyone. The actress doesn't like the curtains that are hanging up; all sorts of things come into it.

It must take a strong personality to deal with all these forces.

You have to tap dance fairly fast sometimes. Also, it's a secondary role; if people notice the sets too much and they're taking over, then the sets aren't good, unless an outrageous set is specifically required. You're really designing an atmosphere, not a set. You're designing a background that seems convincing for the story; what's behind the actor's head seems right for what they're supposed to be saying. It should always be secondary to the actors, but never appear wrong. It should never be an entity in itself. It should never be, "Wow, wasn't that a great set?" Then you know you're in trouble.

Do you think the tendency in the film industry is moving towards more location work rather than shooting in the studio?

Funny enough, it's moving back now. We had that spell where to shoot in the studio was old-fashioned. I don't have any strong feeling; I think what's best for the movie. It might be studio, it might be location; use whichever gives you the best result for what you're trying to achieve. Often it is the studio. Ten or twelve years ago, *Basic Instinct* would have been done all on location, but now we're half on location and half in the studio, and I think rightly so. Paul Verhoeven has made wise choices in bringing certain scenes back to the studio, because things are so much more controllable, whereas outside they're battling against all sorts of inconveniences just to have a real building instead of a translight backing out of a window: it can rain, there is traffic noise. I think gradually other directors are thinking the same and are coming back to the old-fashioned studio system.

Production designers have to deal with both artistic and financial responsibilities. How do you feel about those two parts of your job?

It's very difficult sometimes to equate the two. One does have tremendous financial responsibility because things are so expensive, especially now. When you are building whole streets for *Havana*, you're spending someone else's money. There always has to be a compromise struck with what you think you'd like to do, and what you realize is responsible and practical to do. You have to be aware of that. Often on a big set to gratify yourself you feel, "I could make this better." On the other hand you say, "Well, this particular movie can't stand $10 million in sets." The higher you go, you become more and more an administrator dealing with budgets and schedules and less to do with art comes into your job, which is very sad in a way. I would like to just be doing color sketches, but now production designers hire people to come and do their own color sketches. It's not because they can't do it. It's just because they don't have the time.

What production designers do you feel were influential in creating landmark films in art direction?

Certainly, John Bryan's early films with David Lean, *Oliver Twist* and *Great Expectations*. John Bryan is the mentor of John Box and my mentor. He was a very important figure. Certainly, Perry Ferguson with *Citizen Kane*. Van Nest Polglase, who did the white sets for the early Fred Astaire musicals, was remarkable. Obviously, William Cameron Menzies, for almost everything he did. I think Richard Day was one of the great American production designers. If you look back at some of those old films, he never got the sort of ballyhoo that Cameron Menzies and Cedric

Gibbons did, but he was really something. He did the original *The Razor's Edge* with Tyrone Power. The art direction in that is staggeringly good.

Do you think the new technologies are going to change production design in the future?

I can't see how the computer age can help production designers very much, because it's all imagination and it's all your hand. It's something you cannot get through a machine. Maybe I'm sort of too late for the computer age, but I cannot see how a computer can give you what you get with just a pencil to sow the seed of ideas. I can't see that changing. Some young genius will prove me quite wrong, I'm sure, but I see the future much as we have in the past. I think we'll always be with a pencil and a dream.

11

Ferdinando Scarfiotti

Ferdinando Scarfiotti began his career in the theater in Italy as an assistant to master director Luchino Visconti. Aspiring to the position of designer, Scarfiotti worked on many of Visconti's theater and opera productions, which were highly regarded in Italy. One of Scarfiotti's first film projects was designing the director's adaptation of Thomas Mann's *Death in Venice*.

After ten years with Visconti, Scarfiotti formed a collaborative bond with Bernardo Bertolucci. Together with cinematographer Vittorio Storaro, they created *The Conformist*, a film that helped establish Bertolucci's international reputation and presented an elegant dreamlike look that influenced world cinema. Their second film together, *Last Tango in Paris*, became a *scandale* because of its uninhibited depiction of a sexual relationship. The subtle surrealistic environments in which the story takes place strongly contribute to the mystery and eroticism of the film.

The collaboration between Bertolucci, Scarfiotti, and Storaro reached its artistic summit on the epic *The Last Emperor*. The immense scale and scope of the film presented an enormous challenge to the art department. Drawing upon historic research and a fertile imagination, Scarfiotti created China's Forbidden City in a glory that fulfills the viewer's expectations of that wondrous locale. Scarfiotti won the Academy Award for art direction—set decoration for his fanciful and meticulously realized design.

Scarfiotti has worked on many evocative projects. He designed the elegant *Daisy Miller* for Peter Bogdanovich, the provocatively flamboyant *Scarface* for Brian De Palma, and the stylish *American Gigolo* for Paul

Schrader, a film that echoes Scarfiotti's work on *The Conformist* and in its own right has influenced the look of many contemporary films.

Ferdinando Scarfiotti's work fuses the pictorial beauty of the past with the streamlined visions of the future. His European sensibility and highly developed visual acumen have given the gift of high style to the movies he has designed.

1971   *Death in Venice*
       The Conformist
1972   *Avanti!*
1973   *Last Tango in Paris*
1974   *Daisy Miller*
1980   *American Gigolo*
1981   *Honky Tonk Freeway*
1982   *Cat People*
1983   *Scarface*
1985   *Bring on the Night*
1987   *The Last Emperor***
1988   *Mamba*
1992   *Toys*

**Academy Award for best achievement in art direction–set decoration.

How did you become a production designer?

I became a production designer by first being a designer in the theater for a long time in Italy. I started with Luchino Visconti. He's mainly known in this country as a movie director, but in fact he was maybe even a greater theater and opera director. He directed a huge amount of productions. I started as an assistant, and then I became his designer. I designed opera and stage productions for the last ten years of his life. That was my school. I designed *Death in Venice*, one of my first movies for him, at the very end of his career. After *Death in Venice* he planned to do the first part of Proust's *A la recherche du temps perdu, Swann's Way*, which he wanted me to design, but I turned it down because honestly I did not feel ready for it yet. Visconti and I had a very good working relationship—very important to me—but it was the end of the sixties and I grew a bit rebellious against this quite demanding father figure, so I started working with other directors who were closer to my age. That's when I started working with Bertolucci and other directors.

What are the differences between designing for film and theater?

In theater, nobody can change the designer's point of view, because it's there to be seen by a real person. You design the set from the point of view of the center of the theater. You build it as best you can, and when the curtain rises, the audience sees exactly what you want them to. The visual relationship is a direct one, while in movies this relationship is always altered by the camera, the director's vision, and the editing room. Entire scenes are shot as a close-up on the actors and your set gets lost, or there are entire scenes that end up on the editing room floor and you never see them.

Bertolucci is an extremely visual director. How do you collaborate to interpret his vision of a film?

We really work on symbiosis most of the time. First of all, we grew up together. We are exactly the same age; in fact, Bernardo's birthday is ten days from mine. Bertolucci started working as an assistant to Pasolini, and I started working as an assistant to Visconti. They were brothers in faith, but they were really the two opposite poles of the Communist Party. We left our masters at the same time. We really worked together on *The Conformist*. We were very young and had very little money. We didn't remember the Fascist Era, because we were born in 1941 at the very end of it. So instead of doing our research in books, we decided to watch a lot of movies of that period. Instead of going through newspapers and real footage, which would have been very natural, we looked at American movies, German movies, just to see what the collective unconscious was creating in that time. We decided to get a step further from reality and just take inspiration from what had been done in that period, no matter what the subject. That's why *The Conformist* looks slightly surreal, just a bit off the everyday reality.

What were some of the movies that you screened?

There were so many. One I remember very well was *Angel* by Lubitsch. I can't tell you there was a specific image there that is in *The Conformist*, but I remember the day we saw it and the kind of impact it had on the both of us. Maybe it was the way the lights would hit the costumes and certain faces. The cinematographer, Vittorio Storaro, was a beginner, too, who like Bernardo and I liked to experiment and was full of enthusiasm. It was 1968. Storaro is pretty much the same age; that makes us twenty-seven years old. We were quite young, although not exactly kids, but we already had experience in the field, and we were much more naive than we would be now. You can tell by watching the last thing we did together, *The Last Emperor*, which is so much more mature.

A key image in The Conformist *is of light streaming into an apartment through the venetian blinds. Where did this image come from?*

That probably came from some of those Hollywood movies that we saw. It became the trademark of *The Conformist* and, for a while, of Storaro and me. I used it again in *American Gigolo*. It all goes back to Hollywood in the thirties and forties. When you have an idea, you really have to follow it through, exaggerating a little bit so that it has a visual impact. Otherwise, it only becomes the usual venetian blinds which you see in every office, but if you make this image strong and you move across the room in a very surreal way, that creates a certain unsettling feeling and it becomes something. That's true for every visual idea you might have. You can't leave it there half-dead; you have to make it strong and give it some extra point.

During the opening titles of Last Tango in Paris, *we see paintings by Francis Bacon. Did his work also influence the decor of the film?*

We had already selected the apartment. I had already thought of doing those gradations on the walls, starting with a dark color going gradually into a lighter one but not yet knowing what color we would use. Then we saw the big Francis Bacon retrospective, and we decided that kind of flesh color would be great. I did big cardboard paintings of color tests, starting with burnt sienna, going gradually into a flesh tone, and ending up with a cream color.

In the middle of Brando's apartment is a large object that is covered by sheets, which is never explained. What was the idea behind this?

Remember, it was the early seventies and it was the time when the first Christo sculptures came around. Maybe I placed that object there as a monument to Bernardo's subconscious. He really liked that very much. *Tango* was Bernardo's most personal movie. It was not taken from any book; it was his own personal script. There's a lot of him in it.

Last Tango in Paris *is a film filled with visual ideas. Was a lot of construction necessary to render the sets?*

We didn't build a thing for *Tango*. I went around Paris with Bernardo selecting locations. I had some ideas for the colors, and I knew what to do with the locations, but as far as construction work, it was pretty minimal. The tango scene was shot at the La Salle Pleyelle, a former professional ballroom in Paris now used for concerts. I changed very few things in it. For lighting, I hung from the ceiling around one hundred globes, and they worked amazingly well. When Brando and Schneider spin around dancing, you see all these moon-like shapes over their heads creating a dizzying effect. The rest is the La Salle Pleyelle the way it is— which is already pretty beautiful. *Last Tango* was not a big decorating job. The apartment we found was already quite sensational in itself. Storaro did a great job on balancing the light: the sky outside the window almost looks like a painted backdrop. Instead of having the usual burned-out window, Storaro was able to give us this incredible view of Paris bathed in golden light. It was really a miracle of balancing the light.

How did you come to design American Gigolo, *and how did the look of the film develop?*

It was my first movie in Hollywood, and Paul Schrader wanted somebody who didn't know Los Angeles very well. He wanted a fresh look. In 1978 Los Angeles was on the verge of a big change. Melrose Avenue still didn't exist as such, but there were already some big fashion shops and restaurants that had just opened. So it was a big playground to rediscover and to reinvent. That was the first time I collaborated with Ed Richardson, who's been my art director since then, and we had fun working together. There was some location work, but we built almost everything. We built Richard Gere's apartment, the house in Palm Springs—even the Polo Lounge in the Beverly Hills Hotel was a set, because I felt that that green room was pretty ugly anyway. It's a very glamorous place, but if you photograph it, it's just a very ugly restaurant. So I decided to do something very streamlined and pink instead of green, and it came out nice. We built it at Paramount.

The sequence where Richard Gere lays out his clothes on the bed is a very strong image.

That was fun. Schrader wanted to have all of Richard Gere's clothes exposed behind his bed so that he could pick up everything in a easy way.

Did you work on coordinating what tie would go with what shirt?

Yes, the costumes were a big deal in that movie, because we started with John Travolta, who brought in Armani. Giorgio designed everything down to jeans and overalls, making it right for Travolta. John had to leave the movie. When we switched from Travolta to Richard Gere, we realized that Richard was too real a person to be dressed by one designer. Travolta was a real idol at the time, so you could dress him as such. Richard Gere, on the other hand, was more down to earth, so I had to make a few changes in the apartment that was already being built for Travolta. I changed the colors of the walls, and I told Schrader, "Let's keep Armani, but let's mix it up with other designers, and let's go real American. If he wears jeans, they should be Levi's; they can't be designer jeans." We didn't have a real costume designer, we had a wardrobe person who I was supervising. Plus, we had all these big names like Armani and Basile, who was pretty big at that time.

Was the exercise bar that Gere uses to hang upside down a real piece of exercise equipment, or did you design it?

John Travolta had a gym instructor who was in charge of getting him in shape, and he invented it. I worked with him in redesigning the bar so that it could fit in the set.

The image of the light streaming in through the blinds echoes The Conformist. *How did it come to be used in* American Gigolo?

Schrader and the cinematographer John Bailey were both very big fans of *The Conformist*. They ran the movie three or four times during pre-production. They really studied it well, so it was inevitable that some visual element of *The Conformist* would sneak into *American Gigolo*. I think the reason Paul Schrader called me was because I designed *The Conformist*.

Do you feel you brought a European sensibility to American Gigolo?

That's what Paul wanted, but I don't know whether I achieved that or not. At that time, Italian design was beginning to be very popular. Everybody wanted to have a Memphis chair or an Armani shirt.

You seemed to use a lot of cool colors in American Gigolo.

Yes, I do generally prefer cool colors, but it really varies from movie to movie. Generally, for my house or for myself, I would choose cool colors, but then in my work I might decide to use just primary colors, like I did in *Scarface*. I think it would have been pretty strange to use a refined color scheme with that subject. We had to be bold as the script required.

Did that evolve out of your discussions with Brian De Palma on Scarface?

No, De Palma is not a director who gets very much involved in discussions about colors, shapes, and forms. He does his own storyboarding. He likes to know the exact shape of the room, where the doors are, where the windows are, so he can plan his very accurate camera movements, but his concern stops there. He usually liked what I did, and he's a great director to work with.

What was your design concept of what Miami should look like in the late seventies?

It was the most expensive that the Miami scene had to offer but with a certain element of vulgarity. I developed a Greek and Roman theme in the whole movie, which I already partially found there. I remember visiting a house during a location survey; it must have been the house of a drug dealer. Everything in it was extremely exaggerated. In one room, the walls were done in a Pompeian style with famous Pompeian frescoes turned Cuban. It was very interesting pairing that idea with the decadence of the story. I decided to go for it, and I told Brian, "Let's do Miami like at the time of the decadence of the Roman Empire." Brian liked the idea, and Tony Montana's mansion became the re-creation of the Roman grandeur seen through the eyes of a Cuban drug dealer.

Where did you shoot the exterior of Tony Montana's mansion?

Always keeping this Greek-Roman theme in mind, I found a house in Santa Barbara which was already very Pompeian in structure, and we added an entire floor on top of it to make it really look like a Roman temple with lots and lots of statues scattered around the grounds. It was quite excessive.

Where did you create the disco nightclub?

I found a tourist center near Miami which had this enormous facade that you see briefly in the movie. We used that as an exterior. It was like a Greek temple with statues holding up the roof. We rebuilt the interior on stage with a lot of Greek and Roman statues, columns, and mirrors. It looked like a perfect disco nightmare.

Why did you choose to build the sets on the stage?

They had to be built on stage, because almost every set was going to be completely destroyed by shooting or fire. Even if one gets permission to entirely destroy a real house, it can only be done once. We had five sets of walls for each set, because there is nothing you can do when you have a wall that is bullet ridden. You throw it away and put up another wall. In the final scene, when the whole house gets destroyed, everything was quintupled—furniture, carpets, balustrades, floors, walls, and paintings. Of course, all the bullet hits were preplanned.

Who plans where the hits are going to be?

Special effects with the art department and the director.

What visual concept were you and Paul Schrader going for on Cat People?

We wanted something really Gothic and dark. As a source, I used a lot of surrealistic paintings and some of the French and Belgian Symbolists. The movie takes place in New Orleans. It's very hard not to be stimulated by that city, because it's many things at the same time: it's European, it's deeply American, and it's very Southern.

Were the zoo sequences shot in New Orleans?

Unfortunately for us, the zoo in New Orleans is a very modern Audubon Society environmental zoo. They couldn't even conceive that we would put animals back in cages, so I had to rebuild the New Orleans zoo on the back lot of Universal Studios. That gave me a chance to design this very Gothic Victorian zoo, which probably doesn't exist anywhere in America. It was all rebuilt, exteriors and interiors. We had to build cages strong enough to contain very dangerous animals. The art director, Ed Richardson, was really great on that. I provided the design, and he really worked the whole technical aspect. We shot only the entrance of the zoo in New Orleans. Then through a matte shot, we tied up the two locations. Practically all of the interiors of the film were shot on stage in Los Angeles.

Where were the scenes in the desert filmed?

The red desert and the big tree were done on stage.

How did you create a desert in the studio? Was that all sand?

We used the biggest stage at Universal, which is, in fact, the one they used for the original *The Phantom of the Opera*, and we turned it into a desert with cracked earth to create the effect of the draught. The sand was real sand. It was dyed with a red dye. You couldn't find that color sand anywhere, of course, so I had to mix the sand with different powdered pigments.

That's what Antonioni did for Zabriskie Point. *They sprayed the sand gold.*

Yes, it's one thing to spray something outdoors; it's another thing to be on Stage 18 at Universal. The dye was smelling pretty bad; there were fans going all the time to create sandstorms, so everybody had to wear a mask. Later, a village with mountains and dunes was matted in by Albert Whitlock.

How did you become involved as the designer of The Last Emperor?

The project started out as a ten-hour series for TV. As strange as it might seem, I had been running away from that project for two years. I didn't want to do it. I didn't want to do a ten-hour TV movie on China and spend two years in Peking. So for almost two years I had been hiding from Bernardo. In fact, two other designers had been hired before me, and Bernardo kept coming back to me. When the TV movie became a regular movie, I finally decided to do it.

What was it like to research The Last Emperor? *It must have been massive.*

Massive and fast because, unfortunately, by delaying my commitment to the project, I lost most of the research time. The costume designer was on for a much longer time than I was. Altogether I had not even six months of preparation, which is not much for someone who doesn't know anything about China. I mean all I knew about China was Chinese restaurants in San Francisco. Chinese art is not easy to understand, because it's very static. It hasn't changed in two thousand years. You can tell if a rooftop is Ming or Ch'ing period just because of a certain curve, but the change is minimal. As an Italian, I am used to many art movements through the centuries. From the Renaissance you go to Baroque, and from there, through Rococo, you return to Classicism, and so on. The changes are very visible, and towns have many different but definite styles. The United States is also quite eclectic with an immense variety of styles, forms, and shapes. You go to China, and although it's beautiful to look at, it's very hard to grasp.

What was it like to shoot in the Forbidden City?

It was a very difficult task. We had to build all the interiors on stage, because they wouldn't let us shoot any of the interiors there. We shot the courtyards and the throne room, but they only allowed us inside it for half a day with five people and no lights. We weren't allowed to have any lights, because they were afraid of fire. It's the scene where the little boy gets crowned and then he goes outside through a yellow curtain that opens up becoming a canopy. Using that curtain was the only way we could get some light inside and still have some separation from the outside world. That was the only day that we shot an interior in the Forbidden City. The rest was all built on stage at the Peking Studios and at Cinecitta in Rome. The interiors of the Forbidden City are rather disappointing if you look for grandeur: they are smaller than one expects, and most of the rooms are very tiny. They didn't really give the idea of this little kid living in a grand place. So I practically redesigned and reinvented a lot of the spaces.

It's interesting; in a sense you are dealing with people's perceptions of reality, not reality itself.

Exactly—or expectations. Of course, I don't claim that my China was a faithful copy of the Forbidden City. Certain elements were closer to what people would expect. The hall with all those dragons where the old Empress dies is not to be found anywhere in the Forbidden City.

Were there any records of what the Forbidden City looked like during the time period depicted in the film?

Yes, we had good research. Most of the elements that I used in the sets are real, but they exist somewhere else. For instance, the columns with the dragons exist in another smaller Forbidden City in a city called Shen-Yan in the North near the border of Manchuria, where the Ch'ing Dynasty came from. So I picked up that element and put it in another room I found somewhere else through photographs. I went around China and tried to see all I could of the Ch'ing architecture. Two younger brothers of the Emperor are still alive in Peking; one is a teacher. They are very old, but they still had a good memory. They were able to tell us a lot of stories. They also had a family album. It was absolutely wonderful to look at the real images of Pu-Yi and his family.

What was your crew like?

I found quite a few good Europeans and Americans there who had been studying in Peking and spoke fluent Mandarin. There was an American who had been born in Peking. He was the son of a writer. He went to school in Peking and studied calligraphy there, so I hired him to help me find a good calligrapher who could reproduce the scrolls and calligraphy exercises made by previous dynasties that hang on the walls of the Imperial City. Each dynasty has its own style. You can imagine how impossible it would be for an untrained eye to recognize certain styles of calligraphy.

It was a very difficult job to coordinate all of the these people. I had many people coming from Italy. All the painters, staffers, and sculptors came from Rome with their machinery and materials, so everything had to be shipped by boat months in advance, and a few things didn't arrive on time. We had to set up every single department, including a very large upholstery shop. We bought almost all the fabrics in Hong Kong, since Peking has mostly synthetic materials to offer. Most Chinese rugs in Peking are quite ugly. To get the real stuff, you've got to find out who's the antique dealer who sells rugs to antique dealers in London, Paris, or New York, or go to Mongolia where they still use good materials, old patterns, and vegetable dyes.

There's no structure in China for making movies as we know it. For instance, there are no prop houses. Here in Los Angeles, there are many places whose only business is to rent to the movies. Practically every store rents to the industry. They know how to make a rental agreement. It's all very standard. It's very easy to get everything you want here as long as you have the means. So I guess it would have been not only possible but even easier to build the sets of *The Last Emperor* here than in China, but the cost would have been prohibitive.

There is a dramatic contrast between the look of the Emperor's world in the Forbidden City and the world he enters when he is in prison. What was the idea behind this?

We decided to put all of the colors in the first part of the movie. The moment he leaves the Forbidden City, he leaves this innocent fairy world. Little by little, we go almost colorless. Traditionally in China, only the Imperial Family and the aristocracy were allowed to paint their buildings red and have gold decorations on them. The ordinary people were forced to have their houses painted gray. The old Peking is almost entirely gone now, but still when you leave the Forbidden City you get into a gray world; everything is made of concrete. This man Pu-Yi had never been outside of this world of red and gold. The door opens, and what he sees is a gray world. So that was a decision inspired by what we saw, and we only had to force reality a little bit in order to make the contrast really noticeable.

The costumes were just marvelous. Did you work very closely with the costume designer?

Yes, closely, but it was all the responsibility of James Acheson, who is a very conscientious researcher. He's mad for details even more than I am. He really did a great job. The budget for costumes was immense. I remember Bernardo called him up one day and said, "I need a thousand more extras in the coronation scene." They had miscalculated the size of this huge square outside the Temple of Heaven. They had planned for fifteen hundred extras and fifteen hundred would just have gotten lost in there, so they needed a thousand more costumes to be done in China. Extras don't cost anything, but poor James had to dress them somehow. Of course, he did the best he could. The extras at the farthest end of the square were dressed, but they were wearing sneakers.

Did you coordinate the colors that would be used in the costumes with the colors in the sets?

Yes, I always do that with the costume designer. We work very closely. That's necessary. You can't have certain colors that you don't want, but again, everything in China's art is so predetermined that it's very hard to go wrong.

Is there a major difference between the way production designers work in Italy and the way they work in the United States?

In Italy we tend to work without a budget. We're not given a budget most of the time. One day someone comes to your office and tells you that you've gone over budget. It's much more casual there since there are no unions, and you can hire anybody to work for you as a designer. If I'm a designer in Hollywood and I want to hire you for a union movie, I just couldn't, because you're not a member of the union. In Italy, if you want to, you can collect a bunch of artists and have them work and be part of your project. Sometimes you can have very interesting and creative results, and sometimes not. In Italy making a movie is a much more chaotic and unpredictable experience. Over here it's very departmental, which in a way makes things easier and more orderly.

How do you like to work with cinematographers?

I like to talk to them as early on in the project as I can, so we can plan together a lighting scheme. One of the tendencies of certain cinematographers is to flood the set with light directly from above, which makes everything very flat—a bad TV habit, I believe. I have a tendency to put real ceilings on sets, so that the light has to come in from natural light sources like windows or lamps. I learned that when I was designing for the theater, where if you put a hard ceiling on a set, you can only light from the house or the sides—an extremely challenging job. Luchino Visconti, for instance, only used hard ceilings on his sets and always achieved stunning results. Orson Welles also always put ceilings on his sets. Vittorio Storaro can shoot in a room the size of a closet, and he can light it brilliantly.

Where do you see the future of production design headed?

Just today my art director and I were trying to make this big decision of buying a computer system called Dynaperspective for the project I'm designing now. It's an amazing tool. You just feed it with ground plans and elevations of a room, and it gives you back a three-dimensional rendition of it. You can actually move around that room and see what it looks like from every possible angle. You can practically anticipate every camera movement. I think that computers are going to change somewhat the look of movies. If you look at what commercials and MTV are doing now, they're so technologically advanced that it's scary. But at one point all these new technologies become very unimaginative, and it gets very tiring for the eye and the mind to be bombarded with an enormous amount of images in a very short time. Why not some room for a moment of relaxation and some acting? The Schwarzenegger, *Robocop*-type movies are already setting a trend, but I really do hope that the future of movies is not going to be just that. There must be room for something else.

12

Polly Platt

Polly Platt studied set and costume design for the theater at Carnegie Mellon University. While designing for the theater in New York, she met Peter Bogdanovich, who was directing for the stage, and designed two of his productions. They fell in love and moved to California to follow Peter's quest to become a film director.

On the West Coast, Platt and Bogdanovich wrote and sold two scripts to Roger Corman, both of which were made into movies: *The Gill Women of Venus*, followed by the 1968 cult classic *Targets*, the directorial film debut of Peter Bogdanovich.

In 1971 Polly Platt designed the highly acclaimed *The Last Picture Show*, Bogdanovich's black-and-white elegy to a bygone era. The stark realism and poetic grace of Platt's design meticulously detail the Texas town so eloquently realized in Larry McMurtry's novel and pay homage to American masters John Ford and Howard Hawks. The great success of *The Last Picture Show* was followed by two other collaborations with Bogdanovich, *What's Up, Doc?* and *Paper Moon*. Platt's career as a production designer continued to grow on such projects as *A Star Is Born* with Barbra Streisand and *The Bad News Bears*. In 1977 she wrote a screenplay for Louis Malle, *Pretty Baby*, which was produced at Paramount.

Her long association with James L. Brooks began when she designed *Terms of Endearment*, for which she received an Oscar nomination. She later was the executive producer on Brooks's *Broadcast News* and produced *Say Anything*, on which Brooks was executive producer. Currently, Polly Platt serves as vice president of Gracie Films, a company run by Brooks that produced *The Tracey Ullman Show* for television and continues to produce the highly successful animated series *The Simpsons*.

Polly Platt was the production designer on the unreleased *The Other Side of the Wind*, the last film directed by the legendary Orson Welles. Her flamboyant designs for *The Witches of Eastwick* merged with the vision of director George Miller to create an imaginatively decadent look at a mansion inhabited by the Devil himself.

Polly Platt continues to do it all. She designs for film, theater, and television, in addition to writing and producing.

1967 *The Gill Women of Venus*

1968 *Targets*

1971 *The Last Picture Show*

1972 *What's Up, Doc?*

1973 *Paper Moon*

    The Thief Who Came to Dinner

1976 *A Star Is Born*

    The Bad News Bears

1982 *Young Doctors in Love*

1983 *Terms of Endearment**

1987 *The Witches of Eastwick*

* Academy Award nomination for best achievement in art direction–set decoration.

How did you first become a production designer?

I studied to be a set and costume designer at Carnegie Mellon in Pittsburgh. There I became pretty well versed in the literature of the theater and studied all the periods: the Greeks and Roman theater, English Restoration, Shakespeare. I did a lot of sets and costumes in college, but eventually I dropped out, because there were no women set designers in the theater and they were somewhat uncooperative about my becoming one. So, in the late fifties, I moved to California with my young husband, who was a student of playwriting at Tech. We didn't do very well there. A couple of friends of mine who were graduates of Carnegie Mellon were going to start a theater company in Tucson, Arizona. Their idea was, "We can start a repertory company in Tucson, Arizona, where there are all these retired people from the East Coast who are interested in good theater. We'll do *Thieves' Carnival* by Anouilh and *Camino Real* by Tennessee Williams." They asked me to design the sets and costumes. I did that. Sadly, my young writer husband was killed in an automobile accident in Arizona. Grief-stricken, I intended to give up my ambitions and stay in Arizona and collect Papapo baskets. I was twenty years old. But after a period of time I recovered, and needing a job I moved to New York and designed a couple of plays Off Broadway. I met Peter Bogdanovich, who was a young director. I did a season of stock with Peter. We fell in love. We did a revival of a play in New York; I designed and did the costumes. It was *Once in a Lifetime* by Moss Hart and George S. Kaufman, but Peter wanted to become a movie director. Our production was a critical and financial failure, but I eventually talked him into moving to California. There, Peter and I wrote two scripts for Roger Corman, *The Gill Women of Venus* and *Targets*. We made them with Roger's help, and I ended up designing them. I now realize I also produced them, even though I didn't know what a producer was. I was not only in charge of the locations and stuff, but I also handled the checkbook.

What was it like to make the transition from designing for the stage to designing for films?

That was very funny actually. When you work in the theater, you have a proscenium and a stage. You always have to measure the stage—the height of the proscenium and the fly space you have. When I designed *Targets*, my first movie with sets, we had a whole soundstage. It never occurred to me to measure it, because it just seemed so big compared to what I had to work with in the theater. As it turns out, it was one of the smallest soundstages in L.A. I designed a set for the house where the killer lived with his parents. We prebuilt the set, and as we started to put up the walls, we realized that I had designed a set that was way too big for the soundstage. It just went right off the edge! We had a long hallway, which I had to shorten. I cut five-foot sections out of each wall in the hallway to make the set fit. I also shortened the size of the living room. I didn't get fired, because I handled the checkbook. No one discovered my mistake! That set also converted into the hotel room for Boris Karloff. I saved money by making that set work for both scenes. I just plugged in doors and windows, added gold leaf and some trim for the hotel room of Boris Karloff.

How did you use color to define the killer's character?

I was trying to design a home that might create a murderer. It was bland, and I bought ugly things for the decor. There were no paintings on the walls. It was cold and hard. We used beiges and gold for the Boris Karloff character, and cold colors for the murderer. We wanted to avoid red. When the killer murders his mother, we wanted that to be the first time that you ever saw red. We wanted it to be a big shock psychologically.

The climax of Targets *takes place at a drive-in. Was that an actual location?*

Yes, although I did build a miniature of it for some shots. It was a big landmark near where we lived in the San Fernando Valley. I was driving on the freeway thinking, "How great, we can have him get on the top of the drive-in and shoot at people." Then a director we were talking to—either Sam Fuller or Fritz Lang—had the idea for him to go inside the scaffolding.

Was there ever a discussion of filming The Last Picture Show *in color?*

Everyone assumed we would make it in color, because every picture in the seventies except for *In Cold Blood* was being made in color. Peter and I were very close to Orson Welles at the time. He said, "Well, of course you're going to make in black and white!" And we said, "I guess that would be nice, but nobody will let us." His voice was booming; he yelled at us, "Well, of course you'll do it anyway!" Larry McMurtry also thought it should be in black in white. *Hud* had been made in black and white. We started thinking about it. We had a lot of support from BBS, who produced it. The executive producer, Bert Schneider, decided to poll the exhibitors to see if it made any difference to them whether the picture was in black and white. The exhibitors all came back and said that if the picture was good, they would book it; they didn't care. I said to Peter, "Listen, every picture now is in color. Some are hits, some are flops. Color isn't what makes the difference. So we may as well do something that's unique."

What was your approach to designing in black and white on The Last Picture Show?

I took a lot of color photos and studied those carefully. Then I made black-and-white photos and studied the results. The whole town was brick. I was afraid that all of the brick buildings wouldn't have any dimension, or they would all look the same in black and white. So I painted some brick darker than others. I would heighten the white in the town, dry-brush it to make it hotter. A period film like *The Last Picture Show* in black and white made us all look much better than we really were. It just does something for a style of a picture that is really hard to describe. If you think of *The Last Picture Show* in color, or you see *Texasville*, there's something so devastating about seeing that town in color; you just want to die. I just think that black-and-white photography is awesome. It was one of the most valuable experiences of my life.

What did you do to research what life was like in a small Texas town in the 1950s?

I looked in albums and yearbooks, which belonged to people in the town, and I saw the way people looked then, really. I did not research in *Vogue* magazine. I looked in *Life* magazine; a lot of the pictures were in black and white. I was very influenced by research. It was all there— like those funny angora sweaters the girls wore. When I was a little girl, I had seen movies where nobody looked right to me; they looked too perfect, and no one seemed to have clothes like real people. I had always wanted to make a movie where people didn't have hairdressers, where their hair wasn't perfect all the time. I bought the Levi's off of the men in the town. The amazing thing for me is that people in Italy, France, and Russia have said to me, "That's my hometown."

Where was the town?

Right in the dead center of Texas. It's what we call West Texas, because it's west of Houston and Dallas. It was the town where Larry McMurtry grew up. It had everything we needed—the high school, the lake, the tank dam—so it turned out to be quite right. We were very shocked by how barren the land looked. There's a weed called mesquite that grows there, as big as a tree. Larry McMurtry's dad was a rancher whose hands were literally all gnarled and twisted from arthritis. I began to think that this part of Texas had such a harsh atmosphere and that the people began to look gnarled like their environment. We really showed a lot of that in the movie. It's just a bitter, bitter, hard life, and that's why those young people are so precious, because they had beauty and youth.

How did you transform the actual locations you used into the Texas town that McMurtry wrote about?

I changed that whole street which had the movie theater on it. We put in the marquee. I changed the façades on at least three buildings. I took a supermarket, split it in half, and put a fake wood façade over the brick. That supermarket had been modernized into an awful sort of fifties look. I divided it in two, and in one half I put in the Blue Moon Cafe. I didn't touch the pool room; it was actually a domino parlor. I just put in pool tables and that period Coke machine. It had the stove in there. The paint was peeling off the ceiling; stuff was hanging off from years of cigarette smoke. The windows were so dirty, we just left it alone. That was smart. The biggest thing was to keep the prop man from cleaning the windows, because they had centuries of dirt. I did a lot inside the houses; I had to do the wallpaper. The Texaco station was in really good shape. I took out the Texaco part of the sign from the circle, so it just looked like an empty ring standing in the sky. It really tells you that the town is falling apart. I put in an oil rig next to the theater— it cost a fortune to move it there. It was really hard to find an indoor pool. That was a desperate search. We had to go to Wichita Falls about forty-five minutes away. The Town Hall is still exactly the same. I went back twenty years later; it's still the same; it will never change.

What were the determining factors in deciding where to shoot Paper Moon?

It was adapted from a book called *Addie Pray*, which was set in Georgia. The screenplay still retained a lot of scams having to do with cotton mills. I went to Georgia and it just wasn't right, because there were so many trees. Georgia is all really tall pine trees; you can't get any vista at all. I remembered how flat Kansas was when Peter and I had gone across it in our old Ford on our way to live in California. I had a vision of Ryan and Tatum in this little car against the big sky and I thought, "That's where we'll really relate to them, better than bread lines." Just these two people alone against the world, not the Depression, which didn't interest me.

In Paper Moon *Ryan O'Neal and his daughter travel through many towns. What were the logistics that you had to deal with?*

We had some wonderful locations for that movie. It was in two different areas: Hays, Kansas, and St. Joe, Missouri. We were mostly in little towns in Hays, Kansas. I found these great houses here and there, but I kept them all within a concentric circle. Then we moved the company to St. Joseph, Missouri, which was awesome. The city had not changed since the 1920s. You hardly had to do anything; it was just perfect. The town where they get thrown in jail was around St. Joe, right down the Missouri River. In the original screenplay, they went all the way to New York and stayed at the Plaza Hotel and had a Cadillac. I thought that was wrong. I said, "I don't think we're going to have any sympathy for them if they get so rich and have a Cadillac. Let's keep it little." So we had them go to St. Joe, which was a lot different than going to the Plaza Hotel in New York and having furs. The best they ever did get was a real nice Ford.

Were the hotel rooms practical locations?

Almost all of them were practical. The small actual locations were great, but it was so hard to do camera moves, we ended up using corners of bigger rooms and making them look smaller. The long scene where Ryan and Tatum both look in the round mirror as they are getting dressed was actually done in a cafeteria. I used the place we used to feed people. We really needed a big room to be able to get that distance to show them in the mirror.

Paper Moon *was also photographed in black and white. Did you have to make specific adjustments to get the look you wanted?*

I just made sure to make everything very contrasting—light and dark as I could—especially the little girl's clothes. I designed all of her clothes. I used pink, red, and blue. Red comes out sort of black on the screen; it's really odd what happens to colors in black and white. For the scene when Ryan and Tatum are in the cafe having an argument, I designed a movie theater in pure black and white. It's on the reverse angle opposite the window by the table. I decided to experiment; I figured, "The film is in black and white; I may as well have fun. I'll trying using just white and black only!" I'll never do that again; it was almost a disaster. It didn't look right to me. You can't just paint a set black and white and have it look real.

How did you research The Bad News Bears?

I didn't know anything about Little League baseball. I sent away for the Little League handbook about how to make a diamond and found that bases are sixty feet apart instead of ninety feet as in the big leagues. I laid out the diamond so the sun would go across from first base to third base, so we wouldn't have shade-matching problems. Some macho guy who was working on the movie kept saying, "Why are you letting

Polly Platt design this set? What does a girl know about baseball?" I liked the guy, so when I laid out the baseball diamond, I took him and the director out and I said, "So here's where the diamond is. Here's first base, second base, third base, and fourth base." I actually had it laid out like that so that they would all go, "Oh, my God, she put an extra base!" We had a good laugh. I didn't have to learn anything, except that you need to deal with people who think you have no right to design a baseball diamond if you don't know how to play baseball.

As a production designer, what is your involvement with the screenplays of the films you design?

I enjoy my involvement in the script. The first draft of *The Bad News Bears* had scenes in the homes with the families of the kids. I didn't want to design those sets: I didn't get any ideas, which usually means there's something wrong with the scenes. So I kept saying to the director and the writer, "We should make the diamond the world. We will find out about the parents when they come to watch the games." I felt we should get to know the kids completely on their own. In the end, that was a very big cut. When I don't get any ideas about a set, I know there's something wrong with the scene. Then I start trying to decide what's wrong. That also happened on *What's Up, Doc?* which was actually set in Chicago. I moved it to San Francisco. I knew Chicago was wrong for that movie, although I couldn't say why exactly, except it was like New York City. Peter was great about those ideas. He loved my idea that San Francisco was a ricky-ticky town with hills and dales and anything can happen. Then all the funny chase stuff came in. I told Buck Henry about the escalator in the Hilton Hotel in San Francisco, and then he wrote the very funny scene with Barbra Streisand and Ryan O'Neal. Barbra utilized the stairs brilliantly. In the early drafts, the guy who had all the grant money was written as an older man. I kept thinking, "I don't know how to design this set." I just hated the idea of doing a stuffy sort of set, a walnut-paneled library with leather couches, I hated it. Then I had an idea. We had a friend, Danny Selznick, who was young and had access to a lot of grant money from the Louis B. Mayer Foundation because Louis B. Mayer was his grandfather. I said to Peter, "Let's make him like Danny Selznick, somebody young who has taken a San Francisco house, gutted it, and made it all modern." We had fun with that set with the sculpture and the glass staircase. After I designed it, Peter thought of all the funny business to do with the set, because he loved everything. There would be things that I would do that inspired Peter and things he would say that inspired me. So that's how it works. If it doesn't feel right, I usually try to figure out what it is.

It happened on *The Thief Who Came to Dinner*, which was also set in Chicago. It's a story about a corporate guy who sees all this blue collar crime and decides to become a better thief. He decides to rob houses.

Personally, I was offended that he was going into old mansions in Chicago and stealing people's jewelry. I didn't like him for stealing people's heirloom jewelry. I thought of pearl necklaces that belong to people's mothers and diamond rings that had some family history. Finally we moved it to the then nouveau-riche oil capital of the U.S.A., Houston, where everything is new and recoupable by insurance. So my ideas had those kinds of effects on the movies.

In Terms of Endearment *what was the design concept of the house where Aurora, the Shirley MacLaine character, lived?*

There's a lot about her character and tastes in the book. She came from the East; she was a Bostonian. I come from Boston, so I knew exactly what it should look like. We thought all that lace in Shirley MacLaine's bedroom would be so funny when the astronaut, Jack Nicholson, had to lie on that lacy bed. We painted the whole set a warm pink, and then as she got older, I painted everything gray. We decided that she had an old car. She was tight with money, so we were really trying to indicate that there wasn't a lot of it floating around. Over the years we always had her have the same car. Little things like that helped a lot, because it was upsetting that she wouldn't lend her daughter the money for an abortion. I had to justify it.

What location was used for the daughter's house?

I didn't know Jim Brooks very well at the time. I never thought he would go for the house that I found for Emma and Flap. It was on the second floor of an old garage that was falling apart. I knew it was perfect. I showed him a Polaroid, and he just went for it right away. That's when I knew we were going to get along. We had to shore up the whole place so we could shoot on the rickety second floor. I used warm, earthy colors, a lot of brown and pink for Debra Winger and more peasant, Mexican things. I talked it over with Debra, who was very interested.

What research did you use to determine the design of the interior of the astronaut's house?

I did a tremendous amount of research. I got the idea for the kitchen scene from one of the real astronauts. Jim was having trouble, and I said, "You know, one of the astronauts keeps his stuff from the moon in his kitchen, and this astronaut told me that every once in a while, when he really wanted to snow a woman, he would let her put on the glove that he wore on the moon." Jim loved it. We put all the paraphernalia in the kitchen, including the *Time* magazine picture of Jack Nicholson. I would never have thought of it if I hadn't done the research. You do the research. You visit men's houses who don't have wives, and you see they have no flowers. You just do your research. There's really no substitute for it.

The astronaut's house is next door to Aurora's. What was done to the exterior of those locations?

The two houses had to be next door to each other. Finding those two houses and making them work for both characters was very difficult. I put black shutters on Nicholson's house and covered MacLaine's house with fake flowers. I put wisteria all over and made her house very feminine. That was just a brick back yard; the whole garden was created. We did a lot of work on the house. The woman who owned the house next door didn't want me to cut a hole in the hedge so that Jack Nicholson could stand there and talk to Shirley MacLaine over the fence. Her dead husband had planted the hedge. We ended up extending the fence and moving the scene down so they could speak to each other.

The novel The Witches of Eastwick *takes place in New England. Where was the film shot?*

It was set up to be shot on the northern California coast. There was no locale in the script; it never said Salem or Boston. They were just going to do all of the locations in California. There was no doubt in my mind, I just knew it was wrong. It was hard to convince George Miller to go back East because he didn't know anything about America, but I brought back photos and they talked him into it. The studio was down about that because it cost more money, but once they saw how great the locations were, they were very happy.

Where did you create the houses for the three women?

I found the locations on location and built the sets. All the women's houses are sets inside and actual locations outside. My favorite set is Susan Sarandon's house, because it's the first time I ever designed a set on a soundstage that had a screened-in porch. It was fun; there are so many houses with screened-in porches on the Cape.

Where did you get the ideas for what the Devil's mansion would look like?

It really started with the Devil's bathroom. I kept showing the director, George Miller, local buildings that had rather large rooms because he kept saying, "I'd like the bathroom to be big." I thought that the living rooms I showed him for the bathroom were big enough, but he kept saying, "No, it's too small." Finally, I ended up taking him to the flag room in the Capitol Dome in Boston and saying, "Is that what you had in mind?" and he said, "Well, yes, this would be good." So I realized we were talking much bigger than life. I used the lobby of the Boston Opera House for the living room. You're dealing with the Devil. I really got into designing for the Devil. The Devil's attitude toward life was intoxicating. I enjoyed him and had a wonderful time. We invented that set for the luncheon scene when he tries to seduce Cher. It was never written to be out on that lawn; it was inside in the dining room! I found that location north of Boston—it's called the Crane Estate—and decided to build a tent!

The background in that scene is so vivid. Is that a matte painting?

It's real and so beautiful. It's just one vast lawn that goes all the way to the ocean. It was designed by the man who designed Central Park. We put up a very elegant pink tent and had so much fun with it. I had the greatest property master, Mark Wade. He did *Paper Moon* and *Broadcast News*. We had every kind of food you could possibly have—we had octopi. George Miller and I made up the balloon sequence; it wasn't in the script at all. There was a whole episode where the three women try on Restoration comedy costumes, which I thought was awful and so did George. I said to George, "What are you trying to say here?" and he said, "He's trying to seduce the women, but he's also trying to be nice to the kids." I said, "Well, if I was trying to be nice to kids, balloons have always been my favorite thing." So we started with Jack Nicholson coming in with a lot of balloons, and we shot it. We got more and more balloons until we had fifteen thousand balloons. Then George had an idea that we would get a table on wheels and Jack would be able to dance with all three girls. The women wouldn't do it, so George and I danced using the same music. After the women saw us do it, they decided to do it.

Do you think that production design will always play an important role in filmmaking?

Production design will always be silent, unsung, and one of the most important aspects of filmmaking. When you look at a movie like *Batman* or *Blade Runner*, you say, "Wow, there's no end to the outrageousness of the production designer," but it depends on the economy of moviemaking. The corporate mentality, which is slowly inching its way into our films, is very detrimental to good work, because their economics give us less and less prep time. It's really hard to do good work without adequate prep. I'm just worried about where our young people are going to get their experience, yet you come across something like the movie *Brazil* that's designed by a new designer. He's brilliant. What scope! It was fun to work with George Miller because he thinks big. George is very original. I think that the quality of designing will always relate to what kind of filmmakers we have. As long as we have great filmmakers, we'll always have great designers, because you can do the best work in the world with the great directors, our storytellers, and the writers. As long as they are great, we'll have great designers, because you just step up to it.

13

Lawrence G. Paull

Lawrence G. Paull was trained as an architect and city planner. He left his architectural pursuits to follow a dream to design movies and joined the art department of 20th Century–Fox, where he apprenticed under many renowned art directors, including Walter Tyler and John DeCuir.

Paull's career as a production designer began in 1970, and he firmly established his skill in rendering period films on *The Bingo Long Traveling All-Stars and Motor Kings*. The design provided a comprehensive environment for the story of a black baseball team in the rural back woods of the South of 1939.

In 1982 he designed the landmark film *Blade Runner*, which invoked his training as a city planner and architect to conceive a Los Angeles of the future burdened with fetid atmosphere, retrofitted architecture, and overcrowded streets. The film set a precedent within the futuristic genre and influenced countless films to follow. For his work on *Blade Runner*, Paull was nominated for an Academy Award for best art direction–set decoration.

Working on the Universal back lot, he created the town for *Back to the Future*, which was transformed from 1985 to 1955 through the magic of time travel. The film's period detail is significant in propelling the viewer into the world of the 1950s through Paull's realization of quintessential small town America.

Paull has worked with many directors, including Peter Fonda, Lamont Johnson, Robert Mulligan, John Avildsen, Paul Schrader, Ridley Scott, John Badham, Robert Zemeckis, and Jonathan Kaplan.

The work of Lawrence G. Paull is the sum total of his experience. His architectural background, studio apprenticeship, and wide range of design experience bring a fresh and clarified look to all he designs.

1970 *Little Fauss and Big Halsey*
1971 *Star-Spangled Girl*
       The Hired Hand
1972 *Chandler*
       They Only Kill Their Masters
1973 *The Naked Ape*
       The Last American Hero
1974 *The Nickel Ride*
1975 *W. W. and the Dixie Dance Kings*
1976 *The Bingo Long Traveling All-Stars and Motor Kings*
1977 *Blue Collar*
       FM
       Which Way Is Up?
1980 *How to Beat the High Cost of Living*
       In God We Trust
1982 *Blade Runner**
1983 *Doctor Detroit*
1984 *Romancing the Stone*
1985 *American Flyers*
       Back to the Future
1987 *Project X*
       Cross My Heart
1988 *License to Drive*
       Cocoon: The Return
1989 *Harlem Nights*
1990 *Predator 2*
1991 *City Slickers*
1992 *Memoirs of an Invisible Man*
       Unlawful Entry
       Born Yesterday

*Academy Award nomination for best achievement in art direction–set decoration.

How did you become a production designer?

I'm an architect by training, and I left architecture. I had a fantasy of getting into the film business as a designer. One of the reasons I left architecture was it took so much time from when the drawings left my drafting table to when the building got built. It was really laborious and boring. In film you don't belabor a project for years. I started out in the old studio system at 20th Century–Fox as a set designer, which was basically like an architectural draftsman. I worked at Fox for about a year and a half. I did a few shows as an assistant art director and started doing my own shows.

Who were some of the designers you apprenticed under?

When I started out, I worked for a couple of art directors. Walter Tyler was a gentleman who did a lot of the C. B. DeMille films. Walter came out of USC architecture school, went to Paramount, and spent thirty some years there and would get two weeks off a year; that was it. I worked as his assistant when he was the art director on *True Grit*. He told me stories, and I would say, "God, if I were only around during the studio system, it would have been fabulous," because some of the films the art directors at that studio worked on were mind-boggling in the size, the scope, and the look. Walter did *The Ten Commandments*. I worked with John DeCuir on *On a Clear Day You Can See Forever*. John was brilliant; I sat in awe of that man. He had a library. The books that he used to bring in, I never saw books like this in my life. They'd been out of print for a hundred years or more. John traveled all over the world, and wherever he traveled, he had a sketch pad in his hand. I mean this man did more by accident than most people think about in their life; he was brilliant.

Because your background is in architecture, is it a prime concern of your work as a production designer?

Yes, I think it's the starting-off point, what you reach back into. It's what I spent years in college doing. As I look back on a lot of the stronger designed films I did, the architectural quality of the shows incorporated into the look got stronger as the years went on. Architecture is an important part of it, there are no two ways about it.

It seems as if you could not have designed the drug dealer's penthouse in Predator 2 *without having a strong architectural background. Did the references to Mayan art and architecture come out of your architectural background?*

Yes. Originally, this set was going to be in a real high-rise building downtown just west of the Harbor Freeway. By the time I got done redesigning the existing space, it had one tragic flaw: we were twelve stories in the air, and it was a real bitch to shoot there because of all the stunts we had. As we got deeper and deeper into the effects shots, we kept saying, "Why are we here, why aren't we on a soundstage?" So I took a look at what I was going to do and the money it was going to cost to go onto a soundstage. It wasn't quite the same, but it was close enough that we could make it work and come up with something a lot more interesting. The drug dealers were Colombians, so I wanted to introduce something architecturally that was going to set this apart from every other boring high-rise penthouse apartment. One of the story points is an actor climbs a column to reach up into the ceiling to find something. That's why I gravitated towards Mayan architectural research and made columns and doors with the really heavy-handed type of carving. You can't climb up most columns, so I had to come up with an architectural motif to make it work. The actors could climb on it. We had a huge chromatrans backing outside the windows. Normally, you send a guy to the real building and say, "Shoot out here; this is the angle," and you get the panorama of the city. The panorama of that real building was from hunger, so I selected three or four spots off the rooftops of other buildings and we literally pieced it all together. I had never done something like that before.

So research is a key production design tool.

Yes, but I feel strongly that not everybody could go to the books and get the right information. There are a lot of people who would open up the books and pick the wrong things. What is good or bad cinematically has to do with the tools you have in your head or your eyes. A lot of times, something that is wonderful architecturally may not work cinematically because it's so busy. It's so overwhelming that you want to get rid of the actors, get rid of the scene, and just take a still photograph of it. So the key thing in film design is that the design works within the context of the story and who the characters are. You put all that together, and it's very rare that the design of the show becomes one of the stars. There are films where the sets are one of the stars. It happened in *Dick Tracy,* and it certainly happened in *Blade Runner.* Most of the time the setting would be a supporting player; the setting just enhances whatever goes on storywise. It doesn't say, "Here I am."

The Bingo Long Traveling All-Stars and Motor Kings beautifully captures the deep South of the late 1930s. What was it like to work on?

I would call it the first serious twentieth-century period piece I did. It was just a wonderful period to research and to do all the period billboards. We went out to the first big town which was Monticello, Georgia. They gave us carte blanche, and I took it. We sat down with the city fathers. I told them all the lights, all the parking meters, all the signage, and all the buildings that were inappropriate were going to be reclad as period. We just started from top to bottom on every town and the ball parks that we went into for that show.

The wooden store with the platform where the old gentleman teaches the team to dance the strut epitomized the South in that period. Where was that location, and what was done to it?

That was a broken-down barn on a dirt road. We cut some doors into it, and I put in the platform. At that point, I had been collecting big tin signs, and I went to my decorator and said, "I want to cover the entire building." He looked at me like I was nuts. I pulled out a Walker Evans photograph—Walker Evans was my real bible—and I said, "Look at all these buildings with all these tin signs." I had Dr. Pepper, Coca Cola, and all these other fabulous signs, and we just covered the entire building with them. It just turned the building into magic.

Using the tin signs helped evoke the materials of the era. What other materials were evocative of the period?

Yes, you had to research what they used. We used materials like bakelite on some of the facades, a lot of glass block, and pressed tin that was from the turn of the century to evoke what was in that period and before that period so the audience really buys that you're doing a period film. If you are doing a 1939 period film, which is what *Bingo Long* was, you can't just do 1939 modern; you have to do 1929 and 1920 to make the audience buy it. The audience today cares, because the audience today is much more sophisticated. When you do not design a show well and it doesn't look authentic, the audience snickers.

Many designers have called Blade Runner *a landmark in production design. Do you consider* Blade Runner *a landmark in production design?*

As a matter of fact, I do. Of that genre, in the sixties you had *2001: A Space Odyssey*, in the seventies you had *Star Wars*, and in the eighties there was *Blade Runner*. There are magnificent films that are beautifully designed, like *Chinatown* and *Brazil*, but *Blade Runner* is a really special film because of the way it looks, and it looks that way not because I did it all myself in a dark corner and then let everybody see it. It was a special set of circumstances with myself, the director, Ridley Scott, and an art department team that was fabulous. Some of the best people in Hollywood worked on that film and made contributions to it. I designed it, but I didn't design down to every little thing on every little set; there was no time.

What was the initial design concept for Blade Runner?

When I came on the film, I was told by the heads of production we were going to build the streets and that everything else would be shot practical—offices, Deckard's apartment—everything would be shot in a real locale. "So Larry, we want you to concentrate all your design efforts into coming up with a design concept for the streets and how people will be living forty years from now." I said, "Okay, let's figure out where we're going to do this," and they said, "We have a hold on the back lot of Burbank Studios." You get into the pragmatic stuff real fast, because when I started *Blade Runner* in July, we were going to shoot in September and be done by Christmas.

How much longer than that did you spend on the film?

I was on that film for thirteen or fourteen months. We prepped it for nine months and shot for four. So I went to the back lot, and I had just come back from a trip to Italy. With my background in the history of architecture, I have a special passion for Italian architecture. For the first time in my life, I had been to Milan. On the plane back I said, "I absolutely hate that town, I hate that city. It was built by Mussolini with the aid of Hitler and that's what it looks like." It looked like Albert Speer had stuck his finger in the design of some of the buildings. The Fascism is very, very clear, but what was wonderful about it was in certain parts of Milan the buildings actually came right out to the street curbs, which narrowed up, and you walked under big covered arcades—you could do that for blocks. I said, "That's the concept. Here we are in the back lot of a studio which always looks like shit because the streets are not built to full size, they're too narrow. The buildings are just scrunched together so they're not wide enough. So what I have to do as a designer is take everything and build it out to the curbs, really make it narrow and congested and fill it with people, vehicles, and animals and make it alive with signage and very heavy on graphics." That was the concept, and then you take it one step further. You say, "It's forty years from now." You go back to the script, and the middle classes have left the earth. They're going to off-world colonies and who's left in the center of the city but the working class, the unemployed, the homeless. These people do not have the wherewithal, the education, the skills to fix what breaks in the city. Therefore, when things like heating and air conditioning break down within buildings, they can't go internally and fix it. They discard what isn't really working; they take other generators and machinery and retrofit it to the buildings. They hook it up with other power to serve the same function because there's no room inside the buildings to do it.

All I'm talking about here are two small points of the concept. Then you start really digging. Now all of a sudden you have a concept that the city is dark, there's acid rain, it's overpopulated, it's filled with minorities that are for the most part transient in quality, uneducated, and there are major language problems. Then you start digging in all sorts of other research. I'd never known about Moebius, the French cartoonist, and Ridley Scott showed me these comic books—come on, give me a break! I started to look at Moebius's early work, which is, like, to die from. The whole concept for the streets where we have video monitors that gave public information and traffic signals was a takeoff on a little drawing that Moebius drew, and we just took it and expanded it. So the concept became very involved, very convoluted.

How much information was there in the script about what the locations looked like?

There was no description of anything in the script. I was dealing with a design idea.

Did the script identify the year?

Yes, but it did not identify Los Angeles. The film took place in a large metropolitan city in the United States. It was never L.A.

How did the decision to set the film in L.A. come about?

Primarily, because we were shooting in L.A. and we revamped and shot major Los Angeles landmarks, such as the Bradbury Building downtown and the Ennis-Brown House. The set for Deckard's apartment was based on the Lloyd Wright, Wright House on Doheny Drive. It's not based on the way the rooms look or the layout; it's based on Lloyd Wright's home as a cave. That was my concept of Deckard's apartment: it was a cave, it was his womb, so the rooms were very linear, very overbearing, and the walls bracketed out like a series of contemporary vaults. I had a sixteen-by-sixteen-inch block that had all this wonderful Frank Lloyd Wright design work from around 1922. The advantage I had with the Frank Lloyd Wright architectural theme of the poured concrete blocks is I had a design motif, but I turned it into almost Gothic vaults in a high-rise building. So when you saw Deckard's apartment, you always saw broken surfaces that projected out. When he came in the first time and turned on the lights, you saw a soft glow of light. It was like a soffit, a horizontal surface that projected out from the wall. In this case, there were recessed lights inside projecting down with corbels—brackets that supported it—that broke out into the room. You only saw bits and pieces of this in all the rooms. You saw part of it in the kitchen, a little bit in the bathroom, you got the sense of it in the living and dining area, but there was never a Vincente Minnelli crane shot with the lights on, because it was all shot very, very moodily.

Did you talk to any city planners about what would be projected for Los Angeles in that year?

No, I was the city planner. I went on the premise that I was the production designer on the show; I'm the planner of the show. I'm going to determine what that show is going to look like. All these folks that are collaborating with me, we're going to all go in a direction, and this is the direction we're going in, folks.

It sounds like you had a wonderful sense of confidence about the project.

At the time I preferred not to look at how big this movie was, because if I did, I would go home and throw up every night. So what you do is break it down. I had a huge list of all the things we were doing, and I'd take things one, two, three, four at a time and just tackle what I had to tackle, because you can't tackle everything at once; you can't absorb that much. For the buildings we did, I brought in all the photographs from Milan, and we took photographs of arcades, columns, Classical things, and all the architecture. I brought in just about my entire architectural research library, and we went from Egyptian to Deco to Streamline Moderne to Classical, from Frank Lloyd Wright to Antonio Gaudi. We turned the photographs sideways, upside down, inside out, and backwards to stretch where we were going and came up with a street that looked like *Conan the Barbarian* in 2020. That's basically where we were headed, because it had to be richly carved. I didn't want right angles; I didn't want slick surfaces.

Did you have any one drawing that laid out the entire city you were designing for Blade Runner?

No.

Did you have to see it all together in your mind's eye?

Yes, but I had to see it in the context of what the camera was going to see and what the scene was going to look like. I don't have to see an entire city. So the feeling, the texture, and the look was always there— we always knew where we were headed with that. The streets then became three or four city blocks of this fictitious city, which turns out to be Los Angeles. Another key in *Blade Runner* was not to just do super glistening high-rise buildings; in fact, quite the contrary: get rid of those and show that our society is an eclectic potpourri of looks and styles that somehow all blend together and make up the city. So there were things that were Victorian, there were things that are 1915, 1920, and there was Streamline architecture from the thirties and forties, as well as architecture from the fifties. And that's what made it work. It was paying attention to detail to make sure that all the signage and all the lighting was authentic.

Did you begin with a color palette?

No, there was never a color palette, an overall scheme of the film. The only thing that was discussed was that everything would be in a great deal of urban decay. I used many warm gray tones and a great deal of natural aging, dust and everything. The only time we saw hot color was in the neon at night. Charles Knode and I talked about the costumes. Deckard wore a wonderful shirt that had all these colors in it, but they were so tied into one another that it had a muted plaid effect. Charles found most of the clothes for the actors and extras in used clothing stores. Deckard's coat and jacket, Sean Young's and Joe Turkel's outfits were designed, but a lot of the extras' stuff and a lot of the miscellaneous clothing was found in used clothing stores. It was literally, "Put it in the washing machine, pour a pound of real strong coffee in, and see what happens." That's basically it; everything was very browned over, very heavily aged and crusted over.

How did you and Ridley Scott collaborate on Blade Runner?

I'm trained as an architect and also a city planner. I had a particular take on urban environments. So did Ridley, and the takes melded. The film was so complicated. We had a room just filled with research, and it was everything from paintings to photographers.

Who were some of the photographers?

Irving Penn, Walker Evans—it was sort of diverse, but a lot of fashion work. Sebastian's big apartment at the end of the film was going to be in a high-rise building, and we decided the Bradbury Building was going to be it. My take on it was Sebastian somehow got the presidential suite in this building downtown. He had an elaborate labyrinth of an apartment all done turn of the century, really over the top, moldings and very heavy-handed. I laid out the whole set. It was a simple set to lay out, because it was like laying out a chase sequence. I like to lay them out in almost concentric circles with a lot of arch openings and places that people can double back into one another. It gives the director a lot of ways to go. When the set was designed, Ridley came into my office, threw a magazine on my set, and said, "That's Sebastian's apartment." Here was this blonde fashion model that looked like Irving Penn's wife wearing a long white gown, and she's standing next to this blue-gray wall with these huge heavy moldings on the wall panels, and it's all decaying. It looked like someone had gone in and done a sponge painting on a tenement in New York, and the painting is all peeling back. You could almost sense that there were rats running around at her feet. Here was this woman who looked fabulous against this, and that's how the coloration of that set happened. That's just an instance.

Ridley did what I do in commercials, and there are designers who would say, "I would never work for a director like that," because of just that. There were times in the collaboration where Ridley and I would sit in my office until eight, nine, ten o'clock at night basically saying, "Well, what do you think of this, Rid?" Well, what do you think of this, Larry?" and we'd be, like, topping one another just doing little doodles and little ideas for parts of sets. When I was doing Deckard's apartment, it was very funny. It wasn't all that humorous at the time because we were very tired. I was designing the lobby outside his door, and I had some Frank Lloyd Wright research. I was just working at a drafting table in my room, piddling around with a marker, and Ridley came in one night and said, "Why don't you just turn it upside down. It looks much more interesting that way." I said, "Yes, you're right." So it was that type of thing, because Ridley gets involved in the design process—there's no two ways about it.

When Syd Mead was doing all the vehicles, Syd would come in with sketches of vehicles. We would go into my office. It was like being back in college, where I would do a presentation of a building and I'd have my professors critiquing me. Ridley and I became the critics. So Syd went from doing real slick things like *Car and Track* to what we evolved in the show, which were very gritty, retrofitted, additive types of vehicles that were very strange looking. Syd is a wonderful painter, a wonderful conceptual artist, and he's known for his work on vehicles. If you came to me and said, "Larry, I want you to design a car," I would say, "Hubba hubba, let's get Syd on the phone," because I'm not an automobile designer. I'm not going to kid anybody about that, but if you're talking about the concept of what we wanted this car to look like and feel like for the movie we were doing in 2019, I knew what I wanted. I knew what I wanted on and in the vehicle, and I knew the texture it had to have.

Everything in Blade Runner *works together—the costumes, the vehicles, the physical design. All the elements appear to be one person's creation.*

Yes, but it was done by a number of people. As a designer I usually get into everybody's department—the props, the costumes, the vehicles, everything. I don't care if it's 1939 or 2019, the look and the style has to have a vision. In a show like *Blade Runner*, it's a very tight collaboration. I was very involved in every department, because I had to either add, redesign, bless, or throw out everything that didn't belong. What I didn't like I would redesign and say, "This is what we need to do." It was just too big for one person to sit down at a drawing board and design everything—it was down to the telephones, the glasses, and the vid phones—it never ended. We designed newspapers. I had one fellow, Tom Southwell, whose only job was graphics on the entire show; that's all he did.

It sounds like the nine month preproduction period is one of the reasons the film is so visually rich.

Oh absolutely, it would have been horrific if we had to start filming in three and a half to four months. I don't know how the hell we would have been finished, as I look back on it. It all happened because the director and producer were behind us all the way saying, "Make it better, make it the best. Make it real, real special." The energy was there, the people were there. Every set designer on that show is now at least an art director, and my art director is a production designer. My illustrators are guys who are the best in the business. It was a melding of some of the best young talent around because it was a huge undertaking. Nothing on that film was thrown away. Nobody said, "Hey, that's good enough." Everything had to focus on the design statement we were making about what 2019 was going to be like to live in, but the design evolves. Even though you come up with great concepts at the beginning of the film, more concepts came up. It was a very convoluted, complicated movie. It was also a very long, tenuous shoot. That was the toughest film I've ever done.

A lot of times on a film, crew people are just sort of hanging around having a cup of coffee; it didn't happen on Ridley's set. We might not shoot for four or five hours, but the effects guys are rigging the rain and the smoke and the camera angle, and for the forty-third time the Chapman crane is going through the move it's going to make, and you go to dailies and say, "Yes, it was worth it." It was fabulous; it was really, really exciting, and so those are all the reasons that I think *Blade Runner* was a real special film. And do I want to do another one? I'm not sure. There was an intensity on *Blade Runner* that showed up in the film in the design, in the photography, in the camera moves, in the actors. It was just this very special time, and I'm very glad. I never ever said it was fun; this was not *fun*. It was tough, but it was professionally, aesthetically satisfying. I've worked on tough films before, and a lot of times they are not satisfying. As a designer, you create a setting to do a scene, and when the setting is right the actors get *x* amount off of it because they believe it. The director gets *x* amount off of it because he's buying it, and hopefully when they get in there with the cameras and the lights, they can make magic. On *Blade Runner* Ridley was in my office every day, because he loves that end of picture making. We all knew at the beginning and during the movie that we were doing something very, very special. We didn't know how special, because you never know. I didn't know it was going to be the cult film it turned out to be.

In Back to the Future *we see the same town transformed from 1985 to 1955. Where was it created?*

I had a production meeting, and they said, "We've got a scout down in Texas, and we've got one in northern California. We want you to get on a plane." I said, "Fellas, have you looked at the script?" They said, "Yes." I said, "Well, how many days are you outside in the town square?" They said, "I don't know, three weeks, whatever." I said, "And you're going to start shooting in November in somebody's little town right around the Christmas holidays, and they're just going to let me come in?" I said, "We're not going anywhere; we're doing the whole movie in L.A. Give me a couple of days." So I spent about a day and a half just walking around on the Universal back lot, making funny little drawings and figuring out where to put the corner drugstore. There was a municipal building which obviously needed to be totally revamped for the clock tower. So I went back and brought the director, Robert Zemeckis, out to the back lot with the Amblin folks, and I said, "It's ours, we don't have to fight weather. We're in southern California. We're certainly not going to have problems in November, December, and January for retakes or changing things from 1955 to 1985, because we own it. You don't have to pay people per diem, you don't have to house them, you don't have to feed them, you don't have to have a jillion trucks. This is what I have in mind, and this is what we do." And Zemeckis said, "Oh no, Larry, it's going to look like a back lot," and I said, "Not when I get done with it—you wait."

What was the back lot like before you started construction?

It looked really broken-down, ill-conceived. People had put Band-Aids on various structures to make them work for *Simon and Simon* and other television series.

How did you proceed to create the town?

It just became a huge design job. They brought in all these promotion people. I had a Sherwin Williams paint store; they sent me eight-by-ten glossies of what their stores looked like in the fifties. Texaco paid for the construction of the period gas station. I had period billboards, the Studebaker car dealership—this is what you need to sell the period. After you go through research, you say, "There better be a Texaco station here, there has to be a corner drugstore, there has to be a record store, there has to be the small town jewelry store, there better be all the following items." You bring all the right elements together and get your priorities straight on what's going to sell the period. Zemeckis just loved it, and it really worked. When I was doing the research, I discovered that after the war, in the fifties, everybody had money again and they were spending it. They were restyling their stores. I had period architectural magazines from the early fifties sent to me from research departments. We did buildings over, and took a look at all the older buildings and revamped them to what they should have been. There was a crummy old movie theater that was in really pathetic shape, and we did the marquee over. We built another theater at the end of the street which was Streamline Moderne. I wanted a potpourri of architecture from the teens through 1955.

Where did you get the concept for the vivarium where the chimps are held in Project X?

I called the research department and said, "I want a lot of museum research." My assistant said, "What museum set are we looking at?" I said, "No, I want to see museums by Richard Meier and Michael Graves; I want to see what the big architects from all over the country are doing with big spaces for museums," because I saw the chimps as a series of canvases. These cages were on walls like art. I wanted ramps going up from one level to another, and that got changed because the director, Jonathan Kaplan, couldn't stage it with ramps. It really became tough. I wound up with a room with a huge curved wall and openings which had bars that projected out like paintings. I had a rolling staircase like a library staircase going around to the second level, so they could get up there, open a cage, and do what they do with the chimps. That was a very difficult one to work out.

I also got very involved with the hallway. I wanted the hallway to go on forever; I mean I wanted it to be the longest hallway ever filmed. You can do what Albert Brenner had done on *California Suite*. He did the hallways at the Beverly Hills Hotel in forced perspective. It worked at the Beverly Hills Hotel, because you could reduce the scale of those big painted palm trees. You'd paint them smaller and smaller as you go down the hallway. Well, I'm in an industrial Air Force complex and I don't have wallpaper on the walls, so instead of doing that, I started converging the walls and converging the ceilings. Basically, I started reducing everything about three-quarters of the way down and started to force the perspective. I wound up with a hallway which was 130 or 140 feet long from beginning to end on stage, and it looked like it was almost 200 feet long.

The testing room had a very striking design. The chimp is in a triangular-shaped module which sits on a cube-like structure. Where did this concept come from?

It was basically an exercise in geometry. That has to do with my formal training and a lot of my experience as a designer. You take simple geometric forms, and when they are well integrated, they make an appropriate visual statement. The simplest things in *Blade Runner* were a cube, a sphere, and a tetrahedron—a three-dimensional triangle. We always come back to good geometry. Basically, I think of the settings as an arena in which the actors and the director interact and play a scene out. If the arena is appropriate, it works. I wanted that room in *Project X* to be simple. When I was designing, I was thinking a lot of *2001: A Space Odyssey*, but it had to be minimalistic; I had to keep stripping everything away. Then I put in that little machine the chimp is in and a viewing room up high. You had to look down. You had to see the wall, the screen, and the chimp; it was all laid out for camera angles. That was the one set that was absolutely laid out, "Jonathan, you've got to shoot it with between a 30mm to a 50mm lens. If you don't, it ain't going to work." So the room became longer than it needed to be because of the points of view.

How do you communicate visually with Jonathan Kaplan?

Jonathan Kaplan shoots the storyboards. With someone like Jonathan, I build a model when I design every set, because he doesn't understand the architectural drawings. I've had many directors lie to me that they understand the drawings.

So he needs to see it three dimensionally?

Oh, absolutely. I don't blame him. Jonathan storyboards everything, and you basically design the sets around the storyboards. Most times it works, and sometimes you say, "Gee, I'd better add this, that, and the other, because what if he changes his mind." So we try and give him as comprehensive a set within his reality as possible. For *Unlawful Entry*, which is the second film I've done with Jonathan, I would design something and do the drawings part way; I'd send them over to the model maker, and three days later we would have the models back and have something to discuss. If he wanted changes, we made changes.

Have you gone through stages in your career?

It seems like last week I was the youngest kid in the business. There are all these young guys that are climbing up the ladder just like I was fifteen or twenty years ago. They want my jobs, and some of them are getting shows that I want. A publicist once told me you go through five phases in your career. The first one is, "Who is Larry Paull?" The second one is, "Who *is* Larry Paull?" The third one is, "Get me Larry Paull." The fourth one is, "Get me a young Larry Paull," and the fifth one is, "Who is Larry Paull?" and that's this business, and it's real funny that way. The attrition rate in this business is incredible.

What do you say to young people who ask, "How do I become a production designer?"

It's real tough today to survive. You better have a great deal of tenacity—that's number one, a great deal of ambition. You need to have some sort of artistic background, be it painting, drawing, decorating, designing, or architecture. Yet, I know there are production designers who were carpenters. I know one who was a greensman on sets. You have to have a great deal of focus to find someone who is going to help you along the way. This business needs a lot of godfathering, it always has, and to get started someone usually has to give you a swift kick somewhere in the right direction to get you moving. It's getting connected with the right people and having the tenacity to hang in there and go after what you want.

14

Patrizia Von Brandenstein

Patrizia Von Brandenstein cultivated her design skills in the theater and began a career in film when she was hired by the late Gene Callahan to work in the art department on *The Candidate*. With Callahan's encouragement, Von Brandenstein began to work as a production designer in the vital New York independent feature movement on *Girlfriends* and *Heartland*. She also worked as a costume designer on *Between the Lines*, *A Little Sex*, and *Saturday Night Fever*.

Von Brandenstein's work as a production designer painstakingly renders time and place while layering the design with images that illustrate the inner message of a film. Her work on *Breaking Away* detailed the world of competitive bicycle racing while serving Steve Tesich's screenplay, which clearly defined the class division prevalent in an Indiana town. For *Silkwood* she surmounted the challenge of creating a plutonium plant. The plant's verisimilitude is heightened with ominous cool colors touched with danger messages coded in yellow and red and is a stark contrast to the natural environment of Karen Silkwood's home. *Amadeus* is a brilliant re-creation of eighteenth-century splendor that presents Mozart's glittering world in parallel to the dark brooding orb of Antonio Salieri. In *The Untouchables* sunburst imagery in the floor of Al Capone's hotel suite creates the metaphor of a Sun King, a man around whom everything revolves. In *Working Girl* the Staten Island Ferry and the skyline of Manhattan are visual reminders of the protagonist's journey to a new world.

Von Brandenstein was part of the Oscar-nominated art department for *Ragtime*. She was nominated for her design of *The Untouchables* and won the Academy Award for best art direction–set decoration for *Amadeus*.

Von Brandenstein has collaborated with many accomplished directors, including Joan Micklin Silver, Claudia Weill, Lee Grant, Peter Yates, Mike Nichols, Brian De Palma, Milos Forman, Robert Benton, Richard Benjamin, Costa-Gavras, and Richard Attenborough. She is married to the production designer Stuart Wurtzel.

1978 *Girlfriends*
1979 *Heartland*
       Breaking Away
1980 *Tell Me a Riddle*
1981 *Ragtime* (art director with production designer John Graysmark and art director Anthony Reading)*
1983 *Silkwood*
       Touched
1984 *Amadeus***
       Beat Street
1985 *A Chorus Line*
1986 *The Money Pit*
1987 *No Mercy*
       The Untouchables*
1988 *Betrayed*
       Working Girl
1990 *The Lemon Sisters*
       Postcards from the Edge
       State of Grace (with Doug Kraner)
1991 *Billy Bathgate*
1992 *Sneakers*
       Leap of Faith

* Academy Award nomination for best achievement in art direction–set decoration.

** Academy Award for best achievement in art direction–set decoration.

Was there a crystallized moment when you decided to become a production designer?

I have to say it was my association on *The Candidate* with the late production designer Gene Callahan, who was extremely influential for me. I managed to get a job on *Play It Again, Sam*, which was the first film I worked on. I was a fairly well-developed designer before I ever set foot on a movie set. I'd been working in the theater for years. People were very nice to me on this film, and I was able to do some creative things that were fulfilling. The producers introduced me to Gene Callahan, who was in San Francisco preparing *The Candidate*. His decorator became ill. I literally met him one day, and the next day he called me up and said, "Come out to Marin County tomorrow morning at six o'clock." I showed up on the set, and we were off and running. One night after we had completed a huge series of feats of wonder, Gene said to me, "You can do this. You can do this!" That was the moment when I began to see it. I thought, "Yes indeed, I could do this."

There was a sense of rightness about what I was doing from the very start. That association was very, very important. He even said how to do it, because at that time, there really were no women *at all* who did this—not as art directors, not as production designers. It just wasn't something that was open. He said, "Don't go to Hollywood; go to New York," because the union was open by examination and merit. They were much freer, and in those years there were many wonderful small films being made here in New York. The independent was a vital part of the industry in New York, and it made for some interesting work. We made commercial films with stars for under a million dollars.

There were so many marvelous filmmakers who were involved in the early seventies—Joan and Ray Silver, Michael Hausman—lots of creative people. My association with Michael Hausman was really pivotal, because he gave me the jobs and he did interesting films. *Breaking Away* was a big jump for me. This was considered to be a real coup. Peter Yates is a terrific director, and he took a chance on me. This was the first big commercial film I had as a production designer. We had a very powerful script that had the ring of truth from the get go. We had a great time. We all became athletes; everyone took up running and bicycling.

Did the original script indicate that Breaking Away *would take place specifically in Indiana?*

Oh yes, there are scripts that have great value in terms of story and character—they could be anywhere. But there are other scripts that are specific to the place, that can't be any other place, and *Breaking Away* was one of those. The quarry is in the script. The writer, Steve Tesich, said that the quarry area was very prominent when he was in school; the kids would go there. The image of a Roman bath, that pristine quality, was something we brought to it by sandblasting the whole quarry, which was quite an undertaking. We used pontoon boats and we sandblasted the walls of the quarry. We heaped up tremendous boulders, stacked them up, and cleaned everything so it was as clear as possible. The sand acted like a filter: as it settled to the bottom of the quarry, it cleaned the water so it had that sparkling blue quality.

What did the quarry look like before you started?

Graffiti on the walls, murky, cloudy—just a growth of moss.

The color palette in the house of the Dennis Christopher character was very monochromatic. What was the idea behind that?

The colors in the house were closely valued. I was working greatly on instinct, but I have since discovered that depth and intensity of color and high contrast is richness. Close-valued colors are not as expensive to produce. Everything was washed and bleached. It kept the values close; it made the family less prosperous.

Prior to working on the film, did you have any knowledge about the world of bicycle racing?

I knew nothing at all. One of the most attractive things about this business is the opportunity to become an expert on a lot of different subjects in a very short time. I've discovered many, many worlds over the years. I have often had this conversation with other production designers about how you learn a tremendous amount about a specific subject, but you are a sort of idiot savant: you know everything there is to know about this one thing, but you don't know other things within that context. It is a very valuable quality for a production designer to have a great curiosity about different societies and how the world works.

What was the concept behind the rainbow mural that was on the wall of the stadium for the final race?

The rainbow road race. We thought that this race was a quest, it was a journey, and on this quest is the proverbial pot of gold at the end of the rainbow. So we called it the rainbow road race.

The rainbow mural is the kind of detail that helps to enrich a film. There are certain elements that reach 100 percent of the audience; other smaller details might reach only 1 percent of the audience, but for them it is a special kind of communication.

Yes, but I never think about how many people are going to get it or not get it. You can't, because it's like a big mosaic, a big canvas. I just have to paint it the way it comes to me. As the painter, you're a kind of an emphasizer. You use the structure and the colors in the film the way a painter lays down colors and forms. What you have to worry about is does it form the story? That's the thing. Believe me, if it's formed properly, they'll get it.

Many people don't understand that everything in a film is a conscious choice. Things are put there for a reason.

Film is a choice, and so is design. Every single thing in a film is a series of choices. If a man walks through a door, sits at the table, takes a drink, and lights a cigarette, there are thousands of choices. The man comes through the double door, dutch door, french door, steel door. He is walking, riding, crawling, slithering on his belly like a reptile. He sits at a Flemish table, Gothic table, a conference table. This is an automatic process. Whenever I'm trying to figure something out, I ask that series of questions. If you question every step of the real logic, the real truth, you won't go wrong; it will all be right.

So you are both intellectual and instinctual in the way you work.

Sure, just as the film is. It would be a very static and boring film if it were only appealing on intellectual grounds. To engage us it has to be appealing to the senses in a physical way and emotionally appealing to the heart as well, whatever the story may be. It can be a story about murderers and rapists and still have enormous sensual and emotional appeal, so it's not just intellectual engagement.

Silkwood was based on the true story of Karen Silkwood. How much did you know about the story, and what research did you do?

I read that big *Village Voice* piece and the *Rolling Stone* article. I was aware of the story but just as the public was. The first time I went to see Mike Nichols and the writers, they said, "What do you think about Karen Silkwood?" I had just read a biography of Silkwood in preparation for this, and I said, "I thought she was an unlikely heroine who had seized on this as a way of redemption for a basically wasted life." To this day, I don't know why I said that. They stared at me, but actually, as it turned out, it was exactly their thinking. I didn't judge anything about her at that point. I was very caught up in the mechanics of the plutonium plant. The only thing I knew about plutonium was to stay as far away from it as possible. I knew right away they were not going to let us run around and find a used plutonium plant. Michael Hausman was the producer along with Mr. Nichols, and I knew they would never let us anywhere near a real plutonium or uranium production plant, not even to see it. Not that we wanted to go, God knows! So it was a matter of creating it.

Where was the plutonium plant created?

In the Dallas Communications Complex at Las Colinas in Dallas. It was a studio that was not yet open, built by the Trammell Crow organization as a real estate venture to establish film production. They were in the process of building. We went all over Oklahoma, Texas, and New Mexico to research the plant. We went to Los Alamos. I went down to Washington to the library and the archives of what was the AEC, the Atomic Energy Commission, to see if there were pictures or plans that were in the public domain just to get an idea. It was not possible to find a physical reproduction. When I went to Los Alamos, I met an engineer who was retired from the Army. We spent two weeks together. He talked about the process, and I drew it. I would say, "How long is a plutonium rod?" He would say, "Well, it's about four feet. But now, wait a minute, there are some that are five feet; they have another kind of well." We would talk and I drew the machine, how the material goes through the production line, and the lines of glove boxes as best I could. We built the glove boxes and the other machines. The glove boxes were a very expensive thing to do. Once we figured out a way to physicalize it, we had them built by guys who make Christmas displays. They thought we were pretty strange, but they were used to building technical and mechanical things inexpensively. We found the slugging press that made the pellets in used factories around Dallas. We brought in a couple of pieces from government surplus. There is a huge surplus yard outside of Albuquerque which doesn't have anything used but has surplus that didn't work or never went into the production line. We lugged this to Las Colinas and put it together.

We used Las Colinas itself. They had a very interesting loading dock which was like a triple-height hall that ran the length of the studio. It had offices on one side and studios on the other. It was about forty, fifty feet in height. It was crisscrossed with catwalks, and we used it as part of the factory. I think it was a fabulous decision, because it gave us a scale that we never could have achieved. Using that hall gave us a whole other dimension. It was a big set, but really not a complex one architecturally. It wasn't painted yet. I wanted the gray concrete. The rest was just a matter of building the hallways and the double-height process room. We figured out how to handle the material through the line, the mechanics of the double air filtration system, and those lights that would flash on when the doors opened. I have no idea if it was authentic or not, but I have been told that we did pretty well.

When Karen's house is decontaminated by officials from the plant, it is literally ripped apart. What did this represent to you?

The reason they ripped her house apart was for punishment. When a person is contaminated, they literally scrub off a layer of skin. When they decontaminated the house, I wanted the idea of literally flaying the house as well as flaying her.

So the skin of the house, the wood, is being stripped down. Was it a real house, or were the interiors done in the studio?

It was a real house. It was pretty much a shell. It belonged to a man who had it in his family for a long while. The house had been moved onto this site. One of the things we wanted to do was make the house more permanent. We built additions onto it by adding the porch and the back wing. We closed it in, making it look like it had been there forever and ever. We redid the interiors and made the interior geography more correct for us. When we built the interior walls, we built layers of wall so it could be flayed and ripped apart for the retakes.

How did you determine the color palette of the film?

Working on the plutonium process was an antilife process. We kept the colors industrial, very close in value. There was an absence of color except for the danger colors: red stop, green go. I called that orange-yellow safety yellow, that construction color which denotes danger. Yellow means danger. Those little bits of colors that we used in this industrial grayness really stand out. You notice them in a world where everything is monochromatic and grayed out. In Silkwood's house—the natural world of the green trees, the fields, and the flowers—this is choosing life.

What was the research like on Amadeus? *The world of Mozart is such an expansive subject.*

I had designed several Mozart operas when I was a stage designer and worked around various regional opera companies, so I was familiar with that music, but not as familiar as I got. The crew was very familiar with the artistic history of Mozart. When I started, they knew more than I did. They really knew their subject. Our prop man was very familiar with the music of the eighteenth century. He was the one who copied the printed manuscript in the style. We had whole teams of people copying. I brought the paper and the ink and the pen nibs on my knees from the U.S. It was remarkable. The research libraries at Charles University are phenomenal. There are many facsimiles of Mozart's letters and manuscripts available in the bookshops in Salzburg, lots of information. I like to use tax rolls and letters. You can find out a lot from tax rolls—what they paid, how many times they moved—because people registered. It was how they kept track of the population. Because Mozart was a musician he traveled all over the place, so he had papers of passage, like a passport. You could keep track; you could figure out a lot. From his bills we found out he was the wildest of spendthrifts—all those pink and blue wigs, that was for real. I mean, they were wildly extravagant. Think about sort of a Madonna tour; it was that kind of atmosphere.

Did you feel that you had to understand the whole world of that time period before you could tackle the production design of Amadeus?

Yes, because it's understanding a culture so far removed from us in time and attitude, a world almost impossible for the twentieth century to understand. For example, a world still handmade, before industry and automation took over and communication was on a person-to-person level. A world in which most people could not read or write, but one could reach out through music, poems, or graphics, such as signage that utilized symbols of eye glasses or teeth to convey messages to customers. The wonder of the music was that in some way Mozart reached out to the people who simply loved his tunes, as well as Vienna's more sophisticated and educated elite.

Amadeus *is based on the play by Peter Shaffer. From the designer's point of view, what is the difference between the play and the film?*

Peter Shaffer's plays all have a physical abstraction. The hardest thing in film is abstraction, not intellectually but physically. There is a reality about the film going through the camera that makes everything very real. That's what the idea of cinema is built on. I think those nineteenth-century plays like the Belasco productions with all that thunder, light-ning, and horses on stage were looking for realism—they were looking for cinema. Other centuries are hard to abstract on film; it's damn near impossible. The physical act of taking the picture makes it all real. There we are—we're in the eighteenth century.

Where was Amadeus *filmed?*

Mostly in Czechoslovakia, in Barondov Studios and the Tylovo Di-vadlo, which was where Mozart stood in the pit and conducted *Don Giovanni*—right in the spot where Tommy Hulce stood; that's quite a feeling. It's a wooden theater. The chandeliers were never in that theater; that was a total invention on our part. The dome was never meant to support that. We figured out how to rig the dome, because those chan-deliers were a lot of weight. Let me tell you, when those chandeliers went in the air and were being lit, I didn't sleep for five nights. I was such a wreck you cannot imagine. I mean, one spark. It's so beautiful, who could resist? There is a tremendous amount of description about those theaters. I had read a lot about how they were built and how they worked, so we were able to transfer that. Josef Svoboda, who designed the opera sequences in the film, is a very knowledgeable man, as all of the theater people are in Prague.

The credits state that parts of the film were shot in castles in Czechoslovakia. Which scenes are those?

Several different sequences were actually shot in the big ballroom in Krōmiřiź, which is a complex of the summer home of the Archbishop of Prague. The big opening concert sequence in the ballroom became the ballroom for the French Embassy by the expedience of adding those brilliant yellow nineteenth-century draperies. We filmed that in the same place. The masquerade ball was in the grotto ballroom downstairs.

Was the furniture part of Krōmiřiź?

There were a few things that were there, but we brought in vast quantities of things. We had many different government sources.

Salieri wore a lot of red clothing. What was the concept behind that?

I thought everything about Salieri was dark, Italianate, full of passion, but from an older time, dark and turgid, heavy like the music—like the fabrics he wore, velvet and wool.

How did you see the character of Mozart from a design point of view?

Mozart's world was reflective, bright, silvery, pastel, brilliant, tingling like crystal, faceted like his music. It was the music that drove the design.

What was it like to work on Amadeus?

I wanted to do something violently different, and I did. I felt tremen-dously honored, because I had such respect for Milos Forman. I was honored, because it was so unusual for an American to have that kind of intimate relationship with another culture. It is such an unusual oc-currence in this industry. I felt I had an obligation because of his faith in me to learn as much and to do everything I possibly could to bring that vision to the screen. I did *Beat Street* directly after *Amadeus*. I was so immersed in *Amadeus*, I wanted something to get me out of it so I wouldn't be stuck in the eighteenth century for the rest of my life.

Beat Street celebrates the early days of hip-hop culture in New York. Did the kids connected with the project contribute to any of the graffiti art depicted in the film?

We used some of the kids' designs as inspiration, and we elaborated on them greatly in the art department. That was a commercial, union venture. If it had been another kind of movie, they could have done the actual work. I remember saying to one of the guys, "If you want to give me the idea of it, there would be credit in the film." He said, "I've got a show in Paris, and I have to go prepare for it." I thought, "This kid doesn't need us, we need him."

Where were the scenes that take place inside the subway system created?

There is a section of the subway in Brooklyn, the complex underneath J Street—Borough Hall where the museum used to be—that is always put out to filmmakers, and we used that section. We were given a station and a track section. We changed the looks of the station. We changed the colors and we re-signed it. You can control the track, but it's very difficult; it takes forever. You're limited in terms of time, because it has to be done during the off hours of the train.

Did the art department use spray cans and the same techniques as the real graffiti artists?

We used spray cans, but our paint washed off. We also rented trains that were scheduled for repainting so that we did not take trains out of service. It was important to the Transit Authority that they could continue to use their trains.

How was the third rail electrocution scene done?

We built a piece of third rail for the flash, and the rest of the time it was an unused piece of track that we shut off.

The Mark Hellinger Theater was used for the film adaptation of A Chorus Line. *How was the look of the theater conceived, and what was done to transform it into that vision?*

The director, Richard Attenborough, thought it was important to have all of the mystery and romance possible that comes from the theater. It was the idea of the theater as a church and dance as their religion. We tried to make the Hellinger churchly. We repainted it. We regilded everything we could lay our hands on. We put in the decorate proscenium, which has all that wonderful, mad Beaux Arts architecture. Up on top, you could see little vestiges of the real one, but it had fallen under sad days. It had all been chipped away and boxed in, because various shows through the years had remodeled the place. In terms of the architecture of the building itself, it was just badly painted, so you didn't know it

was there. Ugly plaster holes had very often been made in various parts
of it to let down a cable. There's absolutely no law or restriction against
doing that, so over the years, it had gotten pretty badly banged up. We
changed the curtains, and we put in a painted marble floor which went
into the lobby. We remodeled dressing rooms and the stage door. We
artfully arranged the drapery on the back wall. It was painted so the
folds were enhanced—you could have a real structural quality. We made
the mirrors. I got a mirror wall from an old bar, and we cut it up and
beveled the edges so that we could get some complexity into the imagery.
It has that old-mirror look because it's silvered, it's not electroplated. It
has that warm quality. Because you're only in one place, the theater
needed as much as we could give it.

*I understand that Brian De Palma did his own storyboard drawings on index
cards for* The Untouchables.

Always, that's the way he does it; it's the springboard. The storyboard
is only good if it comes from the director. It is definitely his vision. Brian
De Palma shoots very economically. I think that man is brilliant. I loved
The Untouchables; the metaphor was so clear. It came to me in a vision;
I just knew how to do it.

What is the metaphor?

The idea of using the architecture of Chicago as power and evil, crush-
ing the weight out of the poor. Al Capone was a gangland king who
controlled all of this like a Sun King, a man the world revolves around.
When we first started working on it, Mr. De Palma said, "It is an American myth. People have made this picture before. Our way of doing it
has to explore the mythic possibilities." And that's exactly what we did.

One of the key visuals in Working Girl *is the image of the Staten Island
Ferry, which is seen from both Melanie Griffith's home in Staten Island and the
office where she works in Manhattan.*

So near and yet so far. Yes, the ferry became the image of the photograph of the immigrants approaching the Statue of Liberty. Once we
got that together, then everything else came on strong.

*Were the exterior views from the windows of the office interiors real? Were
any translights used?*

All for real, no translights. That was simply an empty floor; we created
all of those offices on location to take advantage of the harbor view. You
could have built it in the studio, but you would have spent several
hundred thousand dollars on translights, and for what? It really would
not be the same.

Where did you build the office sets?

In a building on lower Broadway with a square corner and a curved
front that faces the harbor. It had an empty floor, and we knew they
would rent to us because there was a glut of office space. It was right
after *Wall Street* had used another floor.

It must have been a major undertaking to build the open office area with cubicals for all the secretaries.

It's a big set, sure, but once you figure out how to do it, it's just numbers. The elevator wasn't real, so the trick was figuring out the geography to get her out of the elevator and through the pool of secretaries. A fake elevator was built there in the building. We used a different building for the lobby. We used the real elevator when you step on in the lobby; when you step off, that was our set.

Do you think comedy requires a different kind of thinking from a designer's point of view?

Yes. I'm not conscious of it when I do it, but Mr. Nichols has certainly taught me a lot about how crucial the geography is for comedy. It has to be exactly right. There are no wasted moments; nothing gets drawn out.

Do you think there is a simplicity in the design of a comedy?

On *Postcards from the Edge* we were originally going to shoot the fight between mother and daughter in the den. They started working on the stairs, and there was no way they were not going to play it there. I was really nervous, because there is nothing on those stairs; it's just the stairs, the wall, and the two actresses. The visual interest starts when you go down or up. I really worried about it. I thought maybe it should be light or dark or have pictures, but that scene needed nothing else. It was absolutely right the way it was. It would have been wrong to put something behind those actresses. So I'm glad there wasn't any time to change it, because I would have been tempted to do something. We prepared this incredible den. It had pictures of the mother all over the place, but it just would have been wrong for the way that scene was rehearsed.

The photographs, paintings, and Life *magazine covers in the den are supposed to represent the mother's career as an actress. Are they from Shirley MacLaine's personal career?*

The pictures are of the real Shirley. They were reprocessed with different names, different posters. All of those pictures and personal papers came from Shirley's archive donated to universities and various schools and family photos that were in her possession. We took those photos, reproduced them with our graphic images, and created our own magazine covers. When she came in, she said, "This is like walking past my life."

Was the painting of her with the hat and the gloves part of Shirley MacLaine's personal collection?

We did it from a photograph of one of those musicals she used to do. We commissioned the paintings for *Postcards from the Edge* from two artists in Los Angeles, so that the pictures would be in character. If Shirley had photographs or paintings like that, it would have been fine, but she just didn't have that kind of thing. So we created the paintings in the spirit of Doris, not in the spirit of Shirley. Shirley is a very intelligent, sophisticated lady; Doris is so wildly extreme.

What was the principal visual inspiration for State of Grace?

We tried to do the lost world, the Celtic world. There was a book that I left for the cinematographer, Jordan Cronenweth, and the director, Phil Joanou, called *Bonnett's Town*. It influenced us very, very much on this film. It's a book of photographs about the country home in Ireland of a man called Edwin Bonnett. It's a ruined house, and it's called Bonnett's Town. It's a great house in ruin, but it's still inhabited.

So you incorporated those images into the bar?

Yes, the Irish immigration, a great house, a great people who degenerated to that bar, and that pitiful group of people, the Westies.

Was the main bar built on location?

Yes, it was a fish market on Ninth Avenue. There were so many bars in this movie; there were about ten bars. We went everywhere. No sooner would we arrive, they would start remodeling the bar. I got so upset because those places are slowly being phased out. They are slowly turning into a kind of nostalgia tourist thing; they're not for real anymore. We needed a really huge bar, and it had to have that geography of the alley. That's why we went to the place on Ninth Avenue. It was a wholesale fish market that was out of business, and it had entrances on two streets, 51st Street and also on Ninth Avenue. You could actually come at it from both directions, and there was an alley. It was really very good for us in many ways.

When does State of Grace *take place?*

It was early to mid-eighties.

The film has a timeless quality.

It is timeless. Phil said he wanted a timeless quality. He said nothing has changed for these people, which is true; nothing has changed. It could be anywhere from 1978 to 1988. Not much changes in that world. It's like going South, not much happened there in the past hundred years.

Is there anything you would like to accomplish as a designer that you haven't yet achieved? I know one of your dream projects would be to design a film version of the Jack Finney novel Time and Again.

The Finney novel is every art director's dream. The proposition that if you create time perfectly enough, you can slip back into it is irresistible to an art director. Of course, there are many things I would like to do as long as they're different from what I have already done. I make heroic efforts to do different kinds of material, but you can't control what you are. You are what you are. You're going to respond to things a certain way; you can't help it. I don't like the direction of all these megabuck movies. When you start spending $40 million on something, you know it's not going to be a risk-taking situation. So I want to work small. There are so many stories to develop that could be done.

Where do you think the profession of production design is going in the future? Will computers play an important role in production design?

This is still a handmade business. The decisions get made with a pencil. Computers are involved as tools, but if they broke down, you could still make a floor plan with a pencil on the back of an envelope. The fact is most of the floor plans are going to get made with a computer. I wish I had the mastery of all of these wonderful tools, but they're just tools; it's the ideas that count. Unfortunately, it's the ideas that are in short supply.

15

Stuart Wurtzel

After studying scenic design at Carnegie Mellon University, Stuart Wurtzel became a theater designer in New York and spent several seasons at the American Conservatory Theater in San Francisco.

Wurtzel worked as a scenic artist for the late Gene Callahan on *The Candidate*. Callahan, a distinguished film production designer, became a mentor to both Wurtzel and his wife, Patrizia Von Brandenstein.

A conscientious and versatile artist, Wurtzel has constructed detailed environments for diverse projects throughout his career. He created Brooklyn in the 1930s for *Brighton Beach Memoirs*, the black-and-white world of a Hollywood movie and the somber palette of the Depression for *The Purple Rose of Cairo*, and the turmoil of revolutionary Mexico for *The Ballad of Gregorio Cortez* and *Old Gringo*. He has portrayed many facets of life in New York City: the Lower East Side of *Hester Street*, the hippie counterculture of *Hair*, and the cosmopolitan milieu of *Hannah and Her Sisters*, which was nominated for an Academy Award for art direction–set decoration.

Wurtzel has worked with many directors, including Joan Micklin Silver, Robert Young, Woody Allen, Milos Forman, Gene Saks, Richard Benjamin, and Peter Yates.

Equally at home with low-budget or large-scale films, Stuart Wurtzel brings the theatrical tradition of story and character to all of the worlds he renders on the screen.

1974 *Hester Street*

1976 *The Next Man* (art director with production designer Gene Callahan)

1977 *Between the Lines*
1979 *Hair*
1980 *Simon*
      Night of the Juggler
      Times Square
1981 *Tattoo*
1982 *The Chosen*
1983 *The Ballad of Gregorio Cortez*
1985 *The Purple Rose of Cairo*
1986 *Hannah and Her Sisters**
      Brighton Beach Memoirs
1987 *Suspect*
1988 *The House on Carroll Street*
1989 *An Innocent Man*
      Old Gringo
      Staying Together
1990 *Mermaids*
      Three Men and a Little Lady
1992 *Mambo Kings*
      Used People

* Academy Award nomination for best achievement in art direction–set decoration.

What is the role of the production designer in the making of a feature film?
To create a visual and emotional world for the story to unfold. You're
there on every single phase. Filmmaking is a big situation; sometimes I
find myself barely having enough time to say yes and no. I come back
to the art department at the end of the day, and my desk is filled. The
art director and the prop person show me pictures. A whole day's work
is gone through in a half an hour or an hour, because that's all the time
I have to do it. You need people around to filter that through to you.
They have to be responsible to themselves, but nothing goes out without
me looking at it or saying yes or no. Aside from being a creative force
in the picture, you become a traffic cop. You have to be on top of so
many elements. I like to be on the set as much as possible. I like to be
there when the camera's rolling, because I feel that's when the film's
being made. If choices are to be made, then I'm part of those choices.
All of a sudden if something changes and I don't happen to be around,
then somebody else is going to make the decision. It's the accumulation
of the small elements that finally add up to the total of what the picture

is all about. What the camera is focusing on becomes a very important element of the total environment of the picture.

The Ballad of Gregorio Cortez *was an independently made film with a very authentic period look. What was the budget on the film?*

Low budget, a $900,000 picture done in the wilds of New Mexico and Texas. It was a six-week shoot.

How many people were in the art department?

Dan Leigh, who had worked with me for a long time in the theater and in film as my associate, came out to be the art director, the decorator, and the lead man. The art department consisted of myself, Dan, and three production assistants—we did the whole picture. We had four carpenters who would also do painting. They went to each location and camped out. I drove out every day. We would push and shove, and then they'd move on to the next location. I would stay with the film company, then leapfrog to the next location. Every morning, we would go to the warehouse and load up the crates and the barrels. It's a period film—barrels, burlap bags, and bags of sawdust cover a multitude of sins. I called it a crate and barrel show.

What was your budget for the art department?

Besides the carpentry budget, I had about $15,000 to dress everything. When we gave the producer, Michael Hausman, the budget for a lobby that was going to cost $3,000, he said, "Well, I guess we're just going to change the location, aren't we?" It became something else. It was a real training situation. The Ballad of Gregorio Cortez was a lesson in how to make things work. If you don't have the money, you can't say, "I still want to shoot it." You have to find another way to do it. You can change the location or shoot in a location that we've dressed already. You can't be in a situation where demands are made that can't be fulfilled, and everybody has to know it. You just have to be very loose. It doesn't mean that it's less of a movie; sometimes the toughest situations make the best movies.

What were the conditions like working on location in Texas and Mexico?

It was a great experience, because we were doing a Western. It was us against the elements. You just hike up your boots, and you shovel it with everybody else—and we definitely shoveled it. The first day shooting, we were in the homestead where Cortez lived. There was a basic building, but we added the porch. We had a wonderful landscape. We had gotten this wonderful little garden from a university. It was going down to below thirty at night when we were going to plant it. It was adobe that was hard as a rock. The Sunday before the Monday we were starting to shoot, there was nobody there with a back hoe, and we started pickaxing. Each one of us was slinging the pickaxe for about fifteen minutes, and finally the back hoe came in—thank God! Then we go to plant the garden, and it's pouring rain in New Mexico on the first day of shooting. The carriage can't get up the hill, because it's so muddy. We found a root cellar that we dug out. We lucked out, because it was the only dry dirt around to lay over the garden to dry it up. The same thing happened the next day, and we did the same thing again; this time the root cellar was two stories deep. *The Ballad of Gregorio Cortez* was just a great experience; I mean it was a killer. You're out there doing it yourself; it's not like you're pointing fingers.

Were most of the locations practical?

The homesteads were practical and augmented. We built on them a lot, then adobed, and painted. The courthouse was real, but completely repainted. The prison was the actual location where Cortez was held in Gonzales, Texas. The room where I built the gallows was a two-story-high room that was completely carved over with graffiti in the fifties and sixties. It was all chiseled out with knives. I said, "We'll just come in here and do a whole plaster job." Then we found out the wife of the mayor was trying to get the prison on the historic register. It had been accepted, which meant that nothing could be done to the exterior or interior of the building, including the graffiti that was on the wall. So we stretched muslin two stories high, attaching it at the top, stretching it at the bottom, taping it around the windows, and painting in place so that nothing would happen to the graffiti underneath. We literally struck it in an hour. We finished shooting the film at three o'clock in the morning.

You have designed two films for Woody Allen, The Purple Rose of Cairo *and* Hannah and Her Sisters. *Had you worked on any of his films prior to this?*

When Mel Bourne was doing *Annie Hall*, I worked as his assistant, and we became good friends. He needed someone for three weeks to draw up the apartment, the ferris wheel out the window, and a couple of other things. When they were doing reshoots for *Broadway Danny Rose*, which was the last picture that Mel did with Woody, he was off doing something else. I supervised the reshoots on *Broadway Danny Rose*; that was my first experience with Woody. I called up Mel and said, "What should I look out for? What do you think I need to know?" He said, "Just do what you think is right."

When you designed The Purple Rose of Cairo, *were you at all influenced by the seven films that Mel Bourne had designed for Woody Allen?*

You have to be your own person. Although I love Mel and I respect his work, I'm also my own designer. Each picture requires something different. If you're good, you're good in each thing that you do. It was, "How would I do it?" not "How would I do it for Woody following Mel?" Each picture is totally different.

*The Purple Rose of Cairo *is a real valentine for anyone who is in love with the movies. What was it like to work on it?*

It was just to die over this script. For me, that was a coming together of everything I ever could have wanted to do. It was the opportunity to work with Woody and to work on a thirties period film, which screwed me up completely for the rest of my life. I mean, what can I tell you, I wanted to be Fred Astaire. It was a color movie; it was a black-and-white movie. I got to design some of those fantasy Hollywood sets like the drawing room and the bedroom. It was such a totally satisfying project to work on from every aspect, and that happens every once in a while; it's not every picture you do. *The Purple Rose of Cairo* was an ideal coming together of everything.

When you were designing the black-and-white film within The Purple Rose of Cairo, *how did you know how those sequences were going to translate to the gray scale?*

I actually did the main penthouse set in grays and blacks, because it was accurate to the time if you were doing a Deco interior. I also felt it would be very helpful to the actors to do it that way. It was wonderful; you walked onto that black, white, gray, and silver set, and the actors were also in blacks, whites, and grays. All of a sudden before us was a black-and-white movie—they all loved it. The crew was respectful. They were very careful about how they treated the set. We were creating our own black-and-white movie. It was fun.

How was the black-and-white movie put onto the screen in the movie house set. Was a matte shot used?

No, nothing was done as a matte. We projected the film. We shot the movie within the movie first, so that we would have it to shoot in the theater. We wanted always to tie in the audience in the theater with the screen. We didn't want any shots of just the proscenium. It's like doing a TV shot and then you matte in the TV; it looks fake. You always sense there's something wrong. When we shot our black-and-white movie and saw the dailies, they were very crisp. I said to myself, "Well, it's all there, but it doesn't look like the old movies." The old black-and-white movies would glow and glitter. I learned that when the initial black-and-white film was shot being projected in the theater it was then another generation removed, and that extra generation made all the difference in what the black-and-white-movie looked like. The cinematographer, Gordon Willis, was doing tests on this. The first time I saw the film projected, then shot again, it was one generation removed. That softened it up and made it absolutely perfect. Gordie knew exactly what was going to happen with it, but not having that knowledge, I didn't know.

How did you use color to contrast the world of the Depression era that the Mia Farrow character lived in with the glamorous world that the movies represented to her?

I was creating a Depression-era town that was meant to be a very sad

place. Her apartment was meant to be very sad. This was a woman who
had an ordinary, mundane life. The contrast was when she went to the
movies, she transcended all of that. The movie theater was a glowing
palace. The choices that were made in that film were very specific. The
real world was all dark, cool, and green; her apartment was heavy and
somber. For the palette of the town, I painted every single building; not
one building was left original. It's like doing a painting on a grand scale.
When she walks into the theater, it glows from the inside; it's amber,
warm, and very comforting. Then she sees a black-and-white movie.
Gordie Willis said that the problem was to create a black-and-white image
more glorious than a world in color. We had to make black-and-white
something unattainable, unreachable, more up on a mountain, because
it is so glorious.

*You have designed several films for director Peter Yates. How did you first
meet?*

I met Peter when Patrizia was designing *Breaking Away*. They needed
the end race sequence storyboarded, and Patrizia said, "Oh, Stuart can
storyboard that." I never storyboarded anything in my life, but I had
the sense of what it was. When they were shooting the big race, I went
out there for the weekend. A tent was set up in the middle of the field
where the storyboards were laid out on all the tables. Peter is a genius
for action work. He's just great with moving the camera; he has a wonderful sense of style with film. They'd get out there, do the shot, come
back in, check it off, and then we'd go back out. It was very exciting to
actually see the storyboard used in that way. *The House on Carroll Street*
was the first picture I did with him as a designer. It was a low-budget
period film in New York—about eleven million. We had the only crew
in New York I know that could have made it work. Everybody knew
each other. We all got in there and pitched in.

*How did you use exterior locations to turn the clock back thirty years on New
York for* The House on Carroll Street?

It becomes more and more difficult. We actually moved a lot of it. The
film was originally called *The House on Sullivan Street*. We couldn't use
that title for legal reasons, but we looked at Sullivan and Bleecker Streets.
Between that block there's a whole interior courtyard. You could see
from one house to the other, but visually it was not very interesting.
The Park Slope area in Brooklyn is much less changed, so that was a
case in point of trying to help the budget. I said to Peter, "Can she be
looking for a job in Brooklyn, because we can get a really great period
look and there's also a lot less to do." So she did end up looking for
this job in Brooklyn. Residential sections have changed less. Businesses
always have to be upgraded with each decade, because they're reflecting
what people are buying. In New York, you can shoot period in any
number of places from the second floor up, except maybe for air con-

ditioners, but it's the ground level that's changed substantially. In filming, you're dealing with an actor on the ground level, and that's a lot
of what you see. So we shot in the Village, which is still very good for
period, and we shot in Park Slope, Brooklyn, for the exteriors. There
was a chase sequence we were originally going to do around the Sheridan
Square area. It would have been a $17,000 bill budgetwise. It was also
a Friday night shooting in the Village, and the cinematographer Michael
Ballhaus said, "Do you know what's it's like to shoot on a Friday night
in Greenwich Village, let alone making it period?" For him, it was an
enormous headache, because he wasn't going to be able to move as fast
as he wanted to. So then it became the chase in the bookstore done in
the Strand Bookstore, which is very period to begin with. I was always
changing book titles, and I hung overhead lights, which Michael loved
because we had all this light.

*In picking the exterior locations, did you find that the compositional framing
was a critical factor in maintaining the period look? At times, if the camera had
moved one degree, would we have seen 1988?*

Oh yes, in a period film you have to do that, because it means it's
going to cost another ten or twenty thousand dollars if you want to slide
the camera.

The climax of The House on Carroll Street *is a complex chase scene in
Grand Central Station. How were the details of the scene worked out?*

It took weeks of going to Grand Central to find all of the locations,
because it's such an enormous place. To make it all work, you're creating
a chase sequence and writing it at the same time. We were trying to
make it as plausible as possible. Once we had all of the locations, then
I storyboarded again with Peter. There were about a 110 different shots.
I sat there and drew it up, and then handed it in. Then Michael Ballhaus
got it. I said, "Michael, it's only a tool; certainly if you want to change
it or move the camera, this is just an idea of how many cuts are needed
to make it work."

*What was physically done to make Grand Central Station look in period for
the fifties?*

The information booth was fine; we just had to change some lettering.
We covered over the electric information sign that had the incoming
trains on it with our own billboard. The clock wasn't there during that
period; it was too modern. We hung a fifty-foot flag in front of it. There
was a Merrill Lynch booth between the information booth and the staircase that was a completely modern, aluminum square with an electric
sign on it. We covered over the upper part so you didn't see the Merrill
Lynch sign. I'm looking at the aluminum booth and I kept saying, "Michael, we're not going to see this, right?" Michael said, "Don't worry,
it's all going to be backlit." We had all the Musco Light coming from
outside through the window, so there was strong backlight. I couldn't

stand it; it was making me nuts. We got two-inch black masking tape and started taping the hell out of this booth to get rid of the aluminum look—at least it went black. When I saw it in dailies, it was okay. We were pretty wide at that point, so you saw something, but you couldn't really tell what it was. You're trying to control a huge location, and it has to be in period.

At the time the film was made, all of the old manual track signs had been replaced by electric ones. How did you deal with this?

We had to change them all back.

Where were the exterior locations for Suspect *filmed?*

We wanted the reality of Washington, D.C. We were planning on shooting it all in Washington, except for the interior of the courtroom, which was three weeks of filming. We opted for Toronto. We moved a couple of weeks of other locations to Toronto as budgetary considerations, but we did shoot five weeks in Washington and got a real sense of the city. We actually shot in some locations that were never filmed before in Washington. We shot at the Justice Department. It's very difficult to film in Washington only because you're dealing with so many agencies.

Much of the action in Suspect *takes place in a contemporary courtroom, which is very different from the kind of classic courtroom more commonly seen in films. How did this come about?*

When I first read the script, I thought we were going to be able to do a wonderful old courtroom with marble and carved wood to surround this poor guy by the weight of justice, but we were shooting in Washington, D.C., and were using the real courthouse. To my surprise, it was a completely contemporary building. Although the interior space is very exciting with escalators, the courtrooms themselves are very small and unassuming; they're almost like screening rooms. The justices all got together and said they wanted smaller space. They wanted to be able to hear better, and they ended up having much smaller courtrooms. There is such a backlog in Washington, they needed so many courts; we could never find one that was big enough for us to use. Once I saw the building as contemporary, I had to rethink the situation. You have to be flexible. We always knew we were going to build the interior of the courtroom as a set. So the courtroom itself was based on the designs of the courtrooms that were in Washington, D.C., but it was much more elaborated. We had some size to it.

If we didn't get an oppressive quality by the weight of history with the mahogany and everything, we got a little bit in the size and the scale. It was an interesting problem to make something like that visually interesting when it's a fairly uninteresting kind of space. When you're doing a period courtroom, you have carvings, pilasters, maybe a window, but I didn't have any of that to draw from. I was always trying to make it visually attractive, so you didn't get bored being there all the time. We did shoot real courtrooms in Washington for some of the chase scene at the end, so I couldn't just go off in left field and do what I really wanted. It still had to feel like it was part of the same building because we intercut a lot. We built a little hallway outside the courtroom itself which matched the real courtroom, so I think the cuts worked very well.

The man on trial in Suspect *is unable to hear or speak. Did you get involved in researching the equipment that was used in the film for him to be able to communicate with the court?*

Absolutely. I was speaking to some people at Gallaudet College in Washington, and it's fascinating because we had to be absolutely true. Part of the problem is it is a time-consuming situation for him writing and then reading. We had heard about this writing pad that was relatively new when we used it. You're always having to wait for the writing and then the screen, so it was a very difficult challenge to make what was right work for the character, the film, and the dynamics of the story. We knew the technique of how to make it work; then it was a matter of how to make it work dramatically. That's partly the reason why the clerk spoke his words, because people had to hear what he was thinking or else there would be endless amounts of silence. Also, it was at a time when you were trying to create a tension and to build a certain momentum.

What location was used for the prison scenes in An Innocent Man?

The jail in *An Innocent Man* was two locations. The interior was in Cincinnati. It was spectacular, because it was every image of a jail that you'd want; it was five stories high. It was an empty prison, which meant we could move a lot faster. We had complete control, but it was completely derelict, so a lot of effort in that location was in bringing it back up to standards—fixing the shower and then augmenting and building it. It was all covered with chain-link fence. If you're raking the camera down the fence, you couldn't see anything, so I had all of that removed. Then I added the guard walkway on the other side, so we could have shots of the guards going back and forth. We built the cell itself in another wing of the prison using a wall outside, so it looked like the same interior wall. The Stallone picture *Lock Up* was shot at the same interior prison. The lieutenant who had run the prison told them exactly how we built it. So that was a big refurbishing job.

We shot the exteriors in Carson City, Nevada, which was a high-security camp. The captain was a very nice guy who helped us out enormously. In fact, he's the one in the movie at the top screaming down at the residents. They loved it, because they just started yelling back at him. The crew all wore orange vests, so everybody knew exactly who was on the crew and that everybody else was a resident. They loved getting down on the ground when the bullets were firing. They were part of the basketball game. I had a key person who ran the paint crew, but there were eight other residents who were painting on that crew. They were being paid fair wages, so they were making a lot more money than they do when they were just working for the prison. In fact, the captain said for the four weeks that we were there, the incident rate went from something like seventy down to twelve. He said, for him and the guys, it was a great opportunity. He was also looking to become warden, so I think it was very helpful to him.

The film editor Jerry Greenberg once told me that "films are a series of details— details within details." Do you find this to be true about production design?

The detail is incredibly important; it all gels together. Painting a palette for a movie is painting the movie from the smallest detail to the grandest skyscraper. For me, it's all-inclusive; I just don't walk out and leave it to somebody else. That's why I like to be around when the film is being made, because those choices are being made when the film is running through the camera. In the grand scheme of things, you're talking about scale, style, and architecture. I can't separate it; it's the total picture. It's the total overview that actually works down to the most minute detail. When you're dealing with something large, what you do is you start dissecting it. You know what the total look is. You wind up breaking it down to very small elements, because you have to solve many different problems and come up with a lot of solutions.

It's like working on the street. It goes from saying, "What's the biggest chunk of work we have to do?" We'll say, "We'll have to change the facade of this, we have to do the color of that, then we have to do the lamppost." It gets smaller and smaller, then it gets down to the bell on the door. So my list of things to do never gets less, it just gets more minute. You start focusing in on the less and less and less as the camera does, so that every point is absolutely perfect. It doesn't mean that accidents don't help. Some of the best things are when all of a sudden something is running across the street and you say, "Grab it quick. Let's do it." But you have to know about it and you have to be there enough to know how it relates to the rest of the movie, so that it can become part of the fabric of the picture.

What responsibility do you feel towards the actors in helping them to create a character?

You try to make the actor feel as comfortable as possible, so their performance can be more accurate. You're not just going to give him a comic book to look at when he's supposed to be reading *Moby Dick*. The detail is also important to the actors. It's a matter of being able to make the choices that support the story and the characters. It builds from the napkin on the table or the smallest thing that an actor relates to. If you have three coffee cups to chose from, which one is going to tell more about the character? I feel it's an important part of my job as the designer. A lot of that comes from my theatrical background. What you try to do is create the world around them. Some of the best compliments I've gotten are from actors who walk onto sets and say, "I feel like this is my home," or "You know more about the character than I do."

How do you feel about films that take place in New York being shot on a Hollywood back lot?

When we were doing *Brighton Beach Memoirs*, Universal suggested the back lot for all the New York streets. I looked at it and said, "This is a joke." Some of it is wonderful, but it's used to death; there is nothing fresh and new. There's no life to it. You know exactly when it's shot on the back lot, so don't tell me it's New York. You can't shoot down the street, you can't shoot the sky, you can't shoot anything. So no matter how good the choices are, you're just nowhere. People know that it's not real; they sense they've seen it before. You're trying to make a unique experience every time you make a different film. In order for it to be unique, the choices on the film have to be different; they can't be the same old thing.

What films do you feel are landmarks in production design?

Certainly, *Gone with the Wind*, *Lawrence of Arabia*, *Dr. Zhivago*, all the David Lean pictures, *Diva*. I thought *Out of Africa* was brilliant. There are always the lush romantic movies that you respond to, but the contemporary ones that are more hard-edged are also really interesting— *Blade Runner* and *Brazil*, which I thought was spectacular. Also, *The Adventures of Baron Munchausen* was wonderful.

What personality traits do you think are necessary to be a good production designer?

Determination, perseverance. It's an incredible sense of energy, being available, being accessible to everybody and anybody. I talk to the grips and the electricians. You have to be flexible in this business. Sometimes a location doesn't work out, so we've got to get another location. It's always keeping your eye on what you want the picture to say, never losing that through all of the of hysteria you go through in getting something ready. Don't worry about the metaphor after you put it in place. It has to become second nature. It's helpful to be able to get along with people. You're only as good as the crew that works with you. You can only do so much on a picture by yourself before you drop dead, because you can't be at all places at all times.

Production designers are artists who have a tremendous fiscal responsibility on a film. How do you deal with this dichotomy?

It's hard, because as an artist, you like not to worry about how it gets done. I don't think you can ever stop dreaming. On *Old Gringo* there was a little official checkpoint on the American side that we were really under pressure to get done. The construction coordinator said, "It's all based on four-by-eight sheets of plywood. I can really knock it out in about a day and a half." I looked at this and said, "You know it's not really right." Then, as we were driving down the road, there was a little shack. I said, "This is really what it should be." So he started bitching and moaning. He finally accepted the challenge and did it. It looked wonderful, and it didn't take that much longer. I said to myself, "I don't design for four-by-eight sheets of plywood." The minute that becomes the dominant focus, then you've got to stop designing. The budget is important; if your only concern is for the budget, then everything is going to be a compromise. What you have to do is decide what you want to do first and design for that. Then it's a matter of making it work, but at least you start with a spark of inspiration. If you start from the nails and the wood, then nothing is going to fly, nothing is going to soar above your heart, because it's all going to be wedded to the ground. You have to start with a hope, a wing and prayer, and a little money, and then adapt it. If you can't adapt it, then you change it. There's not one solution for any one problem.

16

Norman Garwood

In 1967 Norman Garwood became an assistant designer for an independent television station in England. He achieved the position of senior
designer, but his real ambition was to design for motion pictures. This
desire led him to commercials where he had the opportunity to meet
film people. In 1981 he got the break he was looking for when director
Terry Gilliam hired him to assist production designer Millie Burns as art
director on *Time Bandits*.

In 1982 Garwood attained the post of production designer on *The
Missionary*. After designing several films for other directors, he was
asked by Terry Gilliam to design *Brazil*, a landmark film in art direction,
which brought his enormous talent to full bloom. Working in close
collaboration with Gilliam's ingenious vision, Garwood helped to merge
an Orwellian view of the future with the past and present to conceive
a Brazil of the mind. The oppression of bureaucracy is crystallized in
Garwood's design of the Ministry as a labyrinth with endless connecting
duct work. Garwood was honored with an Academy Award nomination
for his contribution to this significant film.

In the 1989 film *Glory*, Garwood demonstrated his ability to re-create
American history by bringing the Civil War to the screen in exacting
detail. After exhaustive research, Garwood designed and built the base
camp, and a brick-for-brick re-creation of Dunker Church, along with
an precise replica of Fort Wagner. The meticulous art direction of the
film brings the sepia-toned photographs of Mathew Brady to life in
veritable color. Garwood received his second Oscar nomination for his
work on the critically acclaimed film directed by Edward Zwick.

Norman Garwood has designed two films for director Rob Reiner with screenplays by William Goldman. *The Princess Bride* was an original fairy tale magically rendered out of Garwood's fanciful imagination. The house in *Misery* is permeated with character detail and generates a chilling setting for the film adaptation of the Stephen King novel.

Garwood was the production designer of Steven Spielberg's *Hook*, and he garnered an Oscar nomination for his work.

Norman Garwood is an illusionist. *Brazil*, *The Princess Bride*, *Glory*, and *Hook* create worlds that reflect the spirit of our faith in movies to affirm dreams.

1981   *Time Bandits* (art director with production designer Millie Burns)

1982   *Brimstone and Treacle* (art director with production designer Millie Burns)
       The Missionary

1983   *Red Monarch*
       Bullshot!

1984   *Water*

1985   *Brazil**

1986   *Shadey*

1987   *The Princess Bride*

1989   *Glory**

1990   *Misery*

1991   *Hook**

1992   *Being Human*

*Academy Award nomination for best achievement in art direction–set decoration.

How did you become a production designer?

I started as an assistant designer in English television for an independent company called ABC-TV from 1967 through 1978, when I got to be what was known as a senior designer. I was very anxious to move on. I had gone full circle with every form of drama and light entertainment show. When I started, guys would be there for five years and then move on to movies, but that seemed to stop; no one left. I really was desperate to work in the movies. I have an amazing wife; she was pregnant and I said, "I can't bear it. I've got to go." She said, "If you don't go, you'll drive me insane." It was pretty nerve-wracking because everyone in TV was saying, "You must be mad. What about your pension scheme?" I mean, I was thirty-three and people were worried about pensions. I just felt, "I've got to do it." There was another world out there. So I left, and I really had very little to go to. I did a couple of commercials, which was a chance to work with film people. Then I got a call from Terry Gilliam regarding *Time Bandits*. He had a production designer, a lovely lady named Millie Burns, so I was taken on as the art director. I remember getting the script and reading it coming home on the train from London. I just thought, "How on earth are we going to do this?" It was my baptism by fire. That was my first break into the movie business, and it was a wonderful opportunity. I thought I might have to rush back into TV if all failed, but it kind of went along and just got better and better and better. After *Time Bandits*, I did another film with Millie, *Brimstone and Treacle*, with the English director Richard Longcrane, who's a lovely guy. Richard did a film straight after that, *The Missionary*, with Michael Palin and Maggie Smith. They were going to bring in another production designer and wanted me to be the art director. I said, "Hey, how about giving me a break. I'm really capable of doing it," and they said, "Oh, right, oh," and they asked me if I'd be the number one man, which was great.

Brazil is a film that many designers consider a landmark in production design. We are told at the outset that the film takes place "Somewhere in the 20th Century." Although Brazil *has a futuristic look, it is also rooted in the style of the thirties. What was the genesis of the design?*

Terry Gilliam had some very strong ideas. Terry and I had lots and lots of conversations about the look of the film. I had a few months prep, and basically the first month was just getting many ideas together. We got wonderful illustrations from comic books of the 1930s and what they thought the future would look like. We went through just tons and tons of research and reference. It was amazing how a style evolved with the clothes, the props, with everything. People got into a *Brazil* mode of thought. When I first took on the prop crew, everyone would say, "Why is it called *Brazil*? Do we go to Brazil?" It was really difficult inasmuch as I couldn't sketch a lot of it. I did sketching, but it evolved from things we collected. They would start putting props together, and I would say, "No, it's got to be a little more like this, a little more like that." Suddenly, they all got into it, and they'd rush up with something and it was Brazilesque. We got a whole bunch of machines, started playing, and then things would grow. It grew in spirit.

There's a very controlled color scheme in the film. The palette is primarily blue, black, gray, and white. Was this a decision made early on?

Yes. In discussions with Terry he said he wanted to keep it quite monochromatic. Everywhere was this grayness. I suppose we were making a statement about what a gray establishment it was. There would not be many highlights of color anyplace except the mother's home, which was wonderful and glittery. She was out of the general standard. It's a bit like the Politburo; there are people who could afford to have a grander lifestyle.

The Ministry is a monolithic labyrinth structure. An endless series of ducts link all the walls and ceilings creating a powerful metaphor of the ultimate government bureaucracy. How did this come to be such a central image?

It was everywhere. It just got to be obsessive. It began to take on a life of its own. It was a starting point in the same way as the glass blocks. We made quite a number of crossovers with different styles of architecture, and the duct work linked everything.

What location was used for the exterior of the Ministry?

Terry had been to Marne La Vallee just outside of Paris. It is a block of apartments which Bofill, the Spanish architect, had designed. I went there with Terry and saw it was a wonderful exterior for the Ministry.

Was the interior of the Ministry created in a practical location, or was it built in the studio?

Originally, we were looking for a location, something very neo-fascist and massive. We looked in France, and there was nothing of that scale. I said to Terry, "Well, why don't I build it?" I did one model, and we pruned it down because *Brazil* wasn't a massive budget movie; it was something like sixteen million, and it was going to cost too much.

The restaurant was an enormous cathedral-sized space connected by a snake-like piping. Was this set created in the studio?

That was a location, a huge, mammoth house for transcendentalists called Mentore House. We went there and Terry said, "I don't think it's going to work," because the gallery was so high. I said, "Well, why don't I just build the floor up, and then we'll start from the central column where we can start all this pipe work again." So we built everything up. These people were terribly nervous about us being there, but when we finished the restaurant, they were so thrilled they actually said, "Gee, could you possibly leave it?" I said, "No, it's just sort of film scenery; it's got to come down."

Did you work closely with the costume designer Jim Acheson?

I worked very closely with Jim, and we're great friends. He's a brilliant costume designer—Double Oscar Jim. I remember the time he came in with the shoe hat and said, "This is stupid." I said, "Jim, it's absolutely wonderful." So we'd encourage each other a lot. I would see what he was doing, and he'd bounce a few ideas off me. There was a lot of collaboration. Jim was the spirit of the costumes. Some of it was so subtle. He would get a pinstriped material for the suits, which obviously should run vertically, and he'd run it the other way. The rims of the hats were an inch and a half bigger than they should be. It worked. I think he did a wonderful job. We used to have hysterical fun with it. I think humor had a lot to do with that movie. Jim's got the most wonderful humor. Terry's got a lovely sense of humor, and supposedly I've got a good sense of humor. I think my humor comes out in my work sometimes, if there is such a thing as a funny set.

Brazil has extraordinary cinematography. How did you work with the director of photography?

I worked incredibly close with Roger Pratt, the lighting cameraman, who's an excellent man. Roger and I spent a lot of time planning when the sets were being conceived and designed, because the lighting was so important in that movie. I'm thinking of the padded cell in which Jonathan Pryce ends up. Roger and I had talked about how we'd light it from the bottom and the top before I even started to really conceive the set.

MCA-Universal put a lot of pressure on Terry Gilliam during the making of Brazil. *Did any of this have an effect on you?*

Oh no, never. I was very fortunate; I never had any pressure whatsoever from anybody. Terry was amazing. The pressure was basically on him all the way through. I think he did remarkably well to survive it.

Did you know a lot about the Civil War at the time you were asked to design Glory?

I didn't. I was thrilled to be asked to do it, because you couldn't get a much more American subject than the Civil War. I knew about as much as anyone from Britain would have. I knew what the causes were, when it was, and who was who. I said to the director, Ed Zwick, "Why have you asked me to do it?" and he said, "I really think it's the quality of detail. I want that authenticity of 1864." I researched *Glory* to the nth degree. Research is really essential in getting the look. *Gone with the Wind* was a wonderful film, but we wanted to avoid that image. I looked at *North and South,* and the women all wore off-the shoulder dresses with their bosoms pushed up. I wanted to get into a sense of authenticity. What was amazing was that the Civil War was so well documented. All the Mathew Brady photographs were incredible. I just spent the first month researching, researching, and researching. I filled a huge room full of every bit of reference I could find. That was my starting point, finding out exactly what went on and what it looked like.

Where did you get all of the uniforms needed to outfit the two armies?

I thought, "This film is going to cost a fortune," because of the sheer numbers of people and the two major battle sequences. We used these men called Reenactors. When they first told me about Reenactors, I said, "Guys dressed as soldiers, I'm not too sure about this," but they said, "Look, we're going to go down to Florida to meet them. Come down and just look at them; they're going to be in uniform." So I went down there to observe and to look at their uniforms, because if we were going to hire them, they came as a job lot—they came to act, to bring the uniforms, to do the whole thing. It was quite remarkable how good they looked. They take the authenticity to limits you wouldn't believe. They have gone into details like the salt stains on the jackets, one button missing off the back of their pants where the braces were, their cuffs are gone, the scuffs on their boots—it was amazing. I would be thinking to myself, "If we had to costume that many extras, God only knows what it would have cost." It was a marvelous solution. Not only did they know how to fight, they knew how to shoot; they brought their own artillery and the cavalry were brilliant horsemen. They were quite remarkable because they were so well drilled.

What did you have to build for the film?

We had to build Fort Wagner. The Audubon Society didn't want us there on Jekyll Island. They were worried about the wildlife, which was quite right, but we were going to put it back to exactly as it was, and in fact, it did go back. What was gratifying to me was that we built that fort and it was so authentic. It was a twelve-week build. It was huge and monstrous—three hundred foot square. The Reenactors were thrilled that we'd got everything so right. I researched Dunker Church, which was the first sequence in the movie. When we finally built it, I tried to get it just right, inasmuch as every brick which was missing was missing. I was getting people coming to me and saying, "We cannot believe how accurate it is." We found this old thirties rail yard, and I made it a Victorian rail yard. Instead of a thirties look, with flat roofs, we put on pointed roofs and the right detail. Everything was built and matched in beautifully with the brickwork which existed. That was great for me, because that's what *Glory* was about—getting it right. You're re-creating a part of history. I didn't want *Glory* to be glamorous, because it was not a glamorous movie. It was really just a joy to be able to create the raw state of that base camp as it was.

Were there any paintings that influenced the look of Glory?

Yes, we used some lovely Victorian paintings which had a style and a palette. We went with the quality of light and shade of the Victorian painters for the interior light. We were really keen on getting the right quality of lighting. As a designer, I tend to try to have a lot of influence over that. A cameraman can make or break you.

Was there a lot of discussion about where the practical light sources should be?

Absolutely. Source lighting was so important because basically it was gas and candle lit. If it was a daytime sequence, the lighting should be through a window, not from a 10-K inside the room. So, for me, that's terribly important.

What was the budget on Glory?

We started off with about twelve million; it eventually ended up at twenty, and a lot of that went into postproduction, because I think everyone realized they had a really lovely movie. Then sound came in and did a beautiful job. They got James Horner to do the music, which was a beautiful score. There was a great spirit on that film. *Glory* was a wonderful film to do.

The majority of the action in Misery *takes place in a bedroom. In many of the shots we can see a beautiful landscape out of the window. There are several scenes where we can see cars and other movement through the window. Was the bedroom set actually built and shot on location?*

We found a wonderful valley, and I built the house on location. I built the bedroom to look out the window at the helicopter flying over, cars arriving, cars leaving. Then from the balcony of the house, we shot a translight, which is a huge photo blow-up. Then I built the bedroom again back on a stage. The translight can be backlit, obviously eliminating outside movement, but if you shoot all the cars arriving and whatever outside movement on location, it goes together very well. No one could see the joiner of reality and studio. Everybody thought, "Oh yes, it's a backing." Suddenly the helicopter goes over and you think, "Oh, maybe it's not a backing."

There are several exterior scenes that take place in deep snow. Did that cause problems?

Oh, it was murder, absolute murder. When you rely on the elements, they never perform the way you want. We were expecting huge snows, and we never got them. We were getting desperate, and when it did snow, six foot of it came down. You can never rely on the weather. You think, snowstorm—that's going to be fine, but what happens in Nevada is it tends to come down so heavy, you can't see a thing. Then the sun comes out and there are blue skies, which is terribly useless to shoot as well. For the whole sequence with the car crash, a lot of artificial snow was being blown as well as real stuff. When the car tipped down, there was timber framework under a lot of the snow to create mounds of snow. Weather pictures are a nightmare.

*You have designed two films written by William Goldman—*The Princess Bride *and* Misery. *Did you have any personal involvement with him?*

When I did *The Princess Bride*, William Goldman and I became very good friends. He said one thing to me that was just remarkable. He came on the stage of the fire swamp, and I could see him walking around and his mouth was open. Rob Reiner saw me, and he said, "Norman, this is Bill Goldman." I said, "Bill, I'm very pleased to meet you." He said, "Norman, I wrote about the fire swamp, but I never knew what it looked like. You created what I wrote about." That was probably the nicest thing anybody has ever said to me. When I wanted to get my H-1 visa to come and work here, he wrote a letter of recommendation to the Department of Immigration which was stunning. Every time I look at it, it fills me up, because he's such a lovely man and such an important person—a great writer.

There are many people and departments who are involved with the look of a film. How do you feel about the production designer's responsibility to coordinate all of these elements?

If you're going to get the title of production designer, you really should be looking after everything that's going to be up on that screen. If it's wrong, it's my fault; there's no one else. That's the end of the line where the buck really stops. You tend to get involved. I go around to every department. Every department that you can think of was involved on *The Princess Bride* from animatronics to prosthetics. On *Hook* there are a lot of departments, model makers, plasterers turning out cannons and miniatures. You can actually spend a day going from each department keeping your eye on it. When you do get lots of departments, it's extra leg work and a lot of input—people want to know from you what you want all the time. You'll get a lot of wonderful engineering from effects departments, but they're not particularly artistic. So the artistic input has to come from the art department. I'm on call every second on *Hook*. It's everything from, "Where do you want this ship?" to "What is the color of this spoon?" We have about 160 construction guys, and there are a phenomenal amount of questions to be answered.

I tend not to dither around. I tend to know what I want, and that's not being conceited. It's best to always be instinctive when it gets into question time about the size, the feel, the look, and you deal with it there and then. If I make a mistake, I'll soon hear about it. If you tend to say, "Can I let you know about that?" it starts to stack up and frustration grows. I've always been known to move along and be fairly positive. With a project the size of *Hook*, you've got to be positive.

Do you think people understand what the production designer does on a film?

People never do. On *Glory* we had a lot of news interest. People would actually come down on that beach and think, "God aren't they lucky; they found that fort just where it was." They didn't realize what went into creating it. In the end I get used to it. Many years ago, I was doing a commercial for a beer in England; we had to have a fish seller opposite a pub. They found the pub they wanted to use, but on the opposite corner was a little news agent shop, which was really ugly. It had a huge plate glass window. So I took this huge ugly piece of glass out, and we built a beautiful bay window. We plastered and painted. We put a marble slab in the window and dressed it with all the fish. It fitted in beautifully with the rest of the building; it looked lovely. The film unit rushed in because we were on a deadline and said, "We'll shoot the fish mongers now." The camera points to the fish monger. "Right, now we're going over to the outside of the pub." I said, "Are you finished with the fish monger?" They said, "Oh yes, you can take the fish out." I said, "It's a whole construction; that's all been built in there." Everybody watched as we took this bay window out and said, "That's amazing!" Again, there was no realization as to what had been created, and they saw that terrible old news agent go back to being a terrible old news agent again. I think people notice when it's wrong rather than notice how good it is when it's right. You see, this illusion-creating is a tough game, because it's great when people do look up and say, "I've suddenly realized that you've built all this."

How would you define the job of production designer?

You're an illusionist. You're paid to create any time capsule anybody needs to go into—that's your job. The funny thing is when I go to the cinema, I believe everything I see, so hopefully the public does exactly the same. I think if you create that illusion well, people will believe what you've done.

Is there anything that you haven't done as a production designer that you would like to do?

Yes, I'd love to do a traditional musical. I'd hate to get typecast as a designer who could only do one thing. I would hope that I could turn my hand to create anything.

How do you do that? What tools do you use? Research?

Yes, if it's a standard thing, it's a lot of research, but if it's fantasy, it's what you can free up and tap up from your mind. Hopefully that's why people ask me to do movies. It's a style and a look they want. I never realized I could produce a look, but I'm told I can and that's what I would love to continue to do. Sometimes I think it would be nice to direct, but I just love being good at what I do, and hopefully I'll get better and better at it.

17

Jane Musky

Jane Musky was a high school student preparing to study fine arts at Pratt Institute when a teacher told her the sets she created for school plays could lead to the profession of designer. A portfolio brimming with theatrical set renderings helped Musky gain entrance to the theater department at Boston University, where she majored in scenic design.

On graduation, Musky worked as a scenic artist in the theater, a period that included two years at the English National Opera. Returning from London, she was offered a job on an *ABC After School Special*. The production manager, Mark Silverman, liked her work and recommended her for several other *After School Specials*. When Joel and Ethan Coen began their breakthrough first feature, *Blood Simple*, Silverman was asked to be associate producer and advised them to hire Jane Musky. Her career as a feature film production designer was launched.

In *Blood Simple* Musky brought the Coens' highly original New Wave Texas noir to life, functioning as a virtual one-woman crew and working on a shoestring budget. The spare interiors are dotted with idiosyncratic character touches, and the ever-present low-horizon exteriors of Texas bring a stylish but grim reality to the sardonic humor of the story.

Jane Musky has built an impressive career since her 1984 debut. The bold visual design for the Coen brothers' second film, *Raising Arizona*, embraces Southwestern culture in a style filled with comic nuances. The town in *Young Guns* moves away from Hollywood clichés and reaches toward an architectural realism of the Old West. The mysterious and threatening secret world of the Symbionese Liberation Army is interpreted vividly in *Patty Hearst*. The splendor of autumn in New York is delicately woven into *When Harry Met Sally* . . . , and the romantic fantasy of *Ghost* is embodied in a loft with a stairway to heaven.

Jane Musky's recent venture as the production designer of David Mamet's *Glengarry Glen Ross* provided her with the opportunity to apply her theatrical frame of reference to the film adaptation of the Pulitzer Prize–winning play.

1984 *Blood Simple*
1987 *Raising Arizona*
       Illegally Yours
1988 *Young Guns*
       Patty Hearst
1989 *When Harry Met Sally* . . .
1990 *Ghost*
1991 *Dice Rules*
1992 *Glengarry Glen Ross*
       Boomerang

How did you become a production designer?

When I was in high school, I did all of the sets for the school plays. I was going to go to Pratt as a sculpture major. A teacher of mine in high school said, "You know, what you do as a designer is a real profession." It never clicked in my head that you could actually do that for a living. I went up to Boston University for an interview in their fine arts department. My art portfolio had renderings of sets. The person in the fine arts department introduced me to the people in the theater department that day; I went in and they accepted me. I trained at B.U. for four years as a scenic design major. When I got out of college, I was a scenic artist for a long time while I was trying to find design work in the theater. Then I ended up going to London for two years as a scenic artist for the English National Opera and other operas in Great Britain. When I got back from London, a friend of mine who was a scenic designer said he needed an assistant on an *After School Special* he was doing in New York. I just looked at him. It never crossed my mind that you could also design for films or television. I said, "Television! I have never done anything like it," and he said, "Neither have I." So the two of us went and did it.

How did you get the job of production designer on Blood Simple?

I got to be good friends with Mark Silverman, the production manager on this *After School Special*, who produced *Blood Simple* and *Raising Arizona*. He liked what I was doing on *After School Specials*, so when he moved onto another one, he said, "You've got to hire Jane Musky as your art director." After I had done two or three *After School Specials*,

Mark got asked by Joel and Ethan Coen to do *Blood Simple*. They asked Mark if he knew designers, and Mark introduced me to Joel and Ethan the summer before we were going to start shooting.

Blood Simple *was your first film as a production designer. It also was the first feature for Joel and Ethan Coen and cinematographer Barry Sonnenfeld. What was the working atmosphere like?*

We were new kids on the block, but we knew what we wanted. Barry and I had the design sense, and Joel and Ethan knew their story. We all knew which direction we should go in; we just had to be clever about how to achieve it. We were all so innocent about the whole process, we'd try anything to the point of going over the top. Everyone always says the blood in *Blood Simple* was hysterical because it was always so gooey. Everyone thought we did it on purpose. We didn't know it was going to look that way. We couldn't afford the blood you buy from prop houses and we didn't know how to mix blood, so that's what we came up with. All those accidents happened along the way, but somehow we were very cohesive in what we thought this picture should look like. The whole neon aspect of my work in *Blood Simple* was because I had no money. I had about $15,000 to do the whole film. I had no crew. I had four people—we were the art department—and I had to find all sorts of ways to figure out a design. I found a guy around Austin called Dr. Neon, and he said, "Listen, I'll do neon for you for nothing if you put my license plate in the film." So I'm thinking, "Okay, neon," and then all of a sudden I thought, "Well, bars are neon; we can do some fun stuff with the bars."

How would you define the visual style of Blood Simple?

It was a modern version of film noir that took place in a certain part of the country. It had to be film noir with a Texas slant, which is what gave it a look people weren't expecting—they think of film noir as something more universal. We knew we had to achieve that hokey Texas cowboy edge in the darkness and evil of a lot of the characters.

Blood Simple *was shot on location in Austin, Texas. Were you familiar with Texas prior to designing the film?*

No, Joel had gone to school there, but none of us knew what to expect. On all of the location pictures I've done, especially with the Coens, you really grab the place. You find what you want and make it feel the way you want for the purposes of the film, and you throw the rest away. That helped in Austin. It was kind of hokey, and there was fun stuff to find there—the same with Phoenix, Arizona, when we did *Raising Arizona*; it was just so bizarre. That's the beauty of film; you go to one of these little pockets all over the world and see how people live there.

How did the Coens relate to you as a production designer?

As a designer, they always allowed me to really go off the edge and never questioned me about it. A lot of other directors don't let you, because they're not sure of their approach; they can't project that far. With the Coens I always felt the most freedom to do what I wanted and have them accept that it might work.

Where were the interiors for Blood Simple *created?*

We couldn't afford a studio. Everything was practical or built within a space that we found. We cleared out an old loft downtown and built Abby's apartment in it. The bar was a real working bar. It was an old dance hall, a roadhouse kind of place. In fact, it was where Elvis Presley played when he first started his career. We did a lot of cosmetic building. We built a window into the bar. We cleared out the back room where they stored all of the soda and built Marty's office within it.

The pièce de résistance of Blood Simple *is the climax when Frances Mc-Dormand traps M. Emmet Walsh by slamming a window down on his arm and stabbing his hand into the frame. Through all this, Walsh manages to fire his gun through the wall of the adjoining room while the bullet holes appear in bolts of laser-like light. How did you create the set for this scene?*

We found a garage in a storage place where we also had production offices. It was really like being in the back room of someone's basement. The outside of the building was the opening of the garage door. I built a brick wall with two windows. There was nothing out there, just open space. We built the interior of the room and the bathroom in the adjacent apartment inside the garage. They were three-walled sets built right next to each other, so the bullet wall was the joining wall. We knew we had to make so many bullet holes and we had to keep doing it. I said, "We've got to use dental plaster, because we can dry it in thirty seconds." I was also the scenic artist on the job with another person. We made an area for the hand to punch through. We filled the holes with dust and plaster, then squibbed them so they would go boom, boom, boom. For each take we would quickly redo the wall with dental plaster, paint it really fast, and then dry it with hair dryers.

The bathroom was just a small set. They were very cheap sets to build. That's part of the storyboard process. We knew what we needed. As you get higher on the ladder, everyone's into the luxury of "Well, we're not quite sure how we're going to shoot this," so you build five extra rooms. The Coens are very precise; you know exactly what you have to do, so you just do it. You save money and do it right.

J. Todd Anderson is credited as storyboard artist on Raising Arizona. *What was your involvement in that process?*

None at all. The Coens don't storyboard the way a set's going to look. It's just a time for them to have some free thought and to block their shots. They just storyboard shot to shot, so they know there's a gun in this shot and he's going to put it down on a table. That helps me. I know the table is very important, but I don't know what the rest of the room looks like from the board.

When does the storyboard process take place?

That's done during the preproduction process at the same time I'm designing sets. Everything is done all at once, which is great, because they might come up with a storyboard idea that is reflected in a location we've found. It's all happening at once; they're off in a room doing the storyboard by themselves, but there are checks every day about what we found, how we're building something, and does it work for the idea. So that whole process is more cohesive than in most filmmaking. Preproduction is so important, and that's the way it should be, because you save money on the back end if you do it well ahead of time.

Why did the Coens set Raising Arizona *in Arizona?*

Ethan and Joel were trying to think of places in America they could go to that had a weird look. The cactus said it was a weird place just with that shape which we used a lot. They knew they wanted a place where this couple could get a starter home. Arizona is the epitome of beginning the American Dream. They knew they had to be near the Sun Belt and had to go someplace that could support a film group coming in. The people of Scottsdale, Arizona, were very, very good to us. Compared to *Blood Simple*, we did a lot of stage work. Almost every interior was a set. The downstairs of the Arizona house was a real house, but almost everything else in the film is a set. We had three stages out in Carefree, Arizona, where *The Dick Van Dyke Show* used to shoot. It was a vacant set of soundstages, and we could afford it. We had a shop set up there, so everything was in one place. It was great for me, because I had sets going on the three stages all the time, and we would just bounce back and forth.

Nathan Arizona is the unfinished furniture king. How did that element of his character influence what his personal space should look like?

He loved Arizona, so we tried to get in that whole Southwest theme. The crib for the babies came out of Nathan's love for raw wood. There were a lot of raw wood trims in the doorways and hallways, but at the same time, it's that tacky nouveau-riche kind of furniture. This is a guy with a lot of money to burn. He was doing the best he could for his wife and wanted her to have all the things that she wanted. They had odd taste, but they spent a lot of money on it. For a lot of the furnishings in their house, we went to the Designer Showcase in Phoenix. It was all there; people really get this stuff. I didn't invent a lot of it; we just put it together in a form to make it funnier than people would in their homes.

Where did you get the idea for the look of the nursery in Raising Arizona?

It's just my wildest fantasy of a kid's room. I was figuring that Nathan and Florence wanted to do the best they could for their children because they waited so long, and they went over the top. Again it was done with no money, trying to find locally what was applicable. We found a toy company that would give us these huge overstuffed toys. There were five kids—five of everything. As soon as you get into that scale, you've got to go over the top.

The nursery is very bright and cheery with the sky and clouds painted on the walls. On the wall behind the large wooden crib that holds all five babies is a mural which at first seems to fit in with the rest of the room with its bright colors, but on a closer look, there are images of tormented baby faces. What was the reason for this?

I found a lot of children's storybooks and went through them. If you pull out ten children's books, some are so pretty and sweet, and some are really kind of mysterious. There's an evil side, and it starts to make you wonder. I found old illustrations that were horrific, but they were in children's books, and I thought that was another whole side to parenthood. I wanted to explain that as much as parenthood is a wonderful thing, kidnapping is a horrible thing. You have wonderful little kids, but you also have the weird point of view from the adult characters— older people projecting their personalities onto babies. Here was this wonderful joyous place, a beautiful, bouncy nursery. Overall, if you looked at the whole mural, it looked just pleasing and colorful, but once you saw these ghostly babies, you realized it was disturbing.

Did the design of the nursery evolve from your original concept?

It's funny, with Ethan and Joel, every original concept I've ever had for an idea always became that place. There was never a question. We all hit it on the nose from the beginning, so we never really moved that far from the original ideas.

Randall "Tex" Cobb plays Leonard Smalls, a larger-than-life villain always dressed in khaki and covered with dirt. He doesn't have a space of his own. He is almost always on his motorcycle, which is also khaki and dirty. What was your involvement with what he and the motorcycle should look like?

I had done a Broadway show with the costume designer, Richard Hornung, who I brought to meet Joel and Ethan on *Raising Arizona*. Richard and I love working together. We both came up with the idea that since this creature didn't have a home, his bike was his home. It was all one thing; whatever the bike was had to be what he was also. He became one organic creature of the desert, wearing animal skins and moving down the road. Everything else in the movie was very surreal. The way people live out there in Arizona is very weird. Everything is dotted like the trailer park; everything is for the moment. Tex was the most organic thing in the movie. He was there driving around in circles for two thousand years. That was the feeling we were going after.

There is a scene where John Goodman and William Forsythe escape from prison by pushing their bodies up through the ground emerging through a sea of mud. How was this achieved?

We dug a hole and put in a big platform. John Goodman and William

Forsythe are big guys, so it was a big hole. We made an opening out of plastic that they could push up through. We got the idea from a dog kennel door. Then we glopped on a foot of special effects goop and mud. The platform was braced, and the guys were underneath. There was enough room in there for people to be under John to push him up, which was no easy feat. They were being pushed up through there, so it gave that feeling of coming out of a woman's uterus and down the canal. The goop has a mucousy base to it, like a cellulose, that helped us with the whole idea of birth. It was raining, and that helped disguise a lot of it. It was harder for them to shoot it than it was to build.

Patty Hearst is the true story of the newspaper heiress who was held captive by the Symbionese Liberation Army. How did you plan the interiors?

We knew where they really were; that's documented. I went to San Francisco at the beginning of the preproduction and looked around. Every place was very boring. I said to the director, Paul Schrader, "They're like apartments that anyone could live in; they're closets anyone could use to hang their clothes." We decided rather than doing the audience's point of view of where she was, we would do her point of view. It was a very easy switch to make, but it took hours and hours of discussion. Once we made that switch, it was very easy to then say, "Now I can do the most bizarre things I want, because we don't know where she is." That worked really well for the whole opening, which was her point of view, but in total confusion. She was brainwashed by Cinque of the SLA. That helped us present the honesty of her point of view. She never knew where she was. She still to this day doesn't know where she was, which we all believed once we did the research.

What was the conceptual thinking behind the look of the first SLA headquarters?

We got into the confusion of where she was. She was blindfolded. The worst problem in the whole film is that she spends the first third of the film in a closet. What do you do? I saw the closet where she was held in a little tract home outside of San Francisco. It had big, yellow, flowered, sixties wallpaper on it. The SLA wanted the closet to be soundproof, so they hung blankets up and down the closet. I thought, "I can't do this; people are going to think I'm out of my mind." That's when we came up with the idea of what is in her mind. What is it that she sees? The door opening was the idea that all she sees is the door opening and someone coming at her. I worked with the costume designer, Richard Hornung, and we did strange things with people's silhouettes, so that as the audience, we were still a little confused—"What is she seeing there?" We tried to throw it back to the audience, so they were with her in the closet with the door opening and closing. We built four closets to accommodate shots. They were all sets with a rear projection screen. We just lit the silhouettes with a bright light. I knew that after a while, as an actress, Natasha Richardson needed something to do in the closet. I kept thinking of what someone could do sitting in a closet for that long that would just keep their mind going. I thought that instead of having the wallpaper, I would give her something to pick at. We came up with a carpeting insulation that was rubberized on the outside and horsehair on the inside, which the SLA easily could have found on the street. There are scenes where you see her picking at it. That's all she could do.

Once they let her take the blindfold off, then we got into a real space where there was some architecture, and that was the first apartment Patty Hearst remembers being in. Prior to that, every place really didn't have an architecture. We tried to come up with notions of what the audience expected the places to look like. People think brainwashing occurs in bunkers, so we came up with the raked room to give the SLA a bunker feeling. The room with the holes is the visual confusion. There's another room where we finally put a pole in the middle, so there was some visual element to grab onto. Then we took the step into the apartment, which was still not all real, but there were some window shapes. Then we progressed architecturally to get into a complete apartment with a kitchen. That's where the SLA cooked, did their calisthenics, and where the majority of the brainwashing happened.

The wall and floor textures were very intriguing and contributed to the mystery of not knowing where she was.

That was a decision that Bojan Bazelli, who did the photography, and I made. As we moved further along, I created more texture to see. A lot of that is my scenic art background. I can come up with a million and one textures that are fun to look at. Of all the things I've done, *Patty Hearst* was the most fun mesh of theater and film. They were like mini-theater sets that we shot. We had them all laid out in a lane all over the soundstage.

You created a good sense of the early seventies period with the materials that were used to cover over the windows.

It was a period of horrible manmade fabrics like polyester. The SLA didn't have any money. The window treatments were junky fabrics they might have stolen, found in the garbage or at the Salvation Army. I picked certain fabrics because of their lighting quality, but also for their period value.

The lighting of a set is always critical, but this film is an excellent example of how lighting and design work together to create a specific environment.

We had to know how much light we wanted to see in each place and how we wanted to see it, because light was so important to her. Part of the problem in *Patty Hearst* was that we were in dark rooms for almost the whole film, so I had to come up with enough choices to keep the audience interested in the spaces. That gets tedious. Window drapes worked for a while, then we started switching to wall colors and just any kind of combination to keep the audience interested, because they get bored very quickly.

What was it like to design the Western Young Guns?

Young Guns was the most fun I've ever had making a film. It was difficult physically, because it's hard to be outside building for that long, but it was everyone's dream come true to be able to do a Western. It was fun to research, because from 1870 to 1910 Mexico was the most active part of our nation in terms of settlements being started. The architectural research had to be accurate.

Did you build that whole town?

We were offered all the wild west towns from *Silverado.* Pure to the research, I said in my rebellious state, "This is not what happened in this part of the country. This is what happened in Colorado." Billy the Kid lived in Lincoln, New Mexico, which was a town where there was some money, and you had the first adobe and concrete influence in America. We couldn't go to Lincoln, because it had been redone and it was a little more modern. We went on the great search for a town in New Mexico, and I found three choices. We ended up with a little town outside of Santa Fe called Cerrios. Dean Semler is such a renegade DP, he's a real road movie guy on horseback. We knew we had to accommodate his camera shots, and Cerrios had a great main street. When we came into the town as a major motion picture, the people were wonderful, but we threw them for a loop. I mean, we just tore their place apart. We took their buildings as a basis, built on top of them, added all around them, and created our town. I had thirty carpenters working in five-degree weather for three months. It was hard, but everyone loved doing it.

The town you designed has a more realistic look than what we usually see in a Western.

Most Western sets are cluttered up with little window shapes. We were being true to the rounder stucco feeling with stonework you could create and surface. It was softer to look at; ours were soft stone faces. Hardwood planking clutters the frame, because there's a lot to look at. We purposely painted and washed a lot of it and kept it soft and monochromatic, so it was all very subtle. We really had no color in that whole film; we usually went up to the costumes for the most color. They were still very muted, but you got a plum or a maroon in there, and they really had to matter. My work was creating the landscape, how poetic and beautiful that part of the country is. Nothing intrudes on the architecture. The basis of what you're finally seeing on the screen is the actor's face; you don't want to get in the way too much.

An important part of your job is dealing with practical light sources. This was a period where there was no electric light. How do you work with the director of photography on what and where the light sources should be?

Dean Semler is a purist, so if we wanted to see daylight, I had to be able to put cracks in things. They didn't have insulation. They stuck rags in between boards for insulation. There was one scene in a bar along the river where we knew we wanted it to be mysterious, so we purposely let the cuts of light come from in between the planks. If we wanted something to be soft and romantic, like Yen Sun's room, we just had one window filled with moonlight. Oil lamps could brighten up the whole room, or they could just create one corner and be very Flemish looking. A lot of it is coordinating the mood with the tone I painted the wall. Dean could just light it with a soft globe of yellow light, and that becomes very intimate. If you want it to be brighter and you don't want that intimacy, you brighten the wall color, and the reflection of the oil lamp against that is a very different feeling.

Was When Harry Met Sally . . . *scheduled differently because it covers several seasons of New York exterior locations?*

Yes. One of the big problems we have in this business right now is L.A. producers saying, "Oh, you can't shoot in New York anymore; you've got to do it all in L.A." When we did *When Harry Met Sally . . . ,* Rob Reiner thought we were going to shoot it all in L.A. and just come to New York for two weeks. It was being done through Columbia, who basically was saying, "No, no, no, you don't want to shoot fall in New York, because the leaves may fall off the trees before you get there. It may be too cold." I said to Rob, "This film is about people in love in New York City, and the most beautiful time in Central Park is in the fall." So the location manager and I brought Rob here in the summer. We took him to all of the most beautiful places in New York and said, "Oh, you should see this in the fall!" Basically, what I did was brainwash him into believing that he had to be here in the fall. The film was being done by Rob's company, Castle Rock. Rob is the boss of the company, and he said, "Okay, we're shooting in New York," and that was that.

What was your design concept for Ghost?

When you read Bruce Joel Rubin's script, you realized that it was a medieval morality play. In Sam, the Patrick Swayze character, Bruce created the "Everyman" that every person wants to be. Our world was heaven and hell and middle earth. Sam and Molly, the Demi Moore character, loved each other so much, they wanted to create a wonderful home together. In their loft they created a step to heaven, so that someday when they both died, they were going to look back and say, "We had the most wonderful life on earth, and now we are on our way to heaven." That's how we came up with the idea of the steps and the

riser going up; those were the steps to heaven. They are strange metaphors, but they gave us something to hang on. We had an enormous
preproduction on that film. My preproduction was four or five months.
The director, Jerry Zucker, knew there was so much to figure out about
this story. Everyone came on early, and we all had dialogue back and
forth. The producers, Jerry Zucker, Bruce Joel Rubin, Adam Greenberg,
the DP, and I would sit and talk and talk about these characters; it paid
off.

*Sam is a ghost through most of the film. This required many special effects
shots created by Industrial Light and Magic. How did you work with them?*

We had to come up with a set that accommodated all of the effects.
ILM and my department had a great rapport. A lot of times we were
able to help them figure something out with an architectural solution,
like sliding a wall out on tracks. It has to be an enormous collaboration.
For me, the more successful projects I've been on have been the ones
when people forget how much money they make and sit down and
collaborate as artists—that's what it's supposed to be about.

Do you have your own research files?

Yes, I have a big library of books at home. I have a dabbling of everything—period, style, and contemporary—so that if I'm starting a project,
I can at least get a jump on the research at home. I have a lot of books
of photographs, which are the basis for almost every film I do. When
you look at photography books, you see the photographer's point of
view. They are dealing with a frame the way we do in film, and they're
also dealing with a real passionate moment. A lot of times you can grab
something from some photograph, and it will give you a feeling you
can then show to a director. It's a frame of reference, and from there I
can see how far a director is willing to go. You could pick a really wild
photograph and then pick something much more conservative and give
the director a balance. I also keep file folders of pictures of rooms I
constantly rip out of magazines. I read a lot of magazines from all over
the world. There may be something in a room like a chair or the way
they painted a wall, and then I think, "Oh, that would be good to do
somewhere, sometime," and lo and behold, it always comes up.

What designers have influenced you the most?

I just looked at Polly Platt's work with Peter Bogdanovich on *The Last
Picture Show* and *Paper Moon* and thought, "This person has created the
environment for this film to exist." That's the epitome of the director
and the designer creating a movie.

*Do you think that technological advances will change the nature of your job
in the future?*

No, a film like *Ghost* states that you can take all this really wonderful
technology and make it accessible and real to people. It's still an ap-

prenticeship profession. It's still a very honest profession for people to get into. The craftspeople I work with are the most honest people I've ever met in my life. The scenic artists, the carpenters are all real crafts-people in their own right. They're what keeps it pure. People still have to do all of it, and that's never going to change. The only thing that will change is what you use for materials; the process is still the same.

18

Wynn Thomas

Wynn Thomas studied stage design at Boston University and worked in the theater for a ten-year period that included several seasons as a designer for the Negro Ensemble Company. After entering the union, he worked as a designer on several *ABC After School Specials* and tried to break into feature film designing. At one of the union meetings, Thomas met Richard Sylbert, who was in New York designing *The Cotton Club*. The relationship led to Thomas's first professional experience in features.

While working as art director for production designer Patrizia Von Brandenstein on *Beat Street*, Thomas met Spike Lee and formed a collaborative relationship that has continued through six films.

Wynn Thomas's production design of *She's Gotta Have It, School Daze, Do the Right Thing, Mo' Better Blues,* and *Jungle Fever* forms a triumvirate with Spike Lee's directorial vision and Ernest Dickerson's evocative cinematography. The design of Nola Darling's altar-like bed, Sal's old-world pizzeria textured with decorative sheet metal, the skyline that rises above the jazz club Beneath The Underdog, and the Taj Mahal of crack houses contribute to the cumulative power of Spike Lee's films.

In addition to his collaborations with Spike Lee, Wynn Thomas has designed two films for Robert Townsend, *Eddie Murphy Raw* and *The Five Heartbeats.* He has worked in the art department on *Beat Street, Brighton Beach Memoirs, The Money Pit, The Package,* and *Homeboy.* Currently he is designing *Malcolm X* for Spike Lee.

1984 *Beat Street* (art director with production designer Patrizia Von Brandenstein)

1986 *She's Gotta Have it*

    The Money Pit (assistant art director with production designer Patrizia Von Brandenstein)

1987 *Brighton Beach Memoirs* (assistant art director with production designer Stuart Wurtzel)

    Eddie Murphy Raw

1988 *School Daze*

1989 *Do the Right Thing*

    The Package (art director with production designer Michael Levesque)

    Homeboy (art director with production designer Brian Morris)

1990 *Mo' Better Blues*

1991 *Jungle Fever*

    The Five Heartbeats

1992 *Malcolm X*

How did you get your start in the film business?

I went to Boston University to study stage design, and when I came out, I worked in the theater for about ten years. Initially, I painted scenery for a couple of years, then I came to New York and worked for the Negro Ensemble Company as a set designer for a few seasons. During that time I was in the process of taking the union exam. I passed the test on my second try, and I began to look for movie work. It took me about two years before I got onto my first film, but during that time I worked on a couple of *ABC After School Specials*. Those are kind of the summer stock of the film industry. I went to a union meeting, and at that meeting was Dick Sylbert. He had been in New York for a few months working on *The Cotton Club*. So the next day, I called him up and said, "Do you remember me? I was the black guy at the union meeting the other day." At that time, there were no black folks doing this kind of work, so of course he remembered me. I said, "Look, I have a proposition for you; I've been trying to work my way into the film industry, and I've had a very difficult time. Could you please just take a look at my portfolio? I would like to volunteer and work on your film, so I can get this as a film credit." I had an interview with him, and he said, "I don't have any positions available at this time, but I'd be happy to bring you on as a volunteer."

I had my interview on a Thursday, and on Monday I went in. They had already started constructing the Cotton Club, and when Dick came in, he took me around the set. He spent a lot of time just talking to me about how things should be done. He gave me a master class. It was really wonderful. We went back to his office, and I started looking through some books to do some research for him. The phone kept ringing. It was Monday, so it's very busy as it is in everyone's life, but particularly in the lives of production designers. I was asked to leave the office for a couple of the calls that came in. I kept saying to myself, "Gee, how's this ever going to work out? It's my first day, and I'm already in the way." The production manager came in and said, "Francis is in Japan, and when he comes back, he's going to want models of the Cotton Club and of the various sets." So Sylbert called in his art director and said, "Find me somebody to build me these models." Meanwhile the conversation is getting very intense; obviously it's something that I shouldn't be hearing. So Dick said, "Wynn, I'm sorry, but you're going to have to leave the office." I went back out to the Cotton Club set. I was standing there, and I was feeling, "God, this is terrible; I feel so in the way." I was completely embarrassed to be there. A few minutes later, Sylbert came out and said to me, "Do you make models?" I said, "Yes, I make models." He said, "Why don't we hire you to make these models." So on my very first day of being a volunteer, I was hired, and a job that was supposed to go on for two weeks stretched into six months. That job led to another job, and I really haven't been out of work since. So that's how I got my start in the film industry—because of Dick Sylbert.

How did you meet Spike Lee?

I was working as the art director on *Beat Street* for production designer Patrizia Von Brandenstein. Spike had come into the office to interview for the coffee fetching position of assistant to the director. He was just one of several people they were interviewing for that spot. A friend of his was a production assistant in the art department, so he had come into our office to visit her. When he saw me there, he said, "Wow, I didn't even know there were any black people doing art direction." I said "Well, there's me. I know that there's me." At that point, we struck up a friendship and stayed in touch with each other. That summer, we started work on a picture called *Messenger*. We had two weeks preproduction but closed on the Friday before the Monday we were supposed to start shooting. The producer pulled his money out of the project. The following summer, we were supposed to do *Messenger* again, but Spike couldn't use the same grant funding and he couldn't raise the money. So he said, "Look, I have this small script called *She's Gotta Have It*. Let's do that instead."

That's how we ended up doing *She's Gotta Have It*. It was hell working on that project because there was no money. There was $800 for the art department. I ended up asking all of my friends to come in and help. It was difficult for me, because at the time I was an assistant art director on *Brighton Beach Memoirs*. Stuart Wurtzel was production designer. I was doing double duty. I would come in and do Spike's work early in the morning. We built everything, painted all the scenery. I sewed drapes—I did everything—then I would rush off to work. The other assistants in the art department on *Brighton Beach Memoirs* kept saying, "What are you doing? You're risking your job here. How can you possibly be going off doing all these other things?" I just had an instinctual feeling about Spike. I knew that he could write, and for me it was an investment. Of course, that movie went on to make history. It was an investment that paid off.

What was your approach toward designing She's Gotta Have It *in black and white?*

I tried to think in terms of grays, blacks, and whites. I worked with contrasting tones. Essentially, most of the things I chose were blacks, whites, and variations of grays, so I could look at something and see if there was enough contrast there.

Was Nola's loft a practical space?

Yes, it was. The building was right at the base of the Brooklyn Bridge. It was a space above the Ferrybank Restaurant, which was owned by a black businessman who was very kind to us but who had no idea of the type of film we were making. In fact, we used to call the film "Nola Darling," because we didn't want him to know that we were making a movie about a woman and her sexual conquests. The room was filled with all of the restaurant's stuff, so we had to get rid of everything. It was a very frustrating space, because there were wonderful large windows which we couldn't open. So it always felt like it was 100 degrees on the inside. We shot there for almost two weeks.

An important design element in She's Gotta Have It *is Nola Darling's bed. How did that concept develop?*

For me, the bed was the most important element in her apartment. It was a very special place for her. I felt it almost had to be like an altar. My design influence was an oriental fan shape for the headboard. There had to be an architectural element that said, "This is where I feel most comfortable, this is my safe haven, this is my place. I love this bed." So I ended up designing a very simple open-framed headboard, and I placed a lot of candles around it.

We can see in the film that the candles were attached to inverted nails in the wooden headboard. Had you gone through other possibilities of how the candles could be attached to the headboard?

No, that was the simplest and most practical thing to do. It was like, "What would Nola do?" You couldn't have been too sophisticated, because it's almost as if she had built the bed frame and put those inverted nails there. So it becomes an extension of the character herself.

Being an artist yourself, it must have been interesting to design a space for Nola, who was a paste-up artist.

It made it easier. Part of the problem on that film was we didn't have any money, so I really could not dress the space the way I felt it needed to be dressed. I brought in all my own art supplies. You have to think what is going to give you the proper impression with the least amount of items. That's what we tried to do on that film. It was difficult; we never had everything we needed. The table in the Thanksgiving dinner scene was never dressed properly. We just couldn't get the stuff, and I didn't have that type of thing in my apartment.

That must have forced you to think in terms of simplicity. Obviously, for Thanksgiving you need a turkey.

Right. We had just the elements essential to make the scene work, but not always the elements that would make it beautiful.

In addition to designing the opening sketch of Eddie Murphy Raw, *what was your involvement with the concert section of the film?*

I chose the curtains that Eddie performed in front of. Actually, it's interesting, because those curtains are very simple, but an army of people were part of that choice. "Is this right? Is this wrong?" I wanted to go with something a little flashier, but they were very afraid that it would be too Las Vegas, so I chose a royal plum to be behind Mr. Murphy. That's not a very big design picture, but what I think people forget is that everything you see is chosen! Someone makes a choice. That's what we do. Even something as simple as choosing some curtains involves other people and sometimes a compromise, as it did in that case.

Where was School Daze *shot?*

We used the main courtyard in front of Atlanta University, which is five colleges sharing a series of different campuses in Atlanta, Georgia. We used actual dorms. I built the frat house interior and several other sets. The set for the coronation sequence was constructed elsewhere and brought into the Martin Luther King Auditorium at Morehouse College.

Did you have an overall color concept for School Daze?

The color concept came about because we were making a musical, and the sets were not going to be realistic. Everything was a stylized realism. Therefore, it was alright to have an extremely colorful palette. Every script affects me from an emotional point of view. My gut emotional response to a script is almost always communicated through my use of color. I can't explain to you in concrete terms how the color choices are made. Those choices vary from job to job. It's just a gut emotional response to the rhythms and feelings in the script. Ironically, color is usually the last decision that I make. The birthing process is difficult. I almost always decide on architectural line and texture before deciding on color.

What research did you do to design the president's office, and where was it created?

We went to a few offices of the presidents of the universities down there, and we chose one that was an actual president's office. We re-dressed it to make it look more like a president's office; they have a tendency to be undressed. There is reality, and then there is movie reality. So we had to come in and put more pictures up on the wall and make things look presidential, as opposed to someone's working office.

Do you find you're dealing more with the audience's perceptions, what they expect to see, rather than the reality, what really is there?

I think so. People do not go to the movies to see reality; otherwise all films would be documentaries. Everything is exaggerated in the film industry. This is how filmmakers alter our perception of ourselves—by controlling the reality that's up on the screen. Sometimes you see unbelievable things when you're scouting locations, and you say, "God, if I were to put that up there, they would never believe it." So it can work both ways. For example, I softened the look of the Italian home in *Jungle Fever*. In most of the research, I found those houses can be very ornate. I simplified the decor in that home, because I didn't want to perpetuate a stereotype. I did not want to say this group of people designed their homes this way all the time. I felt I had to simplify their home so that we would have some information about them and it wouldn't be determined by other people's preconditioned thinking about how working class Italians live. People do come to the movies with their own perceptions, and one of the things you want to work against are those stereotypes.

How did you develop the design of Madame Re-Re's beauty salon for the "Straight and Nappy" musical number in School Daze?

That was a very difficult set to design. Spike's father wrote the music for the film. We were told we were going to get a classic, musical-theater, West Side Story-type number, but instead we got this jazzy musical number that no one expected. The only thing that Spike said to me was that it should be in a beauty parlor and he wanted oversized props, which I rejected right away because they're very expensive to do. I couldn't design a real beauty parlor, because it's a musical number. So I began looking at carnival settings, and the shapes that I chose came out of carnival settings. The color decisions for that set came out of the fact that Spike had already chosen the jerseys the Wannabees and the Jigaboos were going to wear. I hated both of them, but at that point there was nothing I could do about it, so I had to choose a color palette that would complement both costume colors and would help them stand out. As a result, I chose very vibrant colors to work in contrast to those costumes.

Did you screen a lot of musicals prior to designing the set, or did you have a good working knowledge of the genre?

We had a good working knowledge. Spike, myself, and the cinematographer, Ernest Dickerson, all have a very strong sense of those fifties musicals. We did look at *An American in Paris*. Spike and Ernest like looking at other films before they start a movie; I don't. I don't like to have my own thoughts influenced by something else that I've seen. We all borrow from each other all the time in this business, but when I'm about to sit down and do something, I don't want to say, "Oh, I saw this; let me use it here." I like to think that it's either being generated by the research or maybe it's in my sense memory. If it's there, fine, I can still regurgitate it, and the idea becomes mine as opposed to a direct borrow from someone else. If it's in your head, hopefully it's going to come out as your own voice.

Do the Right Thing takes place on the hottest day of the year, which becomes a metaphor for the emotional heat of all the people who live in the neighborhood. How did you translate that metaphor into the design of the film?

I wanted to find a block where people could not escape from the heat. If there were no trees on the block, you couldn't sit under a tree; there's no shade to escape. When it's so hot, most people don't stay in their houses, they sit on the stoops, but even if you sit on the stoop, you're being exposed to all the sun and heat, which lends to the tension. People are all out in the street and observing things that are going on. We tried to find a street that was deserted like a desert. That certainly affects the color choice you make in warm colors or hot colors like red. It affected my choices in making the inside of the pizzeria all warm, desert-type colors. Then of course, there's the red wall, which connotes heat, fire, and many things for many different people.

The three men known as the Corner Men sit on chairs in front of that bright red wall and discuss many of the goings-on in the film. Did you paint that wall red, and how did you arrive at the color?

Oh, yes, absolutely, that's definitely a design choice. Because we were only going to be on this one block for the length of the picture, one of my fears about *Do the Right Thing* was that there wouldn't be enough visual elements to keep the audience interested. So I began to try and find ways to bring color to the picture. I painted the tops of steps. I put a few flowers out on the sidewalk. I painted the wall red as one of those choices. I said to Spike, "I'm thinking of painting the wall red." He said, "Like what, fire engine red?" and I said, "Yes, about the brightest red that we can possibly get." He said, "Oh, great, good idea," and that's how the brightness of the red came about. Who's to say if I would have painted it so red if Spike hadn't said fire engine red. I probably would have painted it red, but with his approval, we made a choice that was blatantly theatrical. It was an effort to sneak some color into the picture, and I think that wall took on a lot of symbolism for people during the course of the film.

Spike's work is very theatrical in its feeling and its intentions. You can't design his films realistically. You can't approach them that way, particularly *Do the Right Thing*, which has such a theatrical premise. It all takes place in a twenty-four hour time period; it was like Elmer Rice's

Street Scene or *Porgy and Bess* in that everything is there and converges during the course of the story towards the climax. Choices have to come out of the need to support the characters visually. Spike's work has always stimulated my theatrical impulses, and a lot of the use of color comes from that. It's like you're flicking a paint brush—"Let me use some color here"—to take the story away from reality.

What was your concept behind the design for Sal's Famous Pizzeria?

My idea on Sal's Pizzeria was that this was something Sal would have constructed with his own hands. His character eventually says, "I built this with my own hands." So it would not have been a place where there were just Formica counters and very simple tables. It had to reflect an environment this man had labored over, nurtured, and cared about for many decades. The choices were made to reflect Sal.

Did the idea of using tin on the walls come out of your research? In the fifties many pizzerias were decorated that way. You don't find it in contemporary pizza places.

Yes, I wanted it to feel like the store had been there for a very long time and that Sal had been there to watch the transition of the neighborhood. That became very important to me. In my research I found using decorative sheet metal is often an element you will see in older neighborhoods around New York. I went up to Coney Island and other sections to look at some interesting pizza places. Some of the stores had that element there. It's also just a wonderful texture to use in a film.

Were the pictures of the Italian celebrities that make up Sal's "Wall of Fame" indicated in the script?

There were a few people mentioned in the script, like Frank Sinatra and Al Pacino. The picture of Rocky Graziano came from John Turturro; he wanted that up there. Spike mentioned a few, and then I went out and gathered the rest of them—people who I thought were appropriate. At the top of the wall were Al Pacino, Liza Minnelli, and Frank Sinatra. When Danny Aiello came onto the set, he came over to me and said, "You know, you've chosen all my very best friends to be at the top of this wall. This is perfect!" For him it was a very telling moment, as if he or Sal had chosen them. It was like I had been to his house and asked him, "Who do you think should be up there?" I'll never forget him coming up to me and saying that.

Was Sal's Famous Pizzeria a practical location?

It was built on Stuyvesant Street and Gates. We needed to have two vacant lots, because I knew I had to build the pizzeria, and the Korean market had to be directly across the street from it in terms of the ground plan. Korean markets don't exist in the Bedford Stuyvesant section of Brooklyn, so we knew that we had to build that. I had to find a street that had two vacant lots with no trees and some architectural elements that would imply that the houses were once very nice but had begun to decay. I was also looking for a street that had many vacancies, because we didn't want to displace too many people, since we were going to be there for a very long time. So we found a street in which almost half the buildings were vacant, and I fixed them all up to make them look inhabited.

Did you have to do a lot of work to refurbish the exteriors of the brownstones?

Yes, because a lot of them looked like they had skin disease. We had to come in and paint the fronts. Some of the detail had fallen away, so it was a major rehab job. There was a lot of work, because there was a lot of structural damage to the exteriors. We ended up fixing all of that and adjusting the color so it was correct. People don't realize that when they look at the film. They're not supposed to realize that.

I'm sure most people think that you found that street just the way it is.

Exactly. The radio station was in an abandoned building. We knocked out some walls, fixed up the ground floor, and completely altered the front of it so the radio station could be there. It was a building with a very leaky roof. Whenever it would rain, it would rain on our set. That was a problem, but the audience never knew it.

The jazz club, Beneath The Underdog, in Mo' Better Blues *is a major set. How did the design come about?*

We didn't start working on *Mo' Better Blues* until the spring, and I got a call from Spike on New Year's Day to talk about the film. He said, "You know, we're doing this jazz picture, and you should start researching jazz clubs." Spike said, "I want to be able to move from one space to another space without interrupting the camera movement, so you should connect all of the rooms." That was essentially my jumping off point. I did go around to several existing jazz clubs. They're all very small, they're very grimy, they're very dark, and I knew I didn't want to do that. I knew I would want to design a club that had lots of color to go against tradition, because jazz films have a tendency to tell stories about people performing in dark basements.

There were a couple of other things that influenced the design decisions. Ernest and Spike love using the Louma crane for high-angle work. I always found that other jazz films were so confining in their use of physical space. Jazz is a fluent music. I decided to do a two-story club, so that the music could breathe and live in the space and so I could move the camera fluently in that space. Beneath The Underdog implies that something is underground. The cityscape around the top of the club came out of the idea that I felt these people would exist beneath the city, and I wanted to supply them with something visual to support that idea. I didn't want to do a mural around them. I said, "Wow, what if I make it into something that we could light and change; that would be interesting." That ended up being the design element that influenced all the color changes you see during the course of the film. I looked at a lot of research of nightclubs from the twenties and thirties, and the key word there is nightclub—I stopped calling it a jazz club and started calling it a jazz nightclub. Generally, I will make up a story about the people I'm designing a set for. This club was owned by Moe and Joe Flatbush, and I decided that they inherited it from their father, which means this club would have come to its peak in the late thirties or early forties. Therefore, it was alright to use an Art Deco influence. I began to look at Art Deco shapes and elements. It was in mixing everything together that I came up with the design.

Although Mo' Better Blues *takes place in a contemporary time frame, it has a period feel about it. There's the Art Deco influence you've mentioned and some of the clothes have a zoot suit look.*

That's intentional, because in addition to the nightclub, each set was from a different time period. Bleek's loft is very much like a sixties loft in the sense that people lived in simply furnished space, and only the essentials were there. I used decor straight out of the fifties to dress Giant's apartment. What I was hoping to do from a conceptual point of view was to mix all these different time periods, which would give the film a sense of timelessness but not confine it to any one period. So it had a period feeling without being stuck in any one period. Also, the screenplay very much felt like a forties movie to me. That was one of the reasons I said, "This feels like a period film, so I'm going to use these elements that are really from another time but put them in a contemporary setting!"

Where was the set for Beneath The Underdog built?

We built it at Empire Sound Stages, which is in Long Island City. We built the club on the main stage there. It took about three months to build.

There are several different parts of the club set. How were they laid out on the stage?

It was all connected. You could literally walk from the top of the club where the owners' offices and the balcony were, walk down the stairs into the bathroom, and then walk into the kitchen. You could descend into the club area and then walk backstage to the dressing room. You could literally travel through the whole set and not ever leave the club. Conceptually, I wanted the audience to come into a space that was darker—the blue hallway—and then enter a space that was filled with lots of color.

That design must have really given Spike Lee a lot of directorial possibilities.

It was a huge toy for him. Everyone was trying to find ways to use the different parts of the set. Once it's there, all you can do is let them exist in it and play with it. It was a fun project; I liked doing it very much.

How did you design the personal spaces of the characters to help define who they were?

Both Spike and myself felt that Indigo, being a proper school teacher, a traditionalist, lived in a lovely, ornate, brownstone-type of space and would have very beautiful things. I did find a wonderful house up in Harlem that didn't need any restoration from us. It was simply a matter of coming in and painting a few things and dressing it so it looked appropriate. It was a space that had lots of architectural sculpture; the moldings and the exteriors walls were all very good. We didn't see very much of Clarke's space, so we really didn't have time to establish much. When you don't see much, I think it's important to say a lot about a character as quickly as possible. Sometimes you have to go with an obvious choice. Since she was a singer, we dressed the apartment with the things a singer would have, like portraits of the people that would have been her influences. I also had to do the same thing with Shadow Henderson. We were going to see his apartment for a very brief moment, and I had to be able to say something about him quick! *Mo' Better Blues* is the story of people who are very different from each other. Bleek, played by Denzel Washington, is coming from a traditional point of view, and Shadow Henderson, played by Wesley Snipes, is a nonconformist who is trying to get what he can get from the business. I chose a space for Shadow Henderson that was more modern. I decided to paint the mural in his bedroom, because it says something about how he felt about his bedroom. It also was a theatrical choice that fit in with the rest of the picture. Hopefully, it made a statement about this man's character—who he was in relationship to his bedroom and the women he brought there.

Where did the concept for the crack house in Jungle Fever *come from?*

Spike originally wanted the crack house to be in a simple, boarded-up, abandoned building, and I didn't agree with that at all. I felt that it had to be in a very large space, a space with more mythical proportions. One of the many good things about Spike is that he doesn't say, "No, it has to be this way." I had written him a letter describing my whole concept of the film. That's actually what I do with him sometimes; I send him a note telling him how I'm going to approach the film. In this note I said, "All right, I will concede to your request to put the crack house in an abandoned building." However, I had my location people scout two things: large spaces and abandoned buildings. The problem with going into abandoned buildings is that all the rooms are much too small; you don't get the Taj Mahal effect—something like you've never seen before. I looked at several abandoned buildings, and I had a difficult time staging the scene. In my head as a designer, I will always stage the scene completely—where the camera angle should be and how the camera should move. I couldn't do it in abandoned buildings. I kept having to bring it outside of the building in order to give it scope. So I had the locations people look for some other large abandoned spaces. We looked at a couple of interesting spaces. We looked at the Audubon Ballroom, we looked at a vacant church up in the Bronx, and we looked at the Renaissance Ballroom, which is where we ended up shooting the crack house.

On the day of the scout, I took Spike to a place he had requested, which was an abandoned building. We went inside and walked around; there were several rooms. He hated it. In fact, he walked away from the location without saying anything. So I went back out to his car, and I said, "Look, I have something else I want to show you which is closer to the way I saw it; why don't we go and see this? I'm going to show you my Taj Mahal choice." I took him to the Renaissance Ballroom, and he absolutely loved it. That's how that choice came about. What I did was to show him his way and then to show him how I saw the scene. I'm not telling this story to say that there was a right or wrong approach, but this was an example of collaboration and of me trying to satisfy a director's vision while at the same time holding onto my own, because I think that's what collaboration is about. When Spike walked into that space, he knew it was right. He said, "This is it!" When we supply the director and the actors with something that is really appropriate and correct, it helps them with their work. It supports their work.

How do you and Spike Lee communicate about what a film should look like?

Unlike a lot of directors who feel that they have to talk through and conceptualize their scripts all the time, Spike has a tendency not to do that. He is a man of very few words. I used to always be curious about why he didn't say more, but I began to realize that Spike is also the writer of the script, and he pours his heart and soul and his passions into the script. He doesn't always feel a need to articulate, because he's already articulated it in the script. He's good enough to allow all of us to interpret the material that is there. So we kind of go and come back and say, "This is what I suggest." It used to worry me a lot, because I will design these pictures based on a ten- or fifteen-minute conversation. I think at this point he trusts my interpretation of the material. So there's no "My concept is this; my concept is that." Those type of discussions usually don't happen here.

The films you have designed for Spike Lee are particularly expressive in their use of color. Where does this generate from?

Production designers are the first people to supply cinematographers with their palette. They work with us to give the film a shape, a look, and its color. Generally, I will decide what colors I want, and I will go to both Ernest and Spike and say, "This is the color I think it should be." Ernest will not come and say, "Oh, I want to put a blue wash on it." He goes and thinks, and his creative juices get going. Sometimes it comes from me, or sometimes it comes from the environment that I supply them with. *Mo' Better Blues* is an example—that whole nightclub changes color from scene to scene. I supplied Ernest with that skylight and said, "I think it should have three color changes," and he said, "Well, let's have more changes." It becomes a collaborative process in the purest sense of the word. People have said that Ernest is responsible for bringing Technicolor back to motion pictures. I would like to get some of the credit for bringing back Technicolor to motion pictures, because it begins here in this department. You work together. As a designer, I am very conscious of light. We just chose a prison for *Malcolm X* which is a space that is dying to be lit. I chose that because I know I'm working with a photographer who's going to come in and be stimulated by the same things that I'm seeing and will use that to light the picture brilliantly.

Do you collaborate with actors?

I always talk to the actors, because they often will know things about the character I do not know. I almost always call them very early on when they are still formulating ideas and say, "Look, if you have any particular ideas or thoughts, please let me know as soon as possible." Generally, I will preface my conversation saying that I have the final veto. I find if you approach them that way, they will be very open to what you have to say. I always find they're more interested in what I have to say about their characters than in giving suggestions to me. They're almost coming to me for information about their characters. I also try to take them onto the set before they start shooting. I did this with Denzel Washington on *Mo' Better Blues*. I brought him over to the space early on to let him "live" there for a while and see all the different elements and textures in the apartment. I do think it's important to ask actors how they feel about things.

Where do you think the profession of production design is heading? Do you think that computers are the future of designing?

I do see it changing. I'm aware I need to go out and start taking classes just so I'm up on the technology of it all. I hope that people do not stop drawing and learning how to figure out things on the drafting board, because I think that will rob this business of the emotion it needs to have. I can only hope that the technology will help when it comes to planning, being efficient, and with the nonartistic elements of the business. I hope it doesn't stilt the creative or emotional elements, because art direction has to have an emotional content. If it doesn't, what good is it? It has to support the characters in the film, otherwise what good is it? Then it's just background, just something pretty.

19

Kristi Zea

A succession of experiences led Kristi Zea to the craft of film production design. After studying journalism at Columbia University in New York, she began working as a photographic stylist to a still photographer in commercial advertising. During her four years at this job, she learned the principles of organization and the myriad skills needed to conceive and execute a project. A series of freelance assignments as a stylist for television commercials led Zea to an assistant's position on *Interiors* with production designer Mel Bourne.

After this introduction to features, Zea began a successful career as a costume designer on many films. She has designed the costumes for *Fame, Endless Love, Shoot the Moon, Tattoo, Exposed, Terms of Endearment, Lovesick, Unfaithfully Yours, Beat Street, Best Defense, Birdy,* and *Silverado* and Diane Keaton's costumes in *The Little Drummer Girl*.

After working as costume designer with director Alan Parker on several films, Zea made a transition to art director on Parker's provocative film *Angel Heart*.

Since 1988, Zea has been production designer on several stylish projects, including Jonathan Demme's *Married to the Mob* and Martin Scorsese's *New York Stories* segment, as well as the critically acclaimed *GoodFellas*. In 1991 she again collaborated with Demme on the box-office smash *The Silence of the Lambs*.

Zea's highly developed color sense enables her to create an endless flow of multicolored patterns with an eclectic postmodern sense of style that has given her work a distinctive flair. Her experience as a costume designer helps to unify the details of a character's wardrobe with their environment to produce a consistent vision of the world they inhabit.

While Kristi Zea continues to develop her career as a production designer, she made her directorial debut with "Domestic Dilemma," an episode from *Women & Men II* for Home Box Office.

1986 *Lucas* (art director)

1987 *Angel Heart* (art director, with Armin Ganz)

1988 *Married to the Mob*

1989 *New York Stories* (Martin Scorsese segment, "Life Lessons")

     Miss Firecracker

1990 *GoodFellas*

1991 *The Silence of the Lambs*

     The Super

1992 *Lorenzo's Oil*

How did you become a production designer?

In the early seventies I was going to school at Columbia. I was studying to become a journalist. Then, the opportunity came across my path to be an assistant to a stylist working at Tony Petrocelli Studios, which at the time was considered to be one of the top still photography studios for commercial advertising. This sounded like a cool job, so off I went and wound up staying there for four years. I learned very quickly how incredibly precise this whole business needed to be and how very important it was to come back with a variety of choices, so the photographer, the account executive, and the advertising people all could sit around and ponder the value of a tie and decide which one they really wanted on their man who was selling soap suds. That job was really the training ground for everything I've done since. I was responsible for the entire running of the studio from the styling point of view— casting, finding locations, set designing, costume designing, and prop procurement. It was the place where I picked up all of my knowledge of organization, style, and what you need to put a picture together.

When you selected several ties to give them a choice, did you always know in your mind which one you thought was right?

Oh, yes. I would have one that I thought was the best, and there would be three or four others I thought would work. If somebody had a particular taste, I would pull a couple of those to show them. Inevitably, I was pretty good at figuring out what kinds of things were necessary— the perfect glass for liquor: there would be some Baccarat glass that they loved, but maybe it was an inch too high so you would have to get it glazed down. There would always be some specific thing they needed— this shirt was good for ring-around-the-collar commercials, but the buttons were kind of funny—"Could we get different buttons?" There was always the minutia; the detail was unbelievable. That stuck with me. I became a freelance stylist for five or six years, and I worked for a whole slew of really good commercial directors who first did print, then moved over into TV commercials, and when they did so did I. That was neat, because that exposed me to the whole film world.

Commercials are baby films. You have the same kind of crew, the same kind of needs. The job necessitated getting clothes for actors and specific props the director knew I could find. When I was doing styling, Mel Bourne, who is a fantastic production designer, was hired a lot by these commercial production companies. He'd be doing the set design. I always admired him enormously, and one day he called me up and said, "I'm doing a Woody Allen movie, *Interiors*, and I need somebody who has access to interior decoration and design showrooms." I knew the world of the D&D building, and in this particular movie one of the main characters, played by Geraldine Page, was an interior decorator. Assisting Mel was an incredible experience; I'll never forget. It taught me an enormous amount.

What do you feel is the key to being a good production designer?

The key is organization. Apart from what visual elements you put into it, it's a big coordinating job. Also, knowing how much things cost— you have to be responsible for money.

Do you like that part of the job?

Well, it's inevitable. Larry Kasdan once said to me, "Kristi, I'd hire you for every movie I do, if you can stick to a budget." There is a lot of pressure put on designers to come up with amazing looks for little money. When you try and tell them, "Well, it's not going to cost three cents; it's going to cost five," and they cannot come up with the other two, then you're faced with a real problem of how to make it happen. In some cases you can't. Oftentimes you get into a situation where the director wants the world but doesn't have the money for it. If you don't give him the world, then later he doesn't say, "Oh, she really did the best job she could for the money." Rather he says, "She's not a very good designer." I learned that on a commercial I was doing for Wisk. The director wanted a kitchen and living room set in an Early American style. The producer told me how much money they had in the budget. It was the first freelance job I had ever done, and I was paralyzed because I knew they didn't have enough money. I told them and they said, "Do the best you can." I went and got Ethan Allen stuff, the reproduction Early American furniture, even though I knew in my heart of hearts the director wanted the real thing. He looked at the furniture and said, "This isn't Early American; why did you bring it?" I said, "Well, that's all I can get with the amount of money you have!" He looked at me and said, "Send it all back." That taught me a big lesson.

What would you do now in that situation?

I would get a piece of Ethan Allen and I would say, "This is the kind of Early American you get for $3.30, but if you give me $30.00, you can get the real thing." Let them share in the responsibility. If you don't, then the onus is on you. You find yourself dancing in this funny world appeasing the money guys, appeasing your own visual needs and the visual needs of the director. On every film I do, the first three or four weeks are spent grappling with the budget. While creation and designing is waiting in the wings, I'm in locked rooms with producers saying, "Okay, it's going to cost you a half a million dollars to do all this. If you don't have that, then we're going to have to start paring back on what the director wants, and you as producers are going to have to tell him what he can have." They'd like to have me go and tell the director what he can and cannot have. Long ago, I learned that's not my job. My job is not to say no to a director. If he wants a certain thing, visually I can do it for him. The person who is in charge of the money is the one who then says, "You can't have this entire street redone into the 1950s; it's going to cost us thirty thousand dollars and we've only allocated fifteen. Pick a side of the street or pick half of the block or redesign your shot, so we don't see the entire street." Everybody's got to help keep the money down, or else it's an unending battle.

When you start on a film, how do you approach the producer about the budget for the art department?

Most of the time I'll say, "Don't tell me what you have in the budget. I'll tell you what I think it's going to cost, and then we'll go from there." If I'm told what they have in the budget, they think I can do it for that, and that's not necessarily the case. I prefer to find the locations, see what's involved in each one, then submit a budget, and say, "Okay, given these locations, the amount of time we have, and what's going on in the script, here's what it's going to cost." If it's way above what they've got, then you go into a room and just hash it out. I figure the best way to placate the producers is if I tell them up front what it's going to cost, and then they can track my expenses. As long as my department stays on target, they can worry about something or someone else, which is exactly what I'd like them to do, because after a certain point, you don't want to have to think about the money anymore. You just want to get down to the business of what you've been hired to do, which is to design. So I like to get all of the messy money stuff out of the way at the beginning. It causes me less anxieties.

Married to the Mob has a very expansive color palette. What was the concept behind this?

The hair, make-up, jewelry, and wardrobe were all designed to intentionally push everything to its farthest extreme, like in a comic book. All of the colors, the variegated patterns, and the palette of downtown New York is just the way downtown is: the more varied the colors, the better.

The women in Married to the Mob *were all outlandish in their clothes, hair, and make-up. Did you draw from reality to establish their look?*

We wanted an extended reality. When we walked around a lot of the supermarkets and malls in Long Island, we saw women with a toned-down version of what these women wound up looking like. All we did was boost it. It was just a magnified version of something that already exists. The costume designer, Colleen Atwood, went out to the malls. I said, "You've just got to get into a car and go out to the Sunrise Highway Mall. You have got to see what these women look like." You know, the nails out to here, the poured-into jeans, the big shirts, big gold earrings, and the bouffant hairdos. Those clothes started out being purchased and were added to. It's just highlighting it; it's putting a circle around it saying, "Look at this."

After Angela's husband is murdered, she moves from her suburban home to a Lower East Side apartment, which is a wonderful contrast to the Long Island house. How did that idea come about?

The concept to go to the Lower East Side had not been in the earlier drafts of the script. Originally, Angela moved to Park Avenue, but Jonathan Demme said, "That's not interesting enough; what we really want is for her to go into a life that is so alien from the one she's been part of." The idea of somebody who lives in the Five Towns moving to the Lower East Side might be terrifying under certain circumstances. It helped everybody understand how desperate she was to get out of the conditions she was in. Also, it underscored how silly it is for people to think this area of town is terrible. It's got more character and charm than anything she had been exposed to. Jonathan is so enamored of the ethnic variety that exists here in New York. He loves Haiti, the Caribbean countries, and their music. That's an important thing for him to have in all of his films.

What location was used for the Lower East Side apartment?

We actually shot her apartment at five different locations. The exterior where she goes into a doorway next to the grocery store was one location. The elevator and the hallway where Dean Stockwell meets up with Matthew Modine was shot in an old, decrepit, fleabag hotel downtown on Chambers Street. The interior of her apartment is the third; looking down from the roof top is four; the interior of the elevator, which we built down in Florida, was five.

That's incredible. It really looks like one place.

It does, doesn't it? You get the feeling that she goes in and goes upstairs and everything happens.

As you're looking for all those locations, are you trying to visually match each component, so that the final result will look as if it is all part of the same place?

Right. The issue really is knowing that it's going to be hard to find it all in one place. Exteriors and interiors are easily split, because you might find a perfect apartment that you could shoot in, but the outside of the building looks like hell, so you go somewhere else for the exterior. To split it more than that, you really have to be very careful how you're shooting, because you can get in a jam.

How did you choose the paintings painted by the Nick Nolte character in "Life Lessons," the Martin Scorsese segment of New York Stories?

Marty had originally not intended to show the paintings at all. The first time he and I talked, he said, "I don't want to see the paintings. I want us to film this entire thing without ever seeing what his work looks like." So we started to find the locations and get everything else organized. Three weeks away from shooting, Marty said, "Kristi, I've made a big mistake; we've got to see what this guy is painting, otherwise I'm going to have trouble with the camera moves." So I said, "Alright, what kind of painter do we want?" It couldn't be just anybody; he had to be a recognized accomplished painter. This story talks about an established painter who has a real following. However, every established painter we sent the script to said, "This is not about me; this is not exactly a flattering portrait of a painter. I'm not interested."

Did you talk primarily to Expressionist painters?

It ran the full gamut. At one point, we talked to Robert Motherwell and David Salle. At one point, Malcolm Morley was a very heavy contender. Malcolm was very interested; then after he read the script, he wasn't so interested. So a lot of these painters felt they would be associated with the story if their work was too recognizable. The other thing to realize was because of Nick Nolte's persona, size, and stature, he couldn't be painting weensie little paintings or ones that were too precise or too analytical—that's just not the kind of guy he is. So we had to cast the paintings like casting a person. On our staff we had a very talented research person who spent a lot of time in the art world. I told her to go out and do extensive research on bold-stroked painters who had a following—ideally, who worked and lived in New York, had a lot of their work available and not locked in museums somewhere, and who would be interested in the project.

Were you also asking the painter to paint on camera?

That evolved. We realized the painter we picked was going to be needed for hand shots. It was sort of like *The Hustler*.

What painter was selected after this search?

Chuck Connelly. I brought Marty down to his studio, and Marty looked at his work and liked it. Nick Nolte liked it. Nick felt it was the kind of work the character would do. Connelly's paintings were bought by the Metropolitan Museum and the Saatchi collection in London. Articles had been written about him being on the cutting edge of the New Expressionistic landscape artists. He was in town, and all of his paintings were in town. Chuck was completely amenable to helping us, and he was willing to be "the hands." He taught Nick how to paint. Nick actually painted a Chuck Connelly-style painting and bought a Chuck Connelly painting when it was over. He was perfect, and I pride myself on insisting on him. I was thrilled about his use of color and the thickness of his paint. There was something almost mesmerizing about how Marty used the close-ups of the painting. "Life Lessons" was about painting; it wasn't just about a relationship that didn't work. It was about what makes an artist function. A lot of the scenic artists on the crew started painting again after they finished working on this film. They were so inspired being around Chuck and his work. Two guys came over to me afterwards and said, "I just want to thank you for being allowed to work on this project. I've started painting again."

There is a principal painting that Nolte creates during the episode. What elements were prepared so that the painting looked as if it were being created in front of our eyes?

Chuck had a finished painting we all liked. We had to do the big painting Nick was working on in stages. Chuck did the different layers, so we were very accurate about the painting process. We had to think in terms of the continuity. We had to map it out, so that each time we saw him in his studio painting, the painting would be at a different stage, to make sure we had stage A, stage B, stage C, so that each time we filmed, there would be a different level of completion.

What was the inspiration for the design of the painter's loft?

We went around and saw a lot of artists' lofts. We looked at photos of de Kooning's studio, which had a lot of the things we liked. He had modular easels on wheels that were like free-floating walls, which was great because you could hide lights behind them. They changed the space; you could make more intimate spaces with them. I saw the basketball hoop in Robert Longo's loft, which I loved. I told Marty about a lot of what I'd seen. I showed him pictures of the de Kooning and Motherwell lofts so he could key off some of the photographs. Francis Bacon had a great bedroom. I incorporated those things visually into the set.

What location was used for the loft?

It was 12,000 square feet of the top floor of a building downtown. I showed it to Marty with the idea of using half of it for Rosanna Arquette's loft and the other half for Nolte's loft. Marty loved everything about it. There was this little room upstairs. Initially I loved it, but I didn't know what to do with that room. The art director, Steve Graham, said to me, "Oh, you ought to put her up there like Rapunzel." I thought, "What a fantastic idea! Just stick her up there like some little princess in the tower." That's just what she was.

That made all those shots of Nolte looking up at the outside wall of her room so dramatically effective.

I knew that it was going to be difficult for them to shoot. They crammed themselves in up there. Marty said, "I can't believe this; we're in a 12,000-square-foot loft and you've got us in a room that's six by eight. What the hell is this!?"

Why was there so much paint splattered on the floor?

The idea was that our artist sometimes painted down as opposed to up. Also, he was such a thick painter with layer upon layer of paint that things could drip on the floor. The floor in de Kooning's loft was wonderful. It was just an unbelievable patchwork of different paintings that he had done. I basically told the scenic artists to have a good time. At one point, they got a little carried away, and the camera couldn't go over it—it was too rough and bumpy. We had to shave it all down, which is what would happen in a studio when you walked over it again and again: the paint would flatten out.

The costumes also had to be treated with paint splatters.

Yes, we loved the idea that he would paint in Armani shirts and let them get all crudded up with paint because he is an established painter. We wanted to say he likes to spend money.

How long did you work on this project?

Because the film was only forty-five minutes in length, it was a short preproduction and was shot very quickly. It was a very intense experience—like drinking cups of espresso.

GoodFellas *begins in the fifties and ends in the eighties. How did the production design approach these distinctly different decades?*

The film presented a challenge for both the costumes and the sets, because there was a need for us to quickly reflect certain trends within each of the time periods. Overall, the make-up, hair, and clothing were more sensitive to time passage than the actual locations were. Of course, cars immediately give you a period. The fifties had a sepia-like, subtle color scheme. The cinematographer, Michael Ballhaus, actually changed the film stock to maximize the chromatic look of the sixties. The early seventies was pretty garish, too. Then the eighties were more somber, more kinetic, more drugged out. If you walk on Mulberry Street and peek into one of those social club windows, it could still be in 1952; nothing's changed. In a certain way, even the people have a period look to them. The interior of the cab stand, the house, and everything from the fifties actually had a late forties look to it. They were poor; they wouldn't have brand-new furniture. So to do a clear-cut fifties look for that section of the film wasn't a good idea, because that's not what these people would have had in their houses. We actually picked a late forties look for all of the early scenes.

For the sixties scenes we wanted to say sixties. All of these guys had new cars. No one would drive around in a ten-year-old car, so that kept us in a very specific period. The only thing that didn't change costumewise were those long, pointy Billy Eckstine collars the mob guys wear throughout the film, which Marty loves. Those collars should have died out at a certain point before the end of the film. I wish we had done something much more modern, because it's such a strong statement. Those collars are very, very pronounced. I think it would have helped the time passage as well as everything else if those collars had been modified somewhat.

Some people never change. It has to do with their perception of the world; new styles don't have any effect on them.

That's absolutely true. In fact, we contacted tailors who actually make clothes for some of the mob guys who say these fellows have clothes in their closets for years; they don't change.

Especially the fabrics.

Fabrics were the biggest headache in the world, because what Marty really wanted were mohairs and they just don't make them anymore. Poor Richard Bruno, the costume designer, went crazy trying to find mohair. He was getting mohair shipped in from Europe and digging around in tailors' back rooms to see if there was an old piece lying around that he could use. In a lot of cases we had to use polyesters, and Marty wasn't happy. Richard found clothes that had not been worn; they were originals. They found incredible sweaters and ties. They had to make all of the shirts, but they dug around and found a couple of sources where the clothes really existed. We had a lot of fun with the women's clothes, too, because women's fashions changed more obviously in a five-year period.

The authenticity of the Italian American lifestyle really brings GoodFellas *to fruition.*

It's fascinating when you're dealing with someone like Marty who wants it to be as right as this. He was actively involved in every single detail. He made us adhere to his needs, because it was so important to him. This film was about a lifestyle that he was familiar with. We needed to be as true to it as we could. Prior to the filming, Marty asked me to come over to his house one day. We sat down, and he took out box loads of pictures of him as a boy growing up. I was seeing little Marty going off to communion and graduation and the first marriage, the first baby. I sat there and literally looked through his entire life. That's what we tried to adhere to.

Did you actually shoot at the Copa?

Yes, we shot it all there. They had renovated the Copa a lot, so we had to fake the interior somewhat. The hallway as you saw it in the film doesn't really exist. You go down that back staircase, and you're smack-bang into the Copa; you don't pass through the kitchen first. That was a whole rigged shot. We created that long corridor when they go down the stairs and into the kitchen, because Marty wanted the sense of going through a long passageway. That was tough. It was constructed so that as the camera was following them through the hallway, there were carpenters off on the right getting rid of two or three of the walls that were going to be in the way when they came into the Copa. I've never seen a shot like that before in my life. It was a Steadicam shot from the time they get out of the car until Henny Youngman says, "Take my wife." They shot it maybe six or seven times, and they had it. It was incredible.

That must have taken a lot of planning.

Oh, Marty plans everything beforehand. His scripts are all annotated with little pencil figures and shot lists. He knows exactly what he's going to shoot before he shoots it—before he's even seen a location. In fact, with Marty, the locations have to be chosen with the shots in mind, which is unusual. I think it's a brilliant way to do it. Sometimes it's very limiting because it may mean there's a location that's terrific, but if it doesn't have fourteen-foot ceilings, you can't get a top shot. Even though everything else about the location could be just perfect, it doesn't have the right element. You realize that's his style so you acknowledge it. In *New York Stories*, Marty wanted a 360-degree shot around Nick Nolte in the scene at an art dealer's party where he's surrounded by everyone standing around talking. Well, a 360-degree shot requires a certain-sized room, and we were having a problem finding it. For some reason they were never wide enough. Every location we showed him wasn't right because of that 360-degree shot he needed, even though there were elements that were fantastic. We finally found it; it was Duke Ellington's old house on Riverside Drive and 103rd Street.

Where did the concept for the last house Henry Hill lived in GoodFellas *come from?*

I went to Roma Furniture down on Grand Street, which is such a wonderful store. I was walking around with the set decorator, Les Bloom, seeing bedroom sets in black lacquer, and I said to myself, "Who buys this stuff?" Somebody buys this stuff and thinks it's beautiful and wants it. This furniture is not inexpensive; that's a lacquering process that takes a lot of time. I said, "Les, just take some pictures of this stuff. Let's have it lying around. For some reason, it belongs in this movie, I don't know where." As we started to put the whole show together, one particular headboard kept coming back and hitting me over the head, and I kept thinking, "Where does that whole look go?" Richard Bruno showed me an outfit that he wanted Lorraine Bracco to wear somewhere in the movie. It was a black and red two-piece bolero top with bell-bottom pants. It was unbelievable, and I said, "Oh Richard, she's got to wear that in the last scene when she's showing off this house." I was going to go with silver, gold, and brass in the house. I thought, "Wait a minute, this outfit is going to key off of the black lacquered furniture.

I'm going to do black at the end; it's going to be black and red." There's something wicked about black; it's very symbolic. You know they're all going to hell. Red and black are hellish colors, and it all seemed so obvious. Seeing that outfit completely hit me over the head and made me realize that's the direction the house should go in.

So you actually used the furniture you had seen in Roma Furniture. Was that ornate entertainment unit also a real piece?

No, we built that. When we were drawing it up, I said to my art director, Maher Ahmad, "We've got to do something that's slightly obscene, but it has to come from someplace in their vernacular, in what they've been brought up to understand. We've got to take some element of the Flintstones and marry it to Italian Rococo Baroque." It was sort of a bizarre reference to religion—it was like an altar, a cathedral, a stained glass window. It's kitsch new-wave modernism. That was something they were very, very proud of. I loved the idea of the strong palette of colors in that room, and I loved the idea of doing glitz. I said, "Let's put sparkle in the grout." People kept saying, "Oh no, oh my God!" When everybody walked into the room and saw this thing on the day we were going to shoot, it was like, "I don't believe you've done this. You've really gone over the top."

Was the interior of that house shot in a practical location?

It was a real house in Fort Lee, New Jersey. The green carpeting was there, and I loved it. Marty wanted to shoot in as many real locations as he could. Building sets in New York is very expensive, and a lot of producers and production managers would much rather you find a location than build.

What was built?

The storefront of the cab stand at the beginning of the film was built. There was nothing there but a lot. What we wanted was contrary to what the real cab stand looked like, which was just a tiny garage. We needed more space. Marty had a lot of camera moves, and he wanted the back room to be more like a warehouse. He had visualized the cab stand itself as a storefront, very much like what you see on the Lower East Side.

It looked like the social clubs that were prevalent in the fifties.

That's exactly what Marty had in mind. He said, "Even though this is a cab stand, I really have social clubs in my head."

Both Manhunter, *based on the book* The Red Dragon, *and* The Silence of the Lambs *have the character of Hannibal Lecter and show him incarcerated in prison. How did you interpret Lecter and his environment?*

Manhunter was a much different visualization. Mel Bourne chose to go a very modern route, a very white, pristine kind of feel, and we went in a different direction. Ours is very moody, Gothic. That was largely dictated by what I was seeing in and around Pittsburgh. It was filled with decrepit steel mills that are collapsing. They're dark, dank, strange buildings that no longer work. It didn't make sense to be modern and nastily clean. It made sense to be more mysterious. I found an incredible photograph of a Nuremberg jail where all of the war prisoners were kept. We used that as a visual guide in designing the corridor set, which was built on a stage in Pittsburgh. It was a forty-foot-high, ninety-foot-long corridor with old craggily rocks. There are visual things that happen to me when I see a picture. In *The Silence of the Lambs*, I used Francis Bacon a lot as a key for the color and the spacial relationships.

How do you determine what city a film is going to be shot in?

Deciding where you are going to shoot a whole movie involves more than me. The production company has to be involved in that because of hotel accommodations, where the nearest airport is, how are we going to move from A to B. It's like Hannibal and the elephants. You are dealing with so many people, you have to be practical or it becomes cost-prohibitive.

After the city is determined, how do you go about finding the practical locations?

First, I have a conversation with the director, and the general look of the picture is discussed. Once that's determined, then I go out with a location scout and usually the location manager. We drive around for days going to a variety of locations that have been found previously, or we start from scratch. I'll say, "Stop here; let's look at this for a second," whether it's a street or a building, a rooftop, a palatial mansion, or a store. Once I like something, then we take pictures and show it to the director. Then we take the director to see it. If he likes it, we go back a third time with the technical crew. They talk about what they need in terms of lighting, electrical equipment, where we're going to house all the necessary back-up personnel, where to put everybody between shots, and if there are enough parking facilities. A deal is struck between the production company and the people who own the property.

You have often worked in people's homes to create sets. Is there a special diplomacy involved under these circumstances?

When you shoot on location, you must be respectful of people's lives. The lady who owned the house where Angela DeMarco and her husband lived in *Married to the Mob* was an interior decorator. The room where all the stolen merchandise was stacked up was yellow and white—some of the furniture in there was hers. She was gradually remodeling every room in the house, and she hadn't gotten to that room. I said, "This is perfect." She said, "Oh God, it's terrible. I can't wait to get rid of all of this," so I felt I was at liberty to say, "Well, that's precisely why we love it." We might go into another house, and the people would be very proud. If that was the case, then obviously we're not going to say, "Oh my God, look at this. This is awful; this is just what we want!"

How do you feel about being in a supervisory capacity?

I coordinate the department. People say, "Oh, she's the designer." I *am* the designer, but I'm the designer of designers. I really feel the make-up artist, hair stylist, costume designer, the scenic artist, the construction coordinator, the property master, the art director—all of those people are designers. They are designers within their field. What a production designer does is to cull all of that into one cohesive unit, and that's the way I like to run things.

Do you get involved with the DP and the director about how your sets are going to be photographed?

There's no sense in building a gorgeous set if you're not going to be able to see it. There are times when I get frustrated, because I know the director and cinematographer have something in mind, but they're looking in one corner and there's an entire world behind them that they're not seeing. The director is worrying about the performance; the cinematographer is worrying about composition, camera moves, and lighting. Sometimes it is just left to me to turn to them and say, "Guys, it would really be nice if you wanted to include this in the film. I think this is the way you should shoot it."

What would you like to do as a production designer that you haven't done yet?

I would love to do a grand period piece, something on the scale of *The Last Emperor*, something where you really are in an amazing space totally different from anything that exists in the real world today, where people just stop and think, "Wow, how did they do that?"

20

Bruno Rubeo

In the 1960s Bruno Rubeo was a student at an experimental high school in Italy where he began to study film. During weekly guest lectures given by Italian cinema masters such as Roberto Rossellini and Michelangelo Antonioni, Rubeo explored the multifaceted process of film-making.

A long-time love of architecture led him to choose art direction as his field. To enter the industry, Rubeo painted, sculpted, and worked without pay on many film-related jobs. His first salaried position was as an assistant to special effects master Carlo Rambaldi. He worked with Rambaldi on many projects, including *Conan the Barbarian* and *Dune*.

His first major feature collaboration as a production designer was with Oliver Stone on *Salvador*. After meeting Stone and reading the script, Rubeo plunged into Mexico to re-create Salvador.

Salvador was the first of four films on which Rubeo and Stone tackled re-creating entire environments. For *Platoon*, the 1986 winner of the Academy Award for best picture, Rubeo re-created Vietnam in the Philippines. Rubeo spent months in the jungle cultivating rice patties, planting trees, and building a military base camp to capture the documentary realism of the film. The challenge of *Talk Radio* was to create an entire high-tech radio station fueled by Rubeo's architectural imagination in a warehouse in Texas. The Massapequa of *Born on the Fourth of July* etches into our memories universal images of small-town America torn apart by the Vietnam War.

Rubeo's detailed rendering of the South in the 1950s and 1960s on Bruce Beresford's *Driving Miss Daisy* was nominated for an Oscar. He has designed *Walker* for Alex Cox and *Kindergarten Cop* for Ivan Reitman and is currently working on a two-part film for director Taylor Hackford.

1983 *Spring Fever* (art director)
1986 *Salvador*
      Platoon
      Walker
1988 *Blood Red*
      Talk Radio
1989 *Old Gringo*
      *Driving Miss Daisy**
      Born on the Fourth of July
1990 *Kindergarten Cop*
1992 *Blood In Blood Out*
      Sommersby

* Academy Award nomination for best achievement in art direction–set decoration.

How did you become interested in filmmaking?
I went to a new experimental movie high school in Rome in the mid-sixties. Rossellini, Fellini, Antonioni, Visconti, De Sica all would come in and do lectures. It was very exciting. I studied a little bit of everything in the film arts—directing, editing, even a little animation. Then I specialized. I took art direction—it just seemed like the right thing. I was always fascinated by architecture, which I think is the universal language of different cultures. Through architecture, you see how cultures manifest themselves and how they live. It's a very important aspect of the human race.
How did you get your first job in the film industry?
I started working for free—just anything that came around. The industry in Italy was much smaller, and there was more competition. You just got in however you could. The first job I got paid for was working for Carlo Rambaldi, the special effects creator of *E.T.*, *Dune*, and *King Kong*. In those days, he had a studio where they did creatures, special effects, animation, and some sets. I got in there and showed him what I could do. I did animation, some sculpting, creatures—all sorts of stuff. I was still very young. I came to New York and lived there for five years. There were not very many movies going on. It was very difficult to get in. I ended up doing advertising; I painted, I sculpted, I did all kinds of things. One day I decided I was going to move to Los Angeles to get into the movies. I took a long trip around North America. The first place I stopped in was Toronto. The next day, I met a guy and became an art director for his brand-new TV station, City TV, which was very avant-garde in those days. I designed sets for different programs. They were

very strange and progressive shows. Then I left the station and started freelancing in commercials. I started doing some movies in Canada. Eight years later, I finally made it to Los Angeles. I went back with Carlo Rambaldi, who hired me to design a futuristic theme park. For a year I was helping him design that, and suddenly they offered him the creatures for *Dune*. He put that project on the side, and I helped him to do the creatures on *Dune*. I also did *Conan* with him.

How did you first meet Oliver Stone?

After I did *Dune*, I got married and went to Italy for a year. I was designing a TV station there, even the offices. One day Gerald Green, a producer who produced small movies with Hemdale, called me. He had a small movie in Mexico, and I speak Spanish. I went to do this movie; then I came back to Italy to finish the station, and Gerald called me again to do *Salvador*. He said, "I want you to meet this guy, Oliver Stone; he's really interesting." I read the script and I said, "This guy's got something to say." Oliver was writing and directing himself. It was very important; it was really a make-it-or-break-it situation, so he was very, very intense. There was hardly any money. It was the hardest movie I ever made. Oliver is always on the edge no matter how many years you've been working with him. He always maintains the tension.

Where was Salvador *filmed?*

In Mexico, we didn't go to Salvador. No film financier would cover that movie in Salvador. In fact, Oliver wanted to do it there. He went down to meet with a contact who said, "Don't worry about it; I can take care of everything here politically." A few hours before Oliver arrived, they shot and killed the guy on a tennis court. Oliver came right back and said, "There goes our contact." We ended up doing it in Mexico.

Was it difficult to make Mexico look like Salvador?

No, it's very similar, but we had to do a lot of work. We had ninety-nine sets, and we did it in six weeks. I had no decorator and no construction coordinator. We were moving like mad. I wasn't sleeping; we had no money; it was a nightmare. Typically, you have enough assistants that if a set has to be ready for tomorrow, people have to work overnight. You go over there from time to time, but you don't have to stay up all night; somebody else will do it for you. I was doing everything. If we were shooting at night, I was preparing during the day. It was very intense, but it was worth it.

I understand that Philippine jungles were used to re-create Vietnam for Platoon. *What work had to be done there to prepare it for shooting?*

We scouted the jungle during the wet season, and it was all green. We chose the place, came back to Los Angeles to do some drawing, and then went back over to start preparing. There was no road there. We had to build roads and dams over two bridges and a river to get to the location. We built about seven miles of road. The moment we built the road, all these local people came to chop wood for fire. They don't go with chain saws, they go with machetes. They prepared little bundles on the side of the road, and a guy with a carriage or a water buffalo comes in and picks it up and takes it away. I would go to the set two or three times a day. I didn't pay much attention; I would see a few bundles here and there. Suddenly, one day I looked around and realized that slowly with their machetes they chopped almost every tree in the valley. We couldn't shoot that part of the valley anymore. Luckily, it was the beginning of the valley, so we moved into it further.

There are many things to a jungle. We made a village and real rice fields. We found a river which was quite far away and had a system of pumps to water the valley down. You need a lot of water for rice patties. It soaks and soaks, and eventually the rice starts to grow. We had to prepare this a couple of months before to have a chance for the rice to grow. We ended up planting thousands of trees. To hike with the entire crew for hours to some rain forest is unrealistic. The dry season came, and things started turning brown. Suddenly, there was no jungle there. One day I was in the middle of the valley talking to a construction guy when all of a sudden I hear, whoosh. It was spontaneous combustion. It was so hot; the valley just caught on fire. Things would be burning out of the blue. We had to keep on pumping water into the valley.

Did you use the same techniques as the military would to create the camp in the jungle?

Absolutely, the military base camp with all the hootches, the bunkers, the tents, towers, lanterns—everything was completely built for real. We had to make something like 200,000 sandbags which still didn't look like anything in this huge field. They sink in. You would do a thousand sandbags, and you would just have a little wall. You'd go, "How many do you think we're going to need over here?" "I don't know, like maybe ten or fifteen thousand sandbags." We prepared the first fifteen thousand, and it was nothing. We could barely cover one bunker with that. We had to make almost 200,000, and even then we started cheating in the very far end of the base camp. Instead of putting double layers, we had to put one layer, and eventually we had to paint them on a piece of plywood, because we couldn't keep on building sandbags. The amount was unbelievable. We ended up planting several thousand banana trees in that movie, and you can hardly tell.

How did you create rain?

With rain towers. We had to build them; they were pretty crude. Ninety-nine percent of the crew on *Platoon* was Filipino. I didn't have any Americans in my entire art department. I was my own construction coordinator, my own decorator—everything. We had to build the towers, and there wasn't much money. We built very high tubes on big tripods with sandbags and sprinklers. We had to hide them behind trees.

Strategically, we had to put them where you wouldn't see them and make a ceiling of water just coming down. Also you shoot it against the light, you can see it better backlit. The other way around, you can practically have a downpour, and you don't even see it.

Did you have military assistance on Platoon?

Yes, we had a retired Marine captain who started a consulting company for action and military movies. He was really helpful. We also had Vietnamese consultants; we had both sides of the fence.

Where did you get the military equipment?

We rented the tanks and helicopters from the Philippine army. We were there right in the middle of the revolution, and we almost folded the picture when they kicked Marcos out. With Marcos, you just went to the right person, gave him the money, and he gave you whatever you wanted—ten tanks, twelve helicopters—whatever. Suddenly, you couldn't do that anymore. We thought we were going to have to stop. It turned out to be a peaceful revolution. We managed to make a deal.

The principle set in Talk Radio *is an ultramodern, high-tech radio station with a view of the Texas skyline. Was that a set or a practical location?*

That was a set.

Was it at all based on a real radio station?

We went to almost every radio station in the United States. We wanted to see some regular ones, and then we wanted to see some high-tech stations. People would send us wherever they thought there were high-tech stations. What was high-tech to them was basically modern decor, some designer type of furniture and that was it. No one had a big studio with glass all around and a view to the streets. We'd never seen a station that high-tech anywhere. We decided to take license. Why not? It's a movie that mostly takes place inside of a radio station.

Where was the set for Talk Radio *built?*

In Texas. We were going to do *Talk Radio* and *Born on the Fourth of July* back to back, so we chose a city that was do-able for both movies. *Talk Radio* was based on the Alan Berg story, so we decided that Dallas was the right place. It was a modern city with a new-look station. Dallas is so modern that we decided it could justify something like that. It just gave us more space to move around.

What criteria did you use to design the radio station set?

First you start from the requirements of the script. From there, you discuss with the director and the DP how they see shooting this. Slowly you come up with a concept of the amount of space, the engineer's room, the green room, the lobby. We decided to have the camera moving all the time, going through walls. So we had parts of sets on hinges going up and coming down, allowing the camera to go in. The wall opened so the camera could go in. It was a very interesting engineering experience. We concentrated all of our money on that one set. We built everything on that movie in four weeks, and we shot in exactly four weeks.

The Dallas skyline appears out of the windows of the interior of the studio. Was that a translight?

Yes, that was a translight, but we also did models. What I did outside of that window was to suggest there was another roof with elements. I forced the perspective. I put in miniatures. I had a series of translights. I added blinking lights for the night scenes to suggest helicopters going by, which disappeared as they met the building and then reappeared as they flew past the building. They suggested that the helicopter went behind the buildings. People might not catch a little touch like that, but subliminally it catches as real. We put real neon lights into the translights; we reproduced real blinking lights. It was fun to do that set; I loved it.

Was all the radio equipment on the set real?

Yes, we had a company come in and install real equipment as a promotional thing. We only needed an antenna, and we could have broadcast.

You used a lot of glass in that set. How did you deal with the problems of photographing the glass?

We tilted the glass so you didn't get the reflection from the camera. It was very difficult and time-consuming, because one piece of glass might be reflecting to another piece of glass and to another and eventually back to the camera.

There are plastic call letters in the lobby of the station which were well exploited by Oliver Stone and the cinematographer, Robert Richardson. They shoot behind them, around them, and even through them. Did you design the letters in plastic to allow the option to do this?

I tried to give as many layers as possible. Since there was basically one set for the movie, I figured I couldn't give them too much of a solid area where the camera disappears, unless it's really called for. So I gave as many layers as possible by creating a series of transparent layers like those letters. The color was very strange; it was like a chartreuse day-glo plexiglass, which is usually a no-no.

Why is that?

Green doesn't look good on faces; it's not appealing. I actually had to push a little for that one because Oliver was saying, "Why are you giving me these green letters? How am I going to light the actors? It's green." I said, "It's only that one area; you can play with it." They eventually ended up loving it. He played a lot of scenes there; there are always people coming by it. Bob Richardson likes to do that also; between the two of them, you're moving all over.

So because of the extensive camera movement, it was necessary to create a real environment and not just a three-wall set.

Absolutely. Oliver is somewhat of the European school in that sense;

they don't want to be limited. If you don't need four walls, why build them? But with Oliver, you can't do that. He doesn't want to be limited as to how he is going to move the camera. Of course, that always becomes a little problem between me and the producer, because Oliver knows I'm trying to give him all of it. Obviously he doesn't say no; he says yes, then the producer says, "No, you don't need that." I'd say, "I'm telling you, we've done a lot of movies together; he's going to turn and shoot this way." And sure enough, he shoots all over the place.

The climax of Talk Radio *is a technical tour de force. In a single take the room repeatedly spins around Eric Bogosian as he performs a very long monologue. How was that done? Were there any optical effects?*

No, that is not an optical; that was shot right on the set. We put Bogosian on a platform with wheels which turned around the set. We dimmed the lights; it just got darker and darker and darker.

So by turning the camera and Bogosian on the same platform, it gave the illusion that he was sitting still and that the background was turning. It must have been very complicated lighting that scene?

Yes, it was turning 360 degrees, and you never wanted the reflections to be wrong. It was very complicated. It worked out well because of the tilted glass. Everything was wild, meaning everything was flexible, adjustable, and movable. You just rehearse. Once you find a position for everything, you just go.

After the completion of principal photography on Talk Radio, *when did you start* Born on the Fourth of July?

We did *Talk Radio*. We stopped for about two weeks, and then we started *Born on the Fourth of July*. Oliver went off editing *Talk Radio*, while I was starting to prepare *Born on the Fourth of July*.

Born on the Fourth of July *is based on the life story of Ron Kovic. Did he take you to some of the real places from his life?*

Yes, I went to Massapequa, Long Island, with him and Oliver.

Was Kovic available to you while you were designing and building the sets?

We had him there quite a bit. I would take him through the sets, and he would give us some advice; he was helpful. We didn't reproduce Massapequa exactly. We didn't put the buildings in the order they were in Massapequa, simply because the streets in Texas didn't allow it and the scene didn't allow it. So you take some license unless you're in the real place. We decided to take all of the buildings that we wanted in Massapequa and put them closer together. We reconstructed four city blocks. We built the main house and the exterior of the garden where they talk at night in a warehouse. That was all a set. We had to reconstruct all those streets for the neighborhood and the parade. That's not Massapequa. We constructed everything in Texas.

All of the scenes that take place in Massapequa in Born on the Fourth of July *were shot in Texas? That is amazing!*

Yes, and we used the Philippines for Vietnam and Mexico. We constructed Mexico there.

What did you use for the exteriors of the houses on both sides of the street of Ron Kovic's block?

We built facades on top of the real houses in Texas, because they have a style of porch in Texas that's definitely not Massapequa. We had to put in a lot of greenery that is typical of Eastern Coast states. You can't find spruce trees in Texas. Whenever you saw Massapequa, we had to import spruce trees from Michigan to Texas. They brought the trees chopped. We planted the trees, and we tried to maintain them green. Eventually they dried out; the leaves and all the needles started falling, so we had to constantly refurbish by adding new branches. When it was supposed to be summer, we placed the trees strategically so they would cover the mesquite trees that are typical of Texas. It was already cold when we were shooting the final parade in Dallas. All the trees had no leaves. That was the Fourth of July parade, so we had to put all the trees in a way that would cover the other forty-footers.

Born on the Fourth of July *spans several decades. How was this represented in the locations built for Massapequa?*

All the various stores changed because the period changed three times: from the fifties through the sixties to the mid- seventies. The crew would have to shoot a place that we had prepared and then allow us to make the change in the street. Some buildings were boarded up, some were painted different colors, some had no canopies, there were different movies playing in the theater, and the billboards changed.

The scenes that take place in Vietnam in Born on the Fourth of July *have a very different look than the ones in* Platoon. *They are very surreal. Was there a conscious effort to make them look different?*

Yes. It was very glary and surreal. That village was supposed to be by a river, and we found a small area of sand dunes in the Philippines which is by the sea. We decided to do a village there. It had a completely different feeling than *Platoon*. The wind is always blowing in the sand dunes.

What was it like to work with Bruce Beresford on Driving Miss Daisy?

He was unbelievably exact. We had so little money. We put it all to the camera; that's why it looks so big and rich. It's the least amount of money I've ever had to make a movie. Bruce said exactly what he wanted. All directors say, "Yes, yes, I'm going to stick with what we decided," and eventually they come back and say, "I want to shoot that way." Bruce said, "I'm going to tell you in advance—do a little sketch, a storyboard," and he stuck to it to the letter. He had such a clear idea of what he wanted to do that when we went to dailies at night sometimes I would see one take. I said, "Did you already select this?" He said, "No, this is it—one take." "One take?" I was thinking, "Either this guy knows exactly what he's doing or we're in trouble over here." It wasn't always one take—sometimes two—sometimes more, but very conservative coverage. The movie was perfect. Obviously, the guy knew exactly what he wanted, but it's very rare, very rare.

How did you choose the house that was used for Miss Daisy?

We went to see a whole bunch of houses. We made a decision on which one, then we gutted, and redid it. We decorated it and brought it back to the period. You can't find anything old anymore in Atlanta; everybody has redone the kitchen. Even if they kept some of the house old-fashioned, all the furniture is wrong, the wallpaper is wrong, the colors are wrong.

Although the film takes place in the fifties, the house is decorated as if Miss Daisy had not changed anything for the last fifteen or twenty years. Why is that?

Exactly, it's preserved from the twenties and thirties. She was conservative. She wasn't going to change. Then you go to her son's house and you see the changes there, because his wife is more modern; she wanted the top of the line, the in-thing at the time.

The car is very important in Driving Miss Daisy. *What was your involvement in selecting the right one?*

It's the transportation captain's responsibility to find it, and it's my responsibility to choose it with the director. You call all the collectors, and they come to a big parking lot for one day. You'll see the most beautiful cars, and they're all there for the grabs. We go through and decide which one. You want more than one of the same car in case something goes wrong. So you can't choose a car if there's only one. If they're not quite in the condition that we want, then we say, "Can you send it out and do a reupholstery?" or the decorator does the upholstery.

Were the interiors actually shot inside the car, or did you create an interior of the car in the studio?

No, we didn't have enough money to do that; in a more expensive movie you do that. They were shot right inside the car. Beautiful car—it was in immaculate condition; it was like a living room inside.

When do you start and when do you finish on a project?

I'm the first to start with the director, the writer, the producer, the production manager—we are the first. I finish with the end of principal photography, and then they continue in postproduction and editing.

How do you feel about the financial responsibilities that are a part of your job?

Art direction is an area that is not clearly understood by money people. The politics are half the battle. You have to be half administrator and half artist. It is difficult to separate it. The only thing the money people are concerned about is money, and so you sometimes have shrewd ones that will cut regardless of the reasons. They never trust designers. The director is very trusting, and sometimes you have unnecessary problems with the production side that could be avoided if they trusted what you're there for, at least until you screw up. They always think we're going to go over budget, which is not true. We always try to do something artistic within the money. It would be very silly not to consider that, because the next thing you know, they don't call you and you stop working. They say, "He's very good, but he goes over budget, so forget it." So money is our concern as well. You're given a budget and between me, the assistant, the construction coordinator, and the set decorator, we work it out and see how much each scene is going to cost. Sometimes it is impossible to do it for that money, and we have to go back to the producer. So either we cut something, or we get more money. Sometimes they say that's it, and I have to go to the director and say, "I won't be able to give you certain things."

What kind of relationship do you like to have with a director?

Taylor Hackford is a director who's very open to visual ideas. We get together all the time, even on a nonprofessional level. We always talk about the movie; we have a good rapport. So it's great because you're always coming up with ideas that way. Oliver and Taylor are always socializing. I like that, because you get to know them and you get to know what they want because you're relaxed and not intimidated; you are free to suggest ideas. Some directors can intimidate you.

One of the mysteries of the craft of production design is determining if something was built or shot on a practical location. Unless you've done the movie yourself, you can't be certain. Are you aware of this when you watch the work of other designers?

I am very much aware, because people ask me all the time if something was real. I asked Dante Ferretti, who is a good friend of mine, about *Hamlet,* which is 99 percent built. I couldn't tell. There is a castle and all kinds of interiors and terraces. Only a small part of the front castle was real; it was a piece of a ruin. They built all the rest of the exterior, which is humongous; you can't believe it. Then they built all of the interiors. The courtyard—everything is a set. People thought we went to a location to shoot *Born on the Fourth of July.* We built every single thing you see in the movie. If you don't tell people, who's going to know? Not even designers know. *Driving Miss Daisy* is a period film; it's so pretty you think the designer has done something, when in fact *Born on the Fourth of July* is where we did a lot. My art department budget on *Driving Miss Daisy* was $250,000. On *Born on the Fourth of July,* I had $3 million.

I believe in trying to get things as realistic as possible. I'm very picky about getting the right scenic artist to age things properly. It's a real art to age realistically so it looks just right. It's very, very difficult. I guess my sets look real, because people don't know they were built. I'm not saying anyone should notice. You can only notice if I did it wrong. It's a question of one's integrity. I don't want anybody to come back to me and say that was wrong. I often use real materials. I don't try to fake it unless it's really far away. Say a building is really far away and it's made of tiles, I'm not going to use real tiles, I'm going to fake it, but if it's close, there's nothing like real tiles. To a lot of designers, it works for them to use fake tile; it's cut masonite and they age it. But to make something so close to the camera work, you would have to know for sure that the camera is just passing by. If I did a bad job, you would have noticed it.

Do you ever work on aging a set that you've designed?

Yes, I've had to do it sometimes. They have great crews in Mexico for just about anything, but they really lack the trade of the film scenic arts. On *Salvador* there was one block of houses with those beautiful rich Mexican colors. They're faded and you see all the colors underneath coming through in different layers; it's just beautiful. We extended this block with other houses that had to be matched. I showed up one day on the set, and it was painted badly. It was beautifully built, but the paint job and the aging was terrible. It was obvious that it didn't match. So I said, "Paint this whole house red, this one yellow, this one blue." They painted and came back, "Now what?" I said, "Okay, now the one that is red, paint it blue, this one you paint green, but now mix some starch in it." So they would paint it, let it dry, and it would start to chip; it starts to show the color underneath. "Now paint another color over this again and put in the starch again." So now it starts chipping again; you see three colors, but it matches. It had to, especially when you're next to the real thing—there's no way that you can get away with that.

In your opinion, what movies are landmarks in production design?

2001 is definitely a landmark; *Blade Runner* and *Brazil* are definitely landmarks. I like Fellini's movies; I love his freedom. He says, "Let's do a plastic sea. Let's do a silhouette of a ship going by with plastic waves." If the mood is right, everybody accepts it. *Casanova* is entirely staged. I remember when I first saw it, it bothered me because I wasn't prepared to see something that was done on the stage. Five minutes later, I completely forgot; I was way into it. It moved me, and you never missed the exterior. It was all sets. He had courage; I like him for that.

Is there anything that you haven't done as a production designer that you would like to do in the future?

Yes, science fiction—only to challenge myself. I think to come up with a new look today in science fiction would be very, very difficult. There are a few examples of innovative ideas. First of all, there's *2001*. There's *Star Wars*, but *Star Wars* is a continuation of *2001*—it's the same technology. They took the same spaceships and made them dirtier. Then there was *Alien*; that was an interesting different look. There is the *Brazil* situation where there's the past, present, and future: a timeless, non-specific kind of time period. *Blade Runner* was a bit like that, too, but you know, after that, there hasn't been anything new, really. It's very difficult to do. What do you do?

Do you think that production design is going to change in the future?

I think it's going to go to computers; it's inevitable. It's going to create some interesting things, but it's going to create some bad things, too. I can't imagine anybody doing a Van Gogh with a computer; I just can't. There is nothing like holding the brush—it's the mood, it's an expression of the heart. That's what art is all about. When it becomes too much of the mind, I think the purity of the art itself is going to suffer. The film industry is becoming more and more of an industry. Today you find some producers are ex-accountants. Instead of opening themselves to the artistic, what they say is, "I'm an accountant; I know how to stay on budget." They don't see that the director is trying to achieve something. What they see is the dollar figure. That's a conflict, and we are going in that direction more and more. The executives at major companies sit around and come up with formulas. They put the puzzle together and make a package deal. There's no integrity anymore. I'm sure in the midst of all this, there will always be somebody who is going to come up with great things. Stages in civilizations have always been criticized—the industrial revolution, the electronic revolution. There are always good things that come, but then there is a danger. The mind becomes more lazy. Progress is inevitable—you can't stop that. Let's have progress, but let's still maintain a certain amount of balance of the heart and the mind. If you completely get rid of your past, you're left with no foundation—you're fooling yourself.

Glossary

aging: Technique of making new materials look older.

architecture: The design or style of a building.

art department: Crew members who work under the supervision of the *production designer*. Includes, *art director, set decorator, scenic artist, property master, costume designer*, and others.

art director: Original title used for person who designed sets and decor for a film. Currently, often means person who works directly under the *production designer* executing the design of sets.

asphaltum: Tar-like substance used in aging process.

backing: A painting or photograph used to create a background for a set.

back lot: Outdoor area in a studio used to build exterior locations.

balustrade: A series of short posts used to support a rail.

blue screen: Process in which a scene is photographed in front of a blue screen so that later a matte painting can be printed into the background to form a composite shot.

buyer: Person who buys or rents props, furniture, or clothing for a film.

CAD: Computer-Aided Design. Software used to generate multiple views of a design so it can be seen from any angle.

camera angle projection: A method used to create a perspective drawing from an architectural plan to see how the completed set will look through a particular lens.

cantilever: A projecting beam that supports a balcony.

carpenter: Member of the *construction crew* responsible for woodwork in the building of sets.

color palette: A series of related colors used by the designer to create the mood and atmosphere of a film.

composite shot: A single shot created from several negative elements printed together.

construction coordinator: Person in charge of overseeing the building of sets working directly with carpenters and other craftspeople.

construction crew: People responsible for physically building sets.

costume designer: Person responsible for designing and executing the costumes for a film.

costumer: Person responsible for the care of costumes on the set.

cover set: A standby set that can be used for shooting when another set cannot be used because of inclement weather or other problems.

cyclorama: A curved seamless backdrop.

diorama: A miniature rendition of a set.

DP: Director of photography. Person responsible for the lighting and photography of a film. Also called cinematographer.

drafting: Technical drawing process used to create a *plan* to build a set.

dress: To decorate a set with furniture and props.

elevation: A *plan* that shows one view of a structure.

exterior: An outdoor location.

façade: The front of a building.

fly: Scenery on ropes or cables above a set.

forced perspective: Technique used to create depth by foreshortening the background.

gantries: A bridgework over a set used to hang lights.

gimbal: A device that cradles an object allowing it to be steady even though what is below it is unsteady.

gray scale: A gradation of tones from black to white.

greensman: Person responsible for the installation and care of trees, lawns, and flowers on a film set.

hard backing: A set *backing* on a hard surface.

interior: An indoor location.

lead man: The assistant set decorator. Person responsible for finding objects needed to decorate a set.

location: Practical space used to shoot a scene in a film.

location manager: Person responsible for finding and securing a location for a film.

matte painting: A painting used in conjunction with *blue screen* process to create a background unobtainable by the filmmakers.

metaphor: An idea that translates into a visualization used to express the themes of a film.

miniature: An identical but small-scale model of a set, object, or location.

model: A three-dimensional reproduction of an object used in a film. Also a three-dimensional representation of a set used in preproduction.

perspective: The illusion of depth on a two-dimensional surface.

plan: A technical drawing used to construct a set.

practical: Something on a set that really works.

practical location: An existing location.

process screen: Technique used to project film from behind a screen to create a background for the foreground action. Also called *rear screen projection*.

production designer: Person responsible for the visual look of a film.

production illustrator: Person who renders illustrations of the production designer's ideas for a set or moment in a film in drawings or paintings.

property master: Person responsible for props and objects used and handled by
the actors.

retrofit: Technical addition to an existing structure.

rig: Piece of equipment used for a specific task.

scenic artist: Person who paints scenic backgrounds, lettering, signs, portraits,
and other things needed to be painted on a set.

scenic loft: Piece of equipment that allows the scenic painter to paint standing
upright as the painting is raised and lowered.

scenic painting: A painting done on canvas or a hard surface used to create a
background for a set.

scrim: A translucent screen used to diffuse light.

set: Place used to film a scene.

set decorator: Person responsible for decorating the sets designed by the *production
designer* and *art director*.

set designer: Person responsible for designing and overseeing construction of sets
based on ideas of the *production designer*.

set dressing: Furnishings used to decorate a set.

stage: Area in a studio used to build sets and to photograph a scene.

standing set: A permanent indoor or outdoor set.

storyboard: A series of drawings that tell the story of a film frame by frame; used
as a guide to design the film.

studio: Production facility where sets are built and scenes for the film are
photographed.

supervising art director: Position held during the Hollywood studio system. Person
who headed the *art department*, assigned the *art director* to each project,
and supervised the design of all the films produced by the studio.

swing gang: Set dressing crew. People who work under the supervision of the
lead man to obtain necessary objects for set decoration.

translight: A transparent photographic blow-up used as a background for a set.

transportation captain: Person responsible for vehicles used in a film.

value: The relative lightness and darkness of a color.

wild: Any part of a set that is movable.

Bibliography

PERIODICALS

American Film. "Dialogue on Film"—Ken Adam. Vol. XVI, Number 2, February 1991.

American Film. "Dialogue on Film"—Richard Sylbert. Vol. XI, Number 3, December 1985.

American Film. "Dialogue on Film"—Richard Sylbert. Vol. XV, Number 3, December 1989.

Corliss, Mary, and Carlos Clarens. "Designed for Film: The Hollywood Art Director." *Film Comment*, May-June 1978. Special midsection devoted to Hollywood art directors includes historical essay, sketches, filmographies, and interviews with many Hollywood designers.

Durgnat, Raymond. "Art for Film's Sake." *American Film*, Vol. VIII, Number 7, May 1983.

Mills, Bart. "The Brave New Worlds of Production Design." *American Film*, Vol. VII, Number 4, January-February 1982.

Stern, Gary M. "Tony Walton at the Beaumont." *Theatre Crafts*, March 1987.

Theatre Crafts. "Designers at Work," May 1987. Profiles of over forty theater designers, including Patrizia Von Brandenstein and Stuart Wurtzel.

Troy, Carol. "Architect of Illusions." *American Film*, Vol. XV, Number 11, August 1990. Article on production designer Patrizia Von Brandenstein.

Vertrees, Alan David. "Reconstructing the Script in Sketch Form: An Analysis of the Narrative Construction and Production Design of the Fire Sequence in *Gone with the Wind*." *Film History*, Vol. 3, Number 2, 1989.

BOOKS

Filmographies

Each of the following books covers a variety of designers and time periods.

Brenner, Debbie, and Gary Hill. *Credits*. Vol. 1 compiled by film title, Vol. 2 by production category, Vol. 3 by individual. Wallington, NJ: Magpie Press, 1985.

The Film Yearbook. New York: St. Martin's Press (published annually).

Monaco, James. *Who's Who in American Film Now*. New York: New York Zoetrope, 1981. Updated edition, 1988.

Pecchia, David. *Cinematographers, Production Designers and Film Editors Guide*. Beverly Hills, CA: Lone Eagle, third annual edition, 1991. Also contains an interview with production designer Lawrence G. Paull.

Technical

Katz, Steven D. *Film Directing Shot by Shot*. California: Michael Wiese Productions in conjunction with Focal Press, 1991. Contains chapters on production design, storyboards, and visualization.

Rose, Rich. *Drafting Scenery for Theater, Film, and Television*. White Hall, VA: Betterway Publications, 1990.

Reference

Albrecht, Donald. *Designing Dreams*. New York: Harper & Row in collaboration with the Museum of Modern Art, 1986. Historical study of modern architecture in the movies.

Barsacq, Leon. *Caligari's Cabinet and Other Grand Illusions*. Boston: New York Graphic Society, 1976.

Behlmer, Rudy. *Memo from David O. Selznick*. New York: Viking Press, 1972. Contains letters and memos concerning William Cameron Menzies's production design of *Gone with the Wind*.

Bordwell, David, Janet Staiger, and Kristin Thompson. *The Classical Hollywood Cinema*. New York: Columbia University Press, 1985. Contains sections on art direction in the Hollywood studio system.

Brouwer, Alexandra, and Thomas Lee Wright. *Working in Hollywood*. New York: Crown Publishing, 1990. Contains interviews with production designer Polly Platt, set designer David Klassen, set decorator Marvin March, property master Emily Ferry, and lead man Paul Meyerberg.

Brownlow, Kevin. *The Parade's Gone by...* New York: Alfred A. Knopf, 1968. Section on art direction in the silent film era.

Carrick, Edward. *Designing for Films*. London and New York: The Studio Publications, 1949.

Carringer, Robert L. *The Making of Citizen Kane*. Berkeley, Los Angeles, London:

University of California Press, 1985. Contains section about Perry Ferguson's production design of *Citizen Kane*.

Chell, David. *Moviemakers at Work*. Redmond, WA: Microsoft Press, 1987. Contains interviews with production designers Eiko Ishioka and Patrizia Von Brandenstein. Also has an interview with production designer Kristi Zea on her work as a costume designer.

Ciment, Michael. *Conversations with Losey*. London and New York: Methuen, 1985. Contains discussions with Joseph Losey on his work with production designer Richard MacDonald.

———. *John Boorman*. London and Boston: Faber and Faber, 1986. Contains discussion with John Boorman on working with production designer Richard MacDonald on *Exorcist II: The Heretic*.

———. *Kubrick*. New York: Holt, Rinehart and Winston, 1980. Contains interview with production designer Ken Adam on his work with Stanley Kubrick on *Dr. Strangelove* and *Barry Lyndon*.

Gottfried, Martin. *All His Jazz*. New York, Toronto, London, Sidney, Auckland: Bantam, 1990. Discussion of production designer Tony Walton's association with Bob Fosse.

Heisner, Beverly. *Hollywood Art*. Jefferson, NC, and London: McFarland & Company, 1990. History of Hollywood art direction during the studio era.

Lee, Spike, with Lisa Jones. *Do the Right Thing*. New York: Fireside, 1989. Contains storyboards, drawings, and discussion and Wynn Thomas's production design of *Do the Right Thing*.

———. *Mo' Better Blues*. New York: Fireside, 1990. Contains interview with production designer Wynn Thomas on designing the nightclub for '*Mo Better Blues*.

———. *Uplift the Race: The Construction of School Daze*. New York: Fireside, 1988. Contains interview with production designer Wynn Thomas on the making of *School Daze*.

Lourie, Eugene. *My Work in Films*. San Diego, New York, London: Harcourt Brace Jovanovich, 1985. Memoir of the production designer Eugene Lourie.

Madsen, Roy Paul. *Working Cinema*. Belmont, CA: Wadsworth Publishing Company, 1990. Contains section on production design with production designer Dean Tavoularis.

Marner, Terrence St. John, ed. *Film Design*. New York: A.S. Barnes and Co., 1974.

Mathews, Jack. *The Battle of Brazil*. New York: Crown Publishing, 1987. Contains sketches and photographs of Norman Garwood's production design of *Brazil*.

Rebello, Stephen. *Alfred Hitchcock and the Making of Psycho*. New York: Dembner Books, 1990. Contains a section about the production design of *Psycho*.

Sayles, John. *Thinking in Pictures*. Boston: Houghton Mifflin Company, 1987. Section on the production design of the movie *Matewan*.

Spencer, Charles. *Cecil Beaton: Stage and Film Design*. New York: St. Martin's Press, 1975.

Taub, Eric. *Gaffers, Grips and Best Boys*. New York: St. Martin's Press, 1987. Contains section on the production designer, art director, and set decorator. Interview with production designer John Muto.

Wiley, Mason, and Damen Bona. *Inside Oscar*. New York: Ballantine Books, 1986. Contains nominations and winners of the Academy Award for interior decoration from 1927 to 1946 and art direction–set decoration from 1947 to 1987.

Index

ABOUT THE AUTHOR

VINCENT LOBRUTTO is the author of *Selected Takes: Film Editors on Editing* (Praeger, 1991). He has a bachelor of fine arts in filmmaking from the School of Visual Arts and has worked as a postproduction coordinator for the ABC television network and as a film editor for the Fox and HBO networks. He has lectured about filmmaking on both coasts and is currently writing his third book for Praeger, *Sound-on-Film: Interviews with Creators of Film Sound*.